Contents

Scotland and Nationalism

By the same author

THE LIGHTS OF LIBERALISM
University Liberals and the Challenge of Democracy
1860–86

Scotland and Nationalism

Scottish Society and Politics, 1707-1977

CHRISTOPHER HARVIE

London
GEORGE ALLEN & UNWIN
Ruskin House Museum Street

First Published in 1977

ISBN 0 04 941006 7 Cloth
0 04 941007 5 Paperback

Printed in Great Britain
in 11 on 13 point Baskerville
by
William Clowes & Sons, Limited
London, Beccles and Colchester

Author's Acknowledgements

The idea for this book originated from a suggestion by Dr Kenneth Morgan of Queen's College, Oxford, some four years ago that I might turn my mind to Scottish nationalism. He in no way bears responsibility for the subsequent division of my life, split mentally between theorising about Scotland's past and reporting on Scotland's present, and physically between Buckinghamshire and Scotland. What has emerged will, I hope, be of some value to people studying either, or both. Some may feel I have stocked the glens with wild generalisations, but there is no close season on them.

My thanks to all those who, while this book was in preparation, have given advice, information, encouragement, criticism and hospitality: to Clive Emsley, Julie Brotherstone, Jack Brand, Neal Ascherson, Graham Martin, Jean Jordan, Gavin Kennedy, Christopher Smout, Tom Nairn, Nicholas Phillipson, Keith Webb, John Simpson, Gordon Brown, Owen Dudley Edwards, Henry Cowper, Joan Christodoulou, Chris MacWhirter, Stephen Maxwell, Bob Bell, Robin Cook, MP, Angus Calder, Ian Jordan, Gwyn A. Williams, Geoffrey Best, Arthur Marwick, Robert Tait, Iain McLean, Alex Aitken, Dr Archie Lamont, W. H. Marwick and Ian MacDougall, to the staff of the Open University Library and the National Library of

Scotland, to John Bright-Holmes, Jackie Baldick and Irene Hatt, my secretary, who achieved wonders with a much-corrected manuscript.

Few will agree with everything in this book, many may dissent completely. One cannot write about present controversies in a totally detached manner. However, at worst, I hope that, if I have been unfair, I have been impartially unfair to everyone.

In memory of
Kenneth MacKenzie

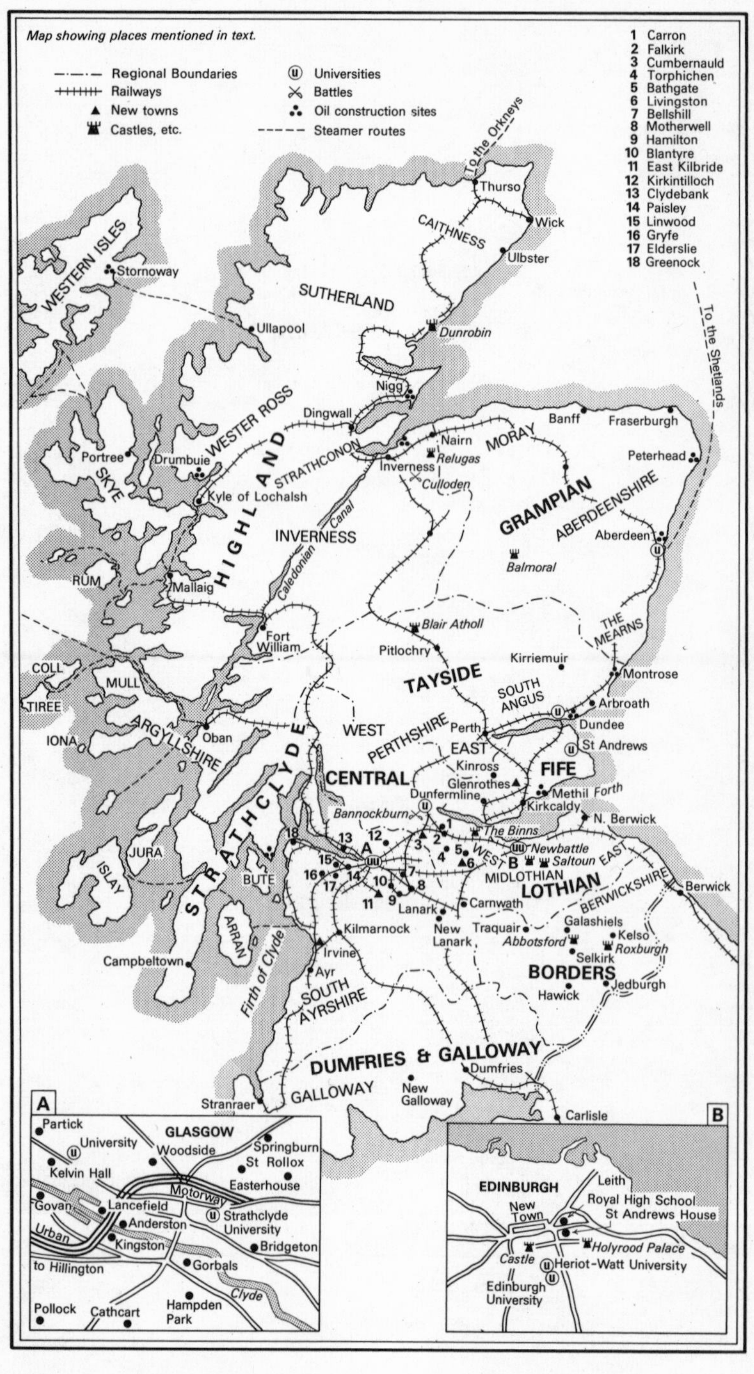
Map showing places mentioned in text.
Regional Boundaries
Railways
New towns
Castles, etc.
Universities
Battles
Oil construction sites
Steamer routes
1 Carron
2 Falkirk
3 Cumbernauld
4 Torphichen
5 Bathgate
6 Livingston
7 Bellshill
8 Motherwell
9 Hamilton
10 Blantyre
11 East Kilbride
12 Kirkintilloch
13 Clydebank
14 Paisley
15 Linwood
16 Gryfe
17 Elderslie
18 Greenock
To the Orkneys
To the Shetlands
Thurso
Wick
Ulbster
CAITHNESS
SUTHERLAND
WESTERN ISLES
Stornoway
Ullapool
Dunrobin
Nigg
Dingwall
WESTER ROSS
Nairn
MORAY
Banff
Fraserburgh
Peterhead
Relugas
Inverness
Culloden
STRATHCONON
Portree
SKYE
Drumbuie
Kyle of Lochalsh
HIGHLAND
INVERNESS
Caledonian Canal
GRAMPIAN
ABERDEENSHIRE
Aberdeen
Balmoral
RUM
Mallaig
Blair Atholl
THE MEARNS
Fort William
Pitlochry
Kirriemuir
Montrose
COLL
MULL
TIREE
IONA
TAYSIDE
SOUTH ANGUS
Arbroath
Dundee
ARGYLLSHIRE
Oban
WEST
PERTHSHIRE
EAST
Perth
St Andrews
Kinross
STRATHCLYDE
CENTRAL
Glenrothes
FIFE
Methil
Forth
Dunfermline
Kirkcaldy
Bannockburn
N. Berwick
The Binns
JURA
ISLAY
BUTE
A
Newbattle
B
Saltoun
WEST
MIDLOTHIAN
EAST
LOTHIAN
BERWICKSHIRE
Berwick
Lanark
Carnwath
ARRAN
Kilmarnock
New Lanark
Traquair
Galashiels
Kelso
Abbotsford
Roxburgh
Selkirk
Campbeltown
Irvine
Ayr
BORDERS
Jedburgh
Hawick
Firth of Clyde
SOUTH AYRSHIRE
DUMFRIES & GALLOWAY
Dumfries
New Galloway
GALLOWAY
Stranraer
Carlisle
A
GLASGOW
Partick
University
Woodside
Springburn
St Rollox
Kelvin Hall
Easterhouse
Motorway
Govan
Lancefield
Strathclyde University
Anderston
Urban
Kingston
Bridgeton
to Hillington
Gorbals
Clyde
Pollock
Cathcart
Hampden Park
B
EDINBURGH
Leith
Royal High School
New Town
St Andrews House
Holyrood Palace
Castle
Heriot-Watt University
Edinburgh University

Introduction

A Sad Nuisance

'We were all assembled to hear Winston make his funeral oration on Roosevelt, but before he started an absurd incident occurred,' Sir Harold Nicolson wrote to his son Nigel in April 1945:[1]

> A young man of the name of McIntyre had been elected as Scottish Nationalist for Motherwell. He refused to be introduced by any sponsors, since he does not recognise the Mother of Parliaments and wishes to advertise himself. He advanced to the Bar without sponsors and the Speaker told him that he could not take his oath, as that was contrary to Standing Orders. At which many Members rose offering to sponsor the cub and put an end to the shaming incident, but he refused. He was therefore told to go away and think it over, which he did, shrugging vain shoulders. Next day he thought better of it and accepted sponsors; but even then, as he reached the box, he said, 'I do this under protest', which was not liked at all. He is going to be a sad nuisance and pose as a martyr.

Sir Harold did not approve of Dr Robert McIntyre. Descended from the gentry of lowland Scotland, his father a former head of the Foreign Office, Nicolson had, in his political gyrations, mirrored the evolution of establishment politics between the wars – from Toryism, through support for the National Government, to membership of the Labour party after 1945. Dr McIntyre, a rather dour young medical officer for the county in which the Nicolsons held their title, Stirlingshire, was a son of the manse, pacifist in outlook, who denied that the Mother of Parliaments had any right to order Scotsmen into the war. The encounter was apposite. It was not only between two men, or two parties, but between two Scotlands.

This book is about both Scotlands – the achieving society, the defensive community – and the relationships between them. It is concerned with political nationalism, the reasons why it remained apparently in abeyance for two and a half centuries, and why it has currently become relevant. But it is also about the Scottish component of the Union which, despite its surface resemblance to the rest of Britain, is a very distinctive one indeed, like a house whose façade looks the same as other houses, but which, internally, is constructed in a quite different manner, for quite different purposes. In the final weeks of Britain's last conflict as a major power, Nicolson did not consider this context at all; McIntyre saw it purely as an instrument of oppression. But for nearly two and a half centuries it had both encompassed and separated two quite different societies. McIntyre's election, however, was a prelude to its most fundamental challenge yet, and one which it may not survive.

Dr McIntyre's career as the first Scottish Nationalist MP lasted only six weeks. Both he and Nicolson were thrown out at the general election. The whole episode had been somewhat eccentric, as McIntyre had only got in through the support of Conservatives, who were not allowed, because of the wartime electoral truce, to run their own candidate. Westminster did not hear about him for nearly twenty years but when he did emerge again it was as president of a movement which threatened to end, once and for all, the supremacy of the House whose patience he had tried, sorely if briefly, in 1945. Over the decade since 1965, the membership of his party, 2000 in 1945, expanded from 16,000 to 80,000, its branches grew from about two dozen to over 500, and in October 1974 it returned eleven MPs to Parliament and secured 30 per cent of the Scottish vote, making it second only to the Labour Party in popularity.

The rise of political nationalism has been the central fact of Scottish politics since 1965. Before then, issues at Scottish elections were generally similar to those agitated south of the border; since then, a new politics has been created which has dramatically reoriented the attitudes of all parties: a dance to the music of nationalism, in which principles and opinions have steadily diverged from the British norm. Divisions between unionists and devolutionists and devolutionists and secessionists have cut across those between right and left, and are made even more complex by the manoeuvring of the ambitious with their eye on power in the eventual political settlement, whatever that may be.

The Scottish National Party has been the prime beneficiary. Its leaders, dismissed as eccentrics for most of its career, now talk confidently about the 'when' of independence, no longer about the 'if'. With their rivals internally divided – not only on devolution – or hopelessly weak, they have the unity and enthusiasm of a new consensus behind them. They have suffered splits and setbacks, but they have retained their membership and momentum. More important, they are no longer alone. Among the other parties, and among non-political groups, growing support exists for extensive measures of devolution, and the probability steadily increases that any failure on the part of a British government to deliver the goods will result in an overwhelming movement for secession.

The Nationalist upsurge and the campaign for devolution have been seen as protest movements, or as a self-interested attempt to grab the revenues from North Sea oil. But the

Nationalists have survived and matured in a way that no protest party would be capable of, while only a minority of the Scottish electorate favour the total separation that such a seizure would require. Yet a political paradox remains. The voters who endorse devolution put it low down on their list of priorities, despite the fact that it has now permeated the language of politics in Scotland.

To what extent, then, does this language reflect reality? Those, mainly on the left, who would brand it as the distortion of some fundamental economic or class reality by 'false consciousness' have been confounded at election after election. Grievances which the Scots have in common with the rest of Britain have fused with those which are peculiar to the country, and both are increasingly articulated in national terms. For political activism is concerned with much more than economics, and the movement for devolution reflects a correspondingly complex social situation. To understand the differences between economic base and political superstructure in Scotland, one has to come to terms with the factors in Scottish history whose development has contributed to this new political situation, and to distinguish between direct responses to specific crises and underlying tendencies. In recent years both have coalesced, but only by disentangling them can one come to any conclusion about the prospects of making any settlement work.

The main thesis of this book is that no understanding of the forces making for a renegotiation of the Union is possible which omits the historical factors which have kept the Union in being, not as the absorption of one nation by another, but as an unique balance of assimilation and autonomy. The Union allowed Scottish nationalism to survive, accompanied by a distinctive pattern of government and society, and the consequences of this relationship were sanctioned by an intelligentsia whose own character was pervaded by a parallel dualism between the cosmopolitan and the native.

This thesis has not been imposed, but has emerged in the

course of writing. Nevertheless, it does underline many of the insights of one European political thinker whose influence on the reorientation of socialist thought has been considerable, not least in Scotland. Antonio Gramsci, leader of the Italian communists until his imprisonment by Mussolini, was a Sardinian – in other words he came from the Italian equivalent of the Scottish Highlands. Influenced by Croce as well as Marx, he challenged the latter's crude generalisations about nationalism. He was preoccupied by the way in which the masses were persuaded to accept the 'civil society' (a phrase originated in eighteenth-century Scotland) which sustained the dominant political and economic groups. and he attributed this critical function to the intellectuals. Intellectual history thus becomes, in Gramsci's view, as in mine, the key to our understanding of why nationalist movements emerge.

Or do not emerge. For the uniqueness of Scotland lies in the power of a 'civil society' divorced from political nationalism, and in an intelligentsia which, lacking a political centre, was divided between two loyalties: the red and the black. The red Scots were cosmopolitan, self-avowedly enlightened and, given a chance, authoritarian, expanding into and exploiting bigger and more bountiful fields than their own country could provide. Back home lurked their black brothers, demotic, parochial and reactionary, but keeping the ladder of social promotion open, resisting the encroachments of the English governing class. Together, they controlled the rate of their own assimilation to the greater world, the balance which underlay the Union.

Since the Second World War, a series of changes in that balance, and the reactions of politicians insensitive to its nature, have brought it to a state in which its stability has fluctuated from year to year, and sometimes from by-election to by-election. But one cannot understand the intricate moves of the current political transactions without casting a backward glance at the politics of two and a half centuries of unionism, and, behind that, at a national history which, although it exercised a profound effect on the idea of nationalism, singularly failed to conform to its orthodoxies. The peculiar history of the Scots has meant that, man for man, they have probably done more to create the modern world than any other nation. They owe it an explanation.

PART I

Chapter 1

The Ballads of a Nation: Political Nationalism, 1707-1945

Oldbuck: I'll supply you with a subject – The battle between the Caledonians and the Romans – the Caledoniad; or, Invasion Repelled. Let that be the title – it will suit the present taste, and you may throw in a touch of the times.

Lovel: But the invasion of Agricola was *not* repelled.

Oldbuck: No; but you are a poet – free of the corporation, and as little bound to truth or probability as Virgil himself – You may defeat the Romans in spite of Tacitus.

Sir Walter Scott, *The Antiquary*

I

In 1704, on the eve of the Union, Andrew Fletcher of Saltoun, the most energetic champion of the doomed Scottish parliament, published anonymously his *Account of a Conversation concerning a*

Right Regulation of Governments for the common good of Mankind. One sentence of this tract was to be prophetic in describing the course of Scottish nationalism over the next two hundred and fifty years.[1]

> I knew a very wise man so much of Sir Christopher [Neville]'s sentiment that he believed that if a man were permitted to make all the ballads, he need not care who should make the laws of a nation.

Nationalist tradition has, to the present day, regarded Fletcher as the parent of Scottish parliamentary democracy. The Scottish National Party equivalent of the Fabian Society is the Andrew Fletcher Society. Fletcher was a man of his unruly time, a talented, choleric soldier, quick to violence and nursing a pet scheme for the economic revival of Scotland which involved the reinforcement of serfdom; his anti-English interventions in the Scottish parliament probably accelerated the Union which he loathed. Yet he had accurately predicted the terms on which Scottish nationalism was to survive, as a movement on the margin not only of British politics, but of European nationalism itself.

Poetic tradition had given a logic of its own to Scottish development during the middle ages. Two national epics treated the War of Independence, 1296–1328, not as a chivalric episode but as a popular struggle for a nationalism which was also libertarian. The myth was underlain by reality. On the edge of Europe, composed of a variety of races and affected by the cultural traditions of Roman and Christian Europe and the Norsemen, Scotland had evolved by the thirteenth century, rather in advance of England and France, a range of institutions which could sustain a national community. These institutions were in the main aristocratic and were derived from Anglo-Norman feudal practice, although their local identity was by the end of the century so secure that when the male royal line of Scotland expired in 1286 the Scottish magnates envisaged with equanimity joining England under a dual monarchy. Instead, the collapse of this scheme, and the English invasions which followed, made patriots of the mass of the population.

In 1320, six years after the defeat of the English at Bannockburn, the Scots nobility, along with 'the other barons and freeholders and the whole community of the realm of Scotland', petitioned the Pope to recognise the independence of Scotland and the kingship of Robert the Bruce. The Declaration of Arbroath, 'the most impressive manifesto of nationalism that medieval Europe produced', culminated with the words:[2]

> We are bound to him (King Robert) for the maintaining of our freedom both by his right and his merits, as to him by whom salvation has been wrought unto our people, and by him, come what may, we mean to stand. Yet if he should give up what he has begun, seeking to make us or our kingdom subject to the king of England or the English, we would strive at once to drive him out as our enemy and a subverter of his own right and ours, and we would make some other man who was able to defend us our king; for, as long as a hundred of us remain alive, we will never on any conditions be subjected to the lordship of the English. For we fight not for glory, nor riches, nor honour, but for freedom alone, which no good man gives up except with his life.

The freedom claimed was an absolute: 'freedom from unfreedom', not the 'liberties' of a privileged class. It reflected the experience of a war sufficiently intense to have involved most classes in society, and the desire of these classes to have a stake in its outcome. The war had in fact produced a type of popular nationalism rarely encountered in Europe before the French Revolution.

It was not to last. There was little popular involvement in the politics of the two grim centuries which followed, disfigured by royal minorities and aristocratic mayhem. After the Reformation of 1559–60, religion was to impose a new set of priorities, in which theology altered concepts both of nationalism and of liberty. But the poets preserved and transmitted the memory of the war and its ideals: the praise of freedom in Archdeacon Barbour's *The Bruce* in 1375:

> A! fredome is a noble thing
> Fredome mays man to haiff liking;
> Fredome all solace to man giffis
> He levys at es that frely levys.

was, a century later, joined by Blind Harry's glorification of Bruce's more obscure predecessor, William Wallace. Both epics were printed in the sixteenth century, and frequently reprinted thereafter. Their echoes carried through to the mobs which rioted against the Union in 1707 and against the Malt Tax in 1713, and which lynched Captain Porteous in 1736. They were picked up by Burns and condensed in 1793 into the powerful stanzas of 'Bruce to his Troops on the eve of the Battle of Bannock-burn':

> Scots, wha hae wi' Wallace bled,
> Scots, wham Bruce has aften led;
> Welcome to your gory bed,
> Or to victorie.
>
> Now's the day, and now's the hour;
> See the front o' battle lour;
> See approach proud Edward's power –
> Chains and slaverie!
>
> Wha for Scotland's king and law
> Freedom's sword will strongly draw,
> Free-man stand, or Free-man fa',
> Let him follow me!

Even at the present day it is to Bannockburn, Arbroath and Wallace's reputed birthplace at Elderslie that the Nationalists make their pilgrimages, not to St Giles Kirk and Parliament House in Edinburgh or Burns's birthplace at Ayr.

Burns's attitude to Scottish nationalism was ambiguous. At the end of the nineteenth century the Glasgow professor John Nichol, the friend of Kossuth and Mazzini, described him as writing the requiem of Lowland Scotland 'as a distinct nationality', while being the prophet of a new and universal democratic order.[3] While his poetry became part of the popular radicalism of nineteenth-century Europe, that same radicalism, allied with industrialisation, was rapidly overthrowing what remained of Scottish political distinctiveness, and with it the basis for any valid nationalist movement.

II

Nationalism has been characterised as an amalgam of the politics of the French Revolution, which vested sovereignty in the people, and the philosophy of German idealism, which announced the liberation of the individual will, and its development in the service of the state.[4] Yet nationalism also drew on earlier tendencies. In the seventeenth and eighteenth centuries absolute rulers had set out to crush aristocratic localism and provincial loyalties, dangerous centrifugal forces during the late middle ages and the wars of religion. It was on the effectiveness of such assertions of royal authority that the shape of future nations depended. Where monarchs suppressed the provincial estates in which local notabilities – clergy, nobles and burgesses – were represented, they created the basis of nationality; conversely, where they failed, or compromised, nationality could develop around what survived. The possession of such institutions, and the traditions and culture which surrounded them, distinguished what mid-nineteenth-century radicals, notably Marx and Engels, called the 'historic' nationalities. Out of aristocratic localism, and in defiance of the conservative multinational empires, groups like the Poles and the Hungarians evolved towards capitalism and democracy.

For the groups which failed to sustain such institutions, or had none to sustain, Marx and Engels had little time. In their eyes the 'peoples without history' were a threat to social progress:[5]

> There is no country in Europe that does not possess, in some remote corner, at least one remnant-people, left over from an earlier population, forced back and subjugated by the nation which later became the repository of historical development. These remnants of a nation, mercilessly crushed, as Hegel said, by the course of history, this *national refuse*, is always the fanatical representative of the counter-revolution and remains so until it is completely exterminated or de-nationalised, as its whole existence is in itself a protest against a great historical revolution.

Amongst Slavs, Basques and Bretons they numbered the Gaels, 'supporters of the Stuarts from 1640 to 1745'. It was one of the few times that Scots as Scots appeared in their discussions, and it exemplified the way in which Scotland escaped from the great generalisations of European history.* The Lowland Scots lacked the constitutional focus – or the determination to secure it – which characterised 'historic nationality'. But if society, language and history separated them from the Highlanders, they were equally distinct from the English, despite the shared parliament. For they had made the *conscious* decision to supersede nationalism by ideology.

From the standpoint of the implicit British nationalism which pervaded nineteenth-century historical writing, the Union of 1707 was analogous to contemporary continental developments: the suppression of a potentially schismatic type of aristocratic politics in the interests of dynastic security. After

* Marx violently attacked the Sutherland clearances in *Capital*, vol. II, but the Duke only seemed to be carrying out his own prescription.

it, in the words of Professor Hugh Trevor-Roper, 'intelligent Scotchmen rejoiced in the removal of their national politics to London' and got on with the apolitical business of improving their country.[6] While accurate enough in portraying the attitude of the English government, this view is as misleading about the Scottish situation as the traditional nationalist myth of a representative assembly cut down in its prime.[7] For, although dominated by aristocrats and their factions, the Scottish parliament had for nearly twenty years claimed to speak for the nation in a way that it had never hitherto done. Its problem was that it was not indispensable to nationality. For a century and a half, it had had a rival – the Kirk.

III

In *The Scot in History*, which remains one of the most perceptive studies of the nation yet written, the American historian Wallace Notestein commented that 'in explaining Scottish character nothing is more important than religion'.[8] But he stressed that this generalisation only applied after the reformation. The events of 1560 created a new politics and a new concept of freedom. Partly because of the corruption of the Catholic Church, partly as a result of a European diplomatic revolution, which allied the great Catholic powers of Europe, Spain and France, against Elizabeth's England, Scotland opted for the most drastic religious innovation possible, along with an agreement with England which would safeguard it. These two events, which brought to an end the French alliance which had endured since the War of Independence, effectively foreshadowed the Union. 'The Kingdom of God which is of this world', the social gospel of Calvinism, rivalled and eventually supplanted the less substantial ideals of national independence and individual freedom which the ballads had celebrated.

Like the Russian Communists after 1917, the Scots Calvinists proclaimed a 'positive' liberty of their own, achieved within a system of total social control. The parallel between the two is not wholly fanciful. In both cases a European crisis coincided with a fatal weakening of central authority in a peripheral and backward state, which an intelligentsia, made cosmopolitan by lack of domestic opportunity, took advantage of to impose its own ideology. The parallel cannot be taken much further, but the combination of intellectual sophistication and social backwardness produced, in Scotland and Russia alike, an equation of liberty with intense political discipline:[9]

> No man may be permitted to live as best pleaseth him within the Church of God; but every man must be constrained by fraternal admonition and correction to bestow his labours when of the Church they are required, to the edification of others [otherwise] discipline must proceed against them, provided that the civil magistrate concur with the judgment and election of the Church.

A hundred and thirty troubled years were to pass before the claims of the Kirk were confirmed by the Revolution of 1688, during which time the Calvinist notion of nationality had been extended to embrace all the dominions of the Stuarts. 1688 was a sort of compromise – 'Calvinism in one country'. But during this time religious ideology had cut across, and weakened, an ideal of political nationalism which had been in advance of its time. 1707 confirmed this victory. So, during the great age of European nationalism, formal Scottish nationalism was a marginal component of a Scottish politics which was fundamentally religious. The writers and singers of the ballads may have provided the closest parallel with European nationalism, and certainly gave the twentieth-century nationalist movement its historical memory, but for the next two centuries they were on their own.

IV

The ideology which triumphed in 1707 was not anti-Scottish. 'Principled' unionists like William Carstares, the leader of the Kirk, and William Paterson, the financier and founder of the Bank of England *and* the Bank of Scotland, recognised that parliament was only one among a range of national institutions. They argued that the safety and effectiveness of the Kirk, the law and the educational system were, in an age of limited governmental activity, worth sacrificing a parliament for. As Sir Robert Rait and Professor A. V. Dicey wrote in their apologia *Thoughts on the Union* in 1920, it was perfectly possible to be both a sincere nationalist and an advocate of the Union: it may even have been essential.[10] A parliament which, without contributing much to the good administration of the country, remained a focus for Jacobite and French intrigue, would not have been allowed to exist for long by any English government, and its suppression – say at the time of the 1745 rebellion – could have been made the occasion for the total assimilation of all the independent Scottish institutions.

The Union was certainly far from popular, even among those who admitted the need for some form of parliamentary incorporation. A loose federation would probably have been preferred by most Scots parliamentarians. Instead they received only nominal representation at Westminster, through MPs who were on the whole government placemen. A more drastic assimilation might at least have brought a competent bureaucracy; but the determination to subordinate Scottish government to English political traditions – of party patronage and local initiative – paradoxically meant that Scottish local and Church government was allowed to go its own way. Coupled with economic depression, 'semi-independence' seemed a poor substitute for a sovereign parliament, but it did satisfy enough power groups in Scotland to inhibit collective action.

Further, nationalist ideology did not develop rapidly enough to unify the distinctive discontents of the two Scotlands. The economic grievances of the Lowlands remained quite separate from the religious and linguistic grievances of the third of the population which lived beyond the Highland line, which found expression in the periodic recrudescence of Jacobite sentiment. This was as near as could be got to the aristocratic localism of Europe. But it was on a dead-end road. After the failure of the last Jacobite bid for power, 'semi-independent' Lowland Scotland embarked on the 'improvement' which was in the space of fifty years to bring it abreast of its southern neighbour in economic performance and ahead in 'enlightenment', and completed the 'de-nationalisation' that Cumberland's guns had begun on Culloden Moor.

By the time of the French Revolution, therefore, the aristocratic tradition which might have produced a basis for a re-invigorated Scottish nationalism had vanished. Jacobitism could still be celebrated by a radical like Burns, but this was really proof of how innocuous it had now become. Were his attacks – and those of his contemporaries – on the Union any more serious? Nationalist historians have insisted that they were, but the evidence is at the very least ambiguous. The French, through diplomatic tradition rather than democratic zeal, periodically toyed with promoting Scots separatism. Some Scots radicals took their cue from them, especially when, as in the case of the radical laird of Huntershill, Thomas Muir, persecution drove them to accept French aid, but on the whole agitation for reform tended to strengthen rather than to subvert the Union. Scottish protests against interference with Scots law in the 1780s managed both to appeal to nationalism and to demand a greater degree of assimilation.[11] The same ambiguities can be detected in the campaign of the Scottish 'Friends of the People' in 1793, whose 'British Convention', held in Edinburgh in November 1793, demonstrated an unprecedented degree of collaboration between Scottish and English radicals, and in the reform agitation which succeeded the peace in 1815, when English agitators like Cobbett and Cartwright were enthusiastically welcomed in Scotland, and the traditions of seventeenth-century English parliamentarianism were celebrated in the foundation of numerous Hampden Clubs. It was thus not altogether surprising that mid-nineteenth-century Scotland was an important centre of 'Anglo-Saxonist' and anti-Irish racialist ideology.

Whatever the views of Scots radicals about the principle of the Union, they preferred alliance with Englishmen to persecution by their native judiciary: the peril in which the Scottish reformers found themselves led to unity rather than separatism. The bourgeoisie, which in Europe after 1789 acted as the main sponsor of nationalism was, in Scotland, either cowed into submission by the power of the government or forced to look for allies in the south.

It was precisely for this reason that its most progressive section, the young Whigs around the *Edinburgh Review*, appealed to English reformers for assistance against a reactionary, but authentically Scottish, ruling group. Some separatist slogans – along the lines of the Irish radicals – were heard from the working-class left. The weavers' rising of 1820 was directed vaguely at securing a 'Scottish Republic'. But these were increasingly unrepresentative. To Scottish liberals and radicals the road to freedom lay through assimilation in general, and assimilation to the English franchise in particular. To Gladstone the Reform Act of 1832 was the 'political birth' of Scotland, 'the beginning of a duty and a power, neither of which had attached to the Scottish nation in the preceding period'.[12] But this metaphor had nothing to do with nationality: it meant in fact the subordination of the remaining Scottish institutions to representative parliamentary government in a British context. Considering their indifferent track record over the previous couple of decades, this was regretted by few. Where the Whigs led, the Chartists – who were very active in Scotland – followed, their eyes fixed on Westminster. For the fifty years the Liberals dominated Scotland, the Union was scarcely ever called in question.

V

The hegemony of 'unionist Liberalism' in Scotland coincided with a profound change in the character of European nationalism. Marx's 'peoples without history' began to acquire national identity, written literature, political programmes. The older nationalists viewed the emergence of groups like the Slavs of the Habsburg Empire with hostility as a gambit of the conservative powers, seeking to create a Jacquerie of reaction. To Marx and Engels a war of genocide waged against the Slav peasantry was preferable. Yet, by destroying the last of the feudal servitudes, the revolutions of 1848 created the basis for the non-socialist populist radicalism which was to dominate the politics of many European states in the last years of the century. The alliance between a freed peasantry coping with the problems of agricultural depression, emigration and urbanisation and a nationalist intelligentsia was potent not only in Continental Europe but in Ireland and Wales, especially against a background of falling prices for farm produce after the 1870s.[13] While in Scotland the agricultural population was smaller, the depression less severe and mitigated anyway by growth in other sectors of the economy, the echoes of this international upheaval made themselves heard, and contributed to the birth of the movement for legislative devolution.

In the early 1880s the 'national refuse' of Gaelic Scotland at last challenged the process of de-nationalisation which it had endured for over a century. Goaded by the example of the Land League in Ireland, crofters in the highlands stood and fought against eviction. The Scottish administration lurched from coercion to conciliation. Gunboats and police were ordered north, and were followed by a Royal Commission, which promised security of tenure, the settlement of rent arrears, and a Land Court. At the same time, using the franchise that they had just been granted, the highlanders expelled the Whigs who had previously represented them and returned five independent 'Crofter' MPs, one of whom, ironically enough, had been a founder with Marx of the International. Highland radicalism was to play some part in establishing the Scottish socialist movement later in the 1880s, and in placing home rule on its programme, but the main pressure for devolution came from more influential and less nationalist sources.[14]

If land agitation paralleled, albeit feebly, European peasant nationalism, the concurrent campaign for a Scottish Secretary (a post which had lapsed in 1746) seemed like a reversion to aristocratic localism.[15] It was headed by the Earl of Rosebery and supported by the Duke of Argyll, the arch-enemy of land reform, and the Earl of Fife, and received consensus support from both main parties. A verbose plutocrat, Rosebery had stage-managed Gladstone's Midlothian campaign in 1880. He then sought to establish himself, like Joseph Chamberlain and Charles Stuart Parnell, as the leader of a territorial interest.

The time was appropriate: the Commons was congested with legislation, made worse by Irish and Tory obstruction. Local government bills, which might have helped by transferring powers to county councils, were themselves trapped, and delays in Scottish legislation gave weight to Rosebery's propaganda. An extra element of urgency was added by the Land War, which seemed to make concession to the representatives of property safer than to risk the Irish malady of nationalism combined with land agitation. In 1884 Gladstone had in fact to legislate for the Secretaryship *against* the opposition of powerful sections of the Scottish administration, who resented the transfer of their authority to a political – and consequently a Westminster – headship. But they could at least be assured that its implications were far from radical. On the fall of the Liberals,

Lord Salisbury completed Gladstone's work and offered the new post to the Duke of Richmond and Gordon, who thought it 'quite unnecessary'. Salisbury's nephew, Arthur Balfour, urged him to persist: 'It really is a matter where the effulgence of two Dukedoms and the best salmon river in Scotland will go a long way.'[16] The Duke accepted and the people of Scotland were suitably enthusiastic.

The agitation for the Secretaryship was, in nationalist terms, as ambiguous as the 'defence' of Scots Law a century earlier. The Secretary effectively increased assimilation by subordinating Scottish affairs to English party politics, a situation which became apparent when the Conservatives (still in a minority in Scotland) stayed in power after 1886. By that time the Liberal Party had split over Irish home rule, and some of its members were canvassing home rule for Scotland. Gladstone uttered a gnomic endorsement of their efforts in 1886:

> Scotland, which for a century and a quarter after her Union was refused all taste of a real representative system, may begin to ask herself whether, if at the first she felt something of an unreasoning antipathy, she may not latterly have drifted into a superstitious worship, or at least an irreflective acquiescence.[17]

He followed it with an equally gnomic disclaimer in 1889, to the relief of most of his front bench. But home rule persisted among the Scottish Liberals, whose central association adopted it as policy in 1888. Only one thing would have been further from their minds in 1883: the thought that they would be supporting Irish home rule in 1886. Whatever credibility Scottish home rule had followed from their ability to swallow Gladstone's new policy.

A Scottish Home Rule association was formed in 1886 to gain all-party backing for the cause, and for twenty-eight years displayed most of the characteristics of later groups dedicated to the same end. Indeed, it provided training for many of their activists. But it courted consensus out of weakness where Rosebery and his colleagues courted it through strength. A cause had to be within sight of success to keep together romantic conservatives like the Marquess of Bute and Professor John Stuart Blackie, Unionists who wanted to direct Scottish home rule sentiment against the Irish, radicals who equated it with land nationalisation and the eight-hour day, and, most significant and most demoralising of all, Gladstonian Liberals who believed that 'Ireland blocked the way'.

Scottish home rule was carried along in the slipstream of Irish home rule: it did not have its motive power. The Irish, as Conor Cruise O'Brien has observed, were not in favour of the principle of home rule; they thought it as good a compromise as they could get, and they were persuaded that the compromise was worthwhile by the opposition to it of men whom they loathed.[18] Subjects of discontent of all sorts – political, religious, linguistic and agrarian – were pulling in more extreme directions: Parnell's commitment to parliamentary agitation provided the necessary means of socialising them and concentrating them behind a movement, a programme and a man.

In Scotland, where such grievances existed they were less acute, like the land problem (only 6 per cent of the Scottish population was employed in agriculture in 1901 against 20 per cent in Ireland), or lacked intellectual focus, like the linguistic issue, or were actually calculated to damage the traditional national institutions, like the campaign, backed by the Liberals after 1887, to disestablish the Church of Scotland. And there was no Scottish Parnell. There could scarcely be when the Scottish Liberals, in their selection of candidates, massively endorsed the Union. Gladstone sat for Midlothian, Morley for Montrose, Asquith for East Fife, Trevelyan for Glasgow Bridgeton. James Bryce, who represented South Aberdeen from 1885 to 1906, would visit his constituency about twice a year 'delivering addresses on political, literary or educational topics and always setting apart one day for callers who might wish to see him on business of any kind.'[19] Such an electorate was unlikely to respond positively to constitutional innovation of any sort.

Scottish Liberalism was conservative and deferential. In the last years of the century it was to suffer for this. 1886, the year in which the Welsh and Irish confirmed their radicalism, was the year in which it started to ebb, with the secession of the Liberal Unionists. Within sixteen years the Conservatives and their Unionist allies had a majority in Scotland. Unlike Wales, there was no large-scale radical nationalist movement: no Tom Ellis, no Lloyd George. New Liberal thinking came from the right, from collectivist-inclined imperialists like R. B. Haldane, who had little time for home rule. Along with antivivisectionism, women's suffrage and disarmament, it became part of the repertory of the party 'faddists', and, further to the left, among the socialists. Sanctioned by the Irish experience, it was, along with land nationalisation, one of few things the fissile components of the Scottish Labour Party could agree on when it came into existence in 1889; and it was a principle that the Party's leader, Keir Hardie, clung to persistently in his awkward transition from Liberalism to socialism. But Scotland remained stony ground for radical politics. The Scottish Labour Party was in sectarian disarray within a year of its foundation, and Hardie headed south to the more promising politics of radical London.[20]

In fact the changes of 1886 drove the Liberal Party further from a logical policy of devolution. The central concern of mid-Victorian Liberalism as John Vincent has identified it was the restructuring of politics to incorporate new classes and interests.[21] In some ways this came close to fulfilment in the radical programme of 1885, with its emphasis on regional government units large enough to sustain the activity and pulling-power of parliamentary politics – a paradigm of latter-day devolution. The abandonment of such radical programmes of reform by Gladstone, in favour of the 'great moral issue' of

Irish home rule (and his own leadership), brought the politics of restructuring to an end. Ireland could not generate support indefinitely, and into the vacuum came socialist and imperialist initiatives. Even with the massive Liberal majority of 1906, and a paper majority for Scottish home rule, the task was so complex as to be beyond the abilities of the government. Only Winston Churchill, characteristically, was prepared to attempt it, with a scheme for parliament for Scotland, Ireland and Wales, and seven English regional councils, all possessing the same legislative powers, but he moved away from the Home Office to the Admiralty in 1911.[22] The Liberal leadership had opted in 1886 for centralisation, party cohesion, and elite control – even at the expense of concessions to collectivism. The momentum of administrative evolution was in its favour, as was the polarisation of politics along class lines. It would take more than motions in favour of Scottish home rule to make it throw these advantages away, but there was no sign that the Scots were tired of passing them.

In the long term, Scottish nationalism was much more profoundly affected by the consquences of an incident at Hampden Park on 30 October 1886 than by anything that happened at Westminster that year. During a third round Football Association Cup match between Preston North End and Queen's Park, Jimmy Ross, a Scots player with Preston, fouled Harrower the Queen's Park centre-forward, before a crowd of 15,000. The pitch was invaded by Queen's Park supporters and Ross had to be smuggled out of the ground. The incident brought to a head differences between the Football Association and the Scottish Football Association, as a result of which the SFA announced on 10 May 1887 'that clubs belonging to this Association shall not be members of any other National Association', and ordered Scottish teams to withdraw from the FA Cup competition.[23]

This declaration of independence came at a crucial moment in the history of the game. The rather aristocratic amateurism which had dominated it since its organisation in associations in the late 1860s was, in England, rapidly giving way to professionalism. Although most of the early professionals were Scots like Ross, the SFA stood out for amateurism. This issue underlay the schism of 1887, and, although the SFA gave in on it by 1893, the organisation of the Scottish and English Leagues had crystallised. The new proletarian, professional game was organised on national, not on British, lines. 'Working class nationalism', James Kellas has written, 'is generally related to culture and football, not politics.' This consciousness stemmed from the 1880s. Had a British League come into operation in that decade, it might have been quite different. Independence in football meant the development of the distinctively Scottish political-religious conflicts of the big city teams. This was paradoxically anti-national, as it promoted sectional rivalries rather than notions of unified community, but, in a nation which always read its newspapers from the back, it ensured that the popular press had a good financial reason for emphasising its Scottishness. To this day, sales of English popular dailies remain very low north of the border.

'Nationalism' in sport in fact paralleled the dualism of the Union settlement. Two years earlier Irish nationalists had created the Gaelic Athletic Association to organise games – hurling and Gaelic football – which the English did not play, and it banned its members from playing football or rugby. Not surprisingly, GAA members were later to become some of the most militant supporters of Sinn Fein. Such was the power of sport. In Scotland, however, the separateness of the society was merged with its economic and political links with England to produce the ritual conflict of two nations playing the same game.

VI

A paradox, however, remains. If, after 1832, Scottish party politics, and most extra-parliamentary radicalism, fitted snugly into the Union mould, what do we make of recurrent agitations which harped on national injustices, and received considerable popular support? In the 1820s, while the Whigs were driving towards assimilation, a campaign headed by Sir Walter Scott, as Malachi Malagrowther, stirred up national sentiment to protect the note-issuing powers of Scottish banks, threatened by a government proposal to grant monopoly rights of issue to the Bank of England. In the 1850s grievances over English heraldic aggressions (always a sensitive area with more romantic Scots) combined with more general social and educational discontents to create a National Association for the Vindication of Scottish Rights. This proved ephemeral, but by the end of the decade national identity was materially commemorated by the Wallace monument on the Abbey Craig at Stirling, which had seen the most decisive clashes in the War of Independence.[24] On a somewhat lower key, similar grievances were ventilated at intervals until the patriotic agitation merged with the home rule movement – such as it was – after 1886. Its impact was variable, but the symbolism which accrued around it is critical to any understanding of the relationship between patriotism and nationalism.

Such outbreaks have been identified as part of an implicit strategy of 'noisy inaction' directed, or at least sanctioned, by the leaders of red Scotland, those committed to a policy of assimilation *on their own terms*.[25] Nationalist emotion, directed at symbolic targets like banknotes or flags, was allowed to surface when it looked as if assimilation might be acquiring a momentum of its own. It was then that a declaration – no more – of nationalism was needed. So the banknote crisis cropped up when the old Scottish system of government was in its death throes after the assault of the Whigs; the Scottish Rights issue became important when the balance of the new settlement was altered, after 1843, by the schism in the Kirk – the Disruption – and the increasing centralisation of government, which caused similar localist reactions in England. In both cases the lowest common denominator of nationalism, resentment of the English, was located and supplemented, intentionally or otherwise, by such historic nationalist ideology as came to hand. This latter was the more unpredictable, and its consequences were frequently to be rather more important than its red Scots sponsors had bargained for.

Patriotic agitation tended to give a continuing legitimacy to groups on the fringes of the Scottish establishment: Jacobites, Gaelic enthusiasts, Catholics, even Tories. While these scarcely promoted political credibility, they were able to tap emotional responses which the ruling consensus neglected. In due course, and with a lot of help from external sources like Queen Victoria and the tourist industry, patriotism evolved into the great Tartan monster, the populist subculture which eventually issued forth in the sentimental literature popularised by J. M. Barrie and other members of the Kailyard school. The political returns to nationalism (in the European sense) may have been small or at least ambiguous, like the Secretaryship, but by the 1870s Scottish towns were sprouting hotels, railway stations and public buildings in the baronial style, all crow-stepped gables and round turrets; the middle classes were wearing highland dress on Sundays; the use of words like Scotch or North British instead of Scots or Scottish, or England instead of Britain, was incurring authoritative disapproval. Throughout the world Burns clubs or Caledonian associations were being formed by the emigrants, and an identification with Scotland was being assiduously cultivated as a means of evading the unpopularity which attached to the British at the zenith of their imperialism. Black Scotland had in fact become an essential complement of red Scotland, a fruitful schizophrenia which enabled the Scots to run with the hare and hunt with the hounds.

The inevitable consequence of the entente between emotive nationalism and effective unionism was the impotence of political nationalism. Not only did it lack the economic grievances on which Irish and Welsh nationalism fed, but the religious and educational institutions of the country, which in Ireland and Wales created a link between economic change and political response, were committed to the Union and through it to the 'Greater Scotland' of the empire. However many radicals identified themselves with left-wing home rule groups like the Young Scots' Society – founded as a pro-Boer pressure group in 1900, which propagandised actively before the 1906 election – the momentum of social and economic development continually frustrated them.[26] There were few rewards in being an anti-imperialist in a community which benefited so much by imperialism.[27]

Home rule stood a chance of success only when the confidence of Westminster faltered, and it came closest to realisation in the imbroglio which surrounded the issue of Irish home rule between 1910 and 1915. This was not a position achieved by radical pressure from within Scotland. The propaganda of the Young Scots had been subdued since 1906; the various Liberal-backed home rule groups had only nominal influence. It owed much more to Conservative fears that without some form of federal settlement a total constitutional breakdown was inevitable. These were voiced, appropriately enough, by an energetic Scots imperialist, F. S. Oliver, in a series of *Times* letters in 1910, and this conception formed the basis of the sort of consensus settlement that Lloyd George and Churchill hoped might avert constitutional breakdown in the troubled years that followed.[28] Had war not broken out, Scotland would very likely have been presented with a parliament. Whether the Scots knew what they wanted to do with it is another, and much more doubtful matter.

The outbreak of war in 1914 merely adjourned the Irish crisis, which resumed with enhanced ferocity in 1918. But it also postponed indefinitely the restructuring of British politics. In 1914 it appeared that if Liberal Britain were to survive, some drastic regional redistribution of political power was inevitable – a repetition of the situation in 1885. Then Gladstone had called into play the 'great moral issue' of Ireland and the centralised organisation of the Liberal Party to frustrate the radicals, but neither option was available in 1914: the issue would have to be tackled. Instead, the war broke out, Liberal Britain died, Ireland ultimately escaped. The cause of devolution had to find its place in an altogether new political order.

VII

Total war – or the problems of sustaining its impact and adjusting to its consequences – dominated British politics for fifty years. Where it did not totally replace old loyalties and institutions it readjusted them in unprecedented ways, both through the adoption of formal war aims which promised adequate recompense for the sacrifices which were being demanded, and through unsanctioned changes engendered by the intensity of the social involvement. Yet the effect of war, even when fought at the level of 1914–18 and 1939–45, was in the long run complex and catalytic rather than absolute and uniform. Nowhere more so than in the relations between Scotland and the United Kingdom. Two examples may suffice as illustration. Devolution was fairly close to becoming a reality in 1914; the war aims of the allies had, by 1918, come to sanction the general principle that autonomy should be granted to national groups; yet Scotland after the war was far more subject to southern control than she had been before it. In the Second World War, by contrast, centralised planning and control was legitimised as the apparatus of a welfare capitalism which would continue into peacetime, yet Scotland ended the war with an unprecedented degree of administrative devolution. Between the aggregate changes that total war unleashed and the development of Scottish politics existed a layer in which detailed political transactions were critically important. It was in this area that the activities of nationalists at last gained relevance.

The First World War effectively closed the option of devolution as a settlement for British political ills. Although a Speaker's Conference examined the problem in 1919, the secession of southern Ireland and the collapse of the Liberal Party fatally weakened the case for it. More fundamentally, the economic and political impact of total war greatly accelerated the assimilation of Scottish institutions, and enhanced the power of British agencies, while the economic upheavals it caused brought an end to the relative prosperity the nation had enjoyed in the British economy. As William Ferguson has written, 'in 1914 the Scottish economy was a reality, but by the 1920s the phrase, while still in use, could be taken to mean only a depressed sector of a none-too-robust British economy'.[29] In the space of six years after 1918 the five railway companies and most of the banks were taken over by English concerns, while a depressed international market afflicted manufacturing industry. Any nationalist movement, if it was to be at all relevant, had to offer solutions to this problem: to combine an interventionist economic and social programme with the traditional arguments for devolution. This the Scottish home rule movement failed to do.

The home rule movement had no power in itself, nor had it a predictable political environment in which to work. Although the subject was much ventilated during the war by many more or less influential Scots, like the Marxist John Maclean and the Jacobite Catholic Aristocrat Ruaraidh Erskine of Mar, there was little or no organisation. The Scottish Home Rule Association lapsed in 1914, along with the various Liberal Party pressure groups, and its revival in September 1918 came only two months before the general election, too late for a sustained propaganda effort. But it was also difficult to plan such a campaign in the unstable politics of post-war Scotland, where an agile electorate voted overwhelmingly for the predominantly Conservative coalition in 1918, swung left in 1922, further left in 1923, then back to the right in 1924. Although most candidates said they favoured home rule in some shape or form, they were never in the same place long enough to do anything about it.

The Labour Party, whose supplanting of the Liberals had been the major political change of the war period, exemplified the ambivalence of the new political order. Its Scottish Council, and the Scottish Trades Union Congress, had traditionally supported home rule, but recent developments, notably the expansion of the membership of non-Scottish trade unions and the growing Britain-wide confrontation between capital and labour, brought this into question and ultimately relegated it to the margin of their programmes.[30] The case of railway amalgamation in 1921–3 was critical. The government had initially proposed to set up a Scottish railway company, but was forced to alter its plans by opposition from Scottish railway shareholders and the trade unions, the first group fearing (with reason) that they would be made responsible for a hopelessly uneconomic system, the second nursing memories of vindictive behaviour by the old Scottish managements. For both, security appeared to lie in unity with the south. As other amalgamations in the textile, chemical and engineering industries showed, this logic was by no means unique.[31]

The home-rulers were not totally to blame for the failure to establish devolution on the party manifestos after the war. For if devolution was to mean collective control, as the railway issue implied, an adequate framework for executive government was necessary. Such a framework was almost totally lacking. Government departments and boards were still divided between Edinburgh and London, and were ill adapted to anything other than the supervision of local government and the traditional institutions, which were themselves badly in need of reform. Devolution before 1914 had made sense in a constitutional context; but no one had been greatly concerned about what a Scottish parliament would actually do. Now different questions, hingeing on social and economic reconstruction, were being posed, and no answer to them was forthcoming. These questions were to dominate the inter-war period: a challenge to nationalism which it rarely met.

VIII

The misfortunes of devolution were aggravated by changes within the nationalist movement itself. The first home rule bill moved by a Labour MP, in 1924, had been a moderate measure of semi-federalism similar to pre-war Liberal proposals. But by 1927, drafting of a bill had fallen into the hands of the enthusiasts of the Scottish Home Rule Association. The bill that emerged, to be briskly dismissed by the Commons in 1927 and 1928, demanded a similar status to that of the Irish Free State. The experience of Ireland and the emergent European nations had not passed unnoticed; neither had the revolutionary discontinuities in Russia and Italy. On the left, younger nationalists were deeply affected by these developments: James Connolly, the martyr of the Dublin Easter Rising of 1916, had been born in Edinburgh and had played an active part in Scottish socialist politics; John MacLean, the pedagogue of revolutionary Marxism in Glasgow, had been appointed Soviet consul in Scotland by Lenin himself. The memory of both – for MacLean died, worn out, shortly after he broke with the British Communists to found his own revolutionary party – was used by publicists like Erskine of Mar to fuse nationalism to the cause of revolutionary politics. The leader of the 'Scottish Renaissance', the poet and critic C. M. Grieve (Hugh MacDiarmid) in his important nationalist manifesto of 1927, *Albyn, or Scotland, and the Future*, went so far as to claim that the death of devolution – 'the last step in the assimilation of Scotland to England' – was an essential prelude to the triumph of real nationalism.[32] In his eyes the rise in the late 1920s of independent nationalist political organisation was less a consequence of the failure to pass home rule at Westminster than an alternative to home rule itself.

In the space of three years, between 1925 and 1927, Grieve produced, besides *Albyn*, 'A Drunk Man looks at the Thistle' and *Contemporary Scottish Studies*, in which the state of Scottish culture was subjected to a sustained and devastating analysis. His standpoint, however, was not that of a traditionalist, on the lookout for traducers of the national myths. He was, almost aggressively, a contemporary European, absorbed by the turmoil of artistic and political revolution, whose attack on Anglicisation stemmed from the conviction that England was provincial. Grieve had been reared in the exotic, cosmopolitan section of the left which centred on A. R. Orage's *New Age*, and he extolled, with little regard for ideological consistency, every force which made for action, be it communism, fascism, nationalism or social credit. He idealised contradiction – the Caledonian Antisyzygy as he christened it, borrowing this monstrous phrase from an academic study of Scots literature – and, in the circumstances, such an intellectual endorsement of inconsistency admirably paralleled the political ambiguities of the national movement he played such a large part in creating.[33]

On 23 June 1928 the National Party of Scotland was formally inaugurated at Stirling. Its creation marked the emergence of nationalism as an independent political movement, distinct from any British political party. In this it paralleled the founding in Wales, three years earlier, of Plaid Cymru. Both depended on the mobilisation of students and intellectuals; both stressed linguistic distinctiveness and the existence of a native tradition of decentralised democracy, currently under threat. But the similarities between the two movements should not be overestimated. The formation of the *Blaid* followed in the wake of a nationalist renaissance in Wales which had lasted for some sixty years and was now on the ebb. Its career was to be bedevilled by its association with forces, like the Welsh language, nonconformist radicalism and temperance, which had once been powerful but were now losing strength, while they still remained capable of frustrating any consensus in favour of home rule.[34] In Scotland the absence of an effective nationalist tradition was a source of strength as well as weakness. In the eyes of its younger and more radical supporters, the new political movement could be seen as a catalyst, from whose actions unprecedented and unpredictable cultural consequences were possible. As MacDiarmid wrote:

O Scotland is
The barren fig
Up, carles, up,
And round it jig!
A miracle's
Oor only chance.
Up, carles, up
And let us dance!

The National Party was a fusion of the sectaries of traditional nationalism, a few Catholic intellectuals, students, journalists, and discontented members of the Independent Labour Party, like Grieve. Its first Chairman and its Secretary, Roland Muirhead and John MacCormick, were likewise refugees from the ILP, which during the 1920s had managed to combine the disparate (and ultimately mutually exclusive) functions of being a nursery of unorthodox radicalism and a training-school for Labour organisers. The ILP legacy – Muirhead's loyalty and cash and MacCormick's organisational ability – was to be crucial in keeping a potentially fissile party together, but it could not resolve the contradictions between political nationalism and the Scottish context.

The recurrent weakness of political nationalism involved an aspect of the situation nationalists persistently complained about: the emigration of talent from Scotland. Even between the wars they could never field anything more than the reserve team of Scottish politics. The forces of assimilation were still powerful enough to ensure that the politically competent – men like Sir Robert Horne and Walter Elliot on the right, Sir Archibald Sinclair in the Liberal Party, and James Maxton and Thomas Johnston on the left – became preoccupied with Westminster politics. This was inevitable, as there was no structure of Scottish politics to which they could relate. Without this the organisational ability and political consistency which individual nationalists showed could easily slip into opportunism on the one hand and eccentricity on the other.

These inadequacies characterised the two men who dominated the pre-war National Party, John MacCormick and Roland Muirhead. Nationalism, still a tender growth, directly reflected their personalities, and both men suffered from isolation from the main political arena. MacCormick, a gifted student politician at Glasgow University, would otherwise have gone into Labour politics, if their focus had not shifted south in the 1920s. He sensed the vacuum and through a series of ably organised publicity coups established nationalism as an alternative focus. Without a parliamentary presence, however, he was incapable of sustaining these initiatives. Instead, he attempted to ally with traditional representatives of Scottish politics, and was branded as an opportunist. Muirhead, on the other hand, was a wealthy tanner of militantly left-wing sympathies, whose memories went back to the formation of Keir Hardie's Scottish Labour Party. A man of simple political faith – in socialism of a rather anarchistic type, pacifism and colonial liberation – he supported with an open purse anyone whose aims tended in these directions, without any serious inquiry as to their effectiveness. In contrast to MacCormick, Muirhead propagated a rather indisciplined radicalism. The coexistence of the two kept the Scottish National Party together in the 1930s, but it also ensured that its achievements were, to say the least, limited.

Ideologically, the National Party was in a position of almost unique awkwardness. During the First World War nationalism took on a new meaning: liberation from imperialism. In Scotland, Muirhead, a veteran of the anti-imperialist cause, welcomed the equation of Scotland with the exploited colonies, but the notion of home rule as a step towards imperial federation still remained persuasive among traditionalists who wanted the restoration of the pre-war balance. Given Scotland's imperial involvement, this course was plausible, but the enthusiasm of the young, and the profits of the Gryfe Tannery, had still to be tapped. The National Party had to contend with its own antisyzygy. The same problem affected its domestic policy. Should it provide collectivist remedies for the economic ills of the country, or should it appeal to the insecurity of the traditional Scottish establishment, worried about the drain of authority to the south? When in the 1930s its leaders opted for the latter course, even sympathetic observers like the poet and critic Edwin Muir found it difficult to forgive them. In the face of the misery of the depression, their politics seemed irrelevant compared with the drastic remedies of the socialists:[35]

> Even if the country were governed by Scotsmen, the economic conflicts within it could still generate the same intestine hatreds as they do now, and would still deserve to do so.

Yet the options before the National Party were limited. The Scottish electorate was conservative, and a move to the left would alienate many potential supporters, particularly former adherents of the Liberal Party. It would also involve a competition – which the Nationalists could never hope to win – with the trade-union-backed Labour and Independent Labour Parties. They, and the Liberals, could still play the home rule card if challenged. The National Party would end up simply as the weakest section of the Scottish left. This was demonstrated by poor results in the 1929 general election, when the party polled less than 5 per cent in two seats. Even in the Glasgow constituency of St Rollox, whose staple industry, locomotive building, had been severely hit by contraction and the transfer of work south, it only managed to poll 15 per cent. After the débâcle of the second Labour government, and the ideological bankruptcy of the left that that revealed, Scottish Conservatism reasserted itself to an extent which made any leftward move by the National Party suicidal. In the 1931 election Labour representation was reduced from 37 to 7 MPs, four of whom shortly seceded with the ILP. The only possibility of success seemed to lie with the cultivation of a traditionalist consensus.

Traditionalists were certainly perturbed enough for such an appeal to succeed – within limits. Besides business amalgamations, much of the Scottish civil service had been put directly under government control and centralised in London, local government had been rationalised, and Church politics had been quieted by the re-union of the Kirk and the Free Church in 1929. The overwhelming victory of the National government in 1931 seemed to demonstrate that assimilation was out of control. The response came from the heartland of the Scots bourgeoisie, the Unionist association in the Glasgow constituency of Cathcart. A solicitor, Kevan MacDowall, led a revolt in favour of a mixture of imperial federation and home rule, 'the Milner programme of the pre-war years with a dash of Lord Beaverbrook added'.[36] (Beaverbrook had just started the *Scottish Daily Express* and supported home rule – for what that was worth, as his support for any cause usually meant the kiss of death.) The rebels were joined by Andrew Dewar Gibb, Regius Professor of Scots Law at Glasgow University and former Unionist candidate for Hamilton, who drew up an appeal to the Duke of Montrose, a convert to Liberalism who was known to look sympathetically on home rule, and Sir Alexander MacEwen, a prominent Highland Liberal. The result was the formation of the Scottish Party.

MacCormick had advised the organisers of the Scottish Party on policy and lost no time in coming to an agreement with them, even at the cost of a split within the National Party and the expulsion of MacDiarmid. In 1934 the two parties merged, with a programme which accentuated home rule and underplayed independence – although it never discarded it completely. The Scottish National Party performed creditably at the 1935 general election, contesting eight seats and polling an average of 16 per cent, and in 1938 MacCormick negotiated a pact with the Scottish Liberals which would give the party a straight run in twelve constituencies of its own choice. Against this, however, the move to a consensus position lost it many activists. From a membership peak of over 10,000 in 1934 it declined to below 2,000 by the outbreak of war in 1939.[37] Respectable and centrist, MacCormick's policy went far towards making nationalism an alternative polarity to socialism in planning Scotland's future. Few of the numerous economic, amenity and social service organisations which were set up in the 1930s by 'middle opinion' in Scotland – like the National Trust for Scotland (1931), the Saltire Society (1936), and the Scottish Council for Social Service (1939) – lacked contact with the nationalist consensus. But it left the activists and the ideologues isolated.

IX

In 1937 the Gilmour Committee recommended the transfer of the Scottish government departments to an Edinburgh headquarters. Although the obsession that 'the bomber will always get through' was probably as influential as political nationalism in securing this devolution, nationalism of a rather conservative sort had certainly played its part. In 1939, St Andrew's House – a formidable building resembling a Central European railway station – was opened as the Scottish Whitehall. Dr James Kellas has seen this as the critical transition which 'accelerated the movement towards political separatism',[38] but in fact it gave Edinburgh only what Dublin had been left with in 1801. St Andrew's House rapidly assumed the persona of Dublin Castle, the impersonal medium of alien government. More significantly, however, the Scottish administration remained concerned with its traditional fields: agriculture and fisheries, law and order, health and education. Devolution had come at the end of a period when economic stagnation coincided with political conservatism, and progressives were envisaging a great expansion in the sphere of government. Would such responsibilities as economic and physical planning also be conceded, or would their centralisation in the south effectively negate Scottish devolution?

The invasion of Poland in September 1939 killed the Scottish National Party's plan for an all-party Scottish Convention to discuss home rule. The Second World War itself ought logically to have been fatal for nationalism *tout court*. In Britain the centralisation of decision making was drastic and sustained; in Europe small nations fell like ninepins. Scottish nationalists, in the early years of the war, reacted to their situation with appropriate gloom. Yet by 1945 they had played a prominent part in wartime politics, and the devolution of executive authority had managed to keep pace with the expansion of government activity. No single group played a critical role. The context of wartime politics was more important than the actors, and its disappearance exposed their relative immaturity. But the line had been held: a combination of political agitation, non-political nationalism and executive determination had at last brought nationalism to terms with the reality of collectivism.

The strength of political nationalism was remarkable, considering the eccentric behaviour of the Scottish National Party. With its dwindling membership, it was scarcely in a position of organisational strength before the outbreak of war. MacCormick had staked all his options on achieving an entente with the parties of the left, a policy which the appointment of Thomas Johnston, Labour MP for West Stirlingshire, as Secretary of State in February 1941 seemed to endorse. But, within sight of success, MacCormick was challenged by the Party's remaining fundamentalists. In 1937 they had managed to pledge the Party to oppose conscription, save when carried out by a Scottish government. When the war came this commitment was put to the test by the chairman of the Aberdeen branch, Douglas Young. Educated at public school (Merchiston Castle) and Oxford, poet, socialist and lecturer in Greek at the university, Young was a picturesque and charming eccentric in the tradition of Erskine of Mar. Privately, he had come to the conclusion that the allies would lose the war and that the Scots should prepare to conclude a separate peace:[39]

> The Germans will look around for aborigines to run Scotland, and it is to be wished that the eventual administration consist of people who have in the past shown themselves to care for the interests of Scotland.

However treasonable those views were, Young was actually charged with refusing to register either for military service or as a conscientious objector, on the grounds that the conscription by the United Kingdom government of a Scottish subject was a violation of the Act of Union. In 1940 and 1941, through a protracted legal battle, Young began to attain the status of a martyr.

If MacCormick exploited the possibility of gaining home rule through wartime consensus politics, Young attracted the support of those who believed themselves penalised by the arbitrary acts of wartime government. Memories of a disproportionately high Scottish death-rate in the First World War were revived; the conscription of Scottish women to work in midlands munitions factories seemed to add insult to the injury of the inter-war depression. Both sides of the dialectic surfaced at the SNP annual conference in June 1942, when MacCormick proposed that the party cease to contest elections and concentrate instead on cultivating an all-party commitment to home rule at the end of the war. He was defeated and angrily withdrew from the conference to found his own movement, Scottish Union, later Scottish Convention. Its time was to come, but not yet.

The splitting of one small movement into two could not be expected to enhance the nationalist cause, yet it did. In February 1944 Young nearly won Kirkcaldy Burghs; the following April the Party's secretary, Dr Robert McIntyre, won Motherwell. With the exception of one election, North Midlothian in early 1943, the main English third force, Common Wealth, made no significant impact north of the border. Criticism of the way the war was being run was seen as nationalist criticism, which the Scottish Secretary, Thomas Johnston, shrewdly orchestrated to gain increased freedom of action.

After the war the Home Secretary, Herbert Morrison, recorded his admiration of the way Johnston used the nationalist threat in cabinet committee to extort from the government what was, in the circumstances, a remarkably advanced social programme.[40] Yet the nationalists were not simply a useful component of his political repertoire. Johnston had for long been associated with the home rule cause, and his programme differed little from what MacCormick had been trying to achieve in the years before the war. In many ways Johnston remains an enigma. He left few personal papers and only a slight volume of reminiscences. Yet by fusing nationalist convictions to administrative acumen and political opportunity, Johnston created for the first time, in Scotland, the institutions on which bourgeois nationalists could build.

The factors which made up Johnston's political background were those which led Scottish radicals of earlier generations – and most of his own contemporaries – to quit the country. He was born into a lower middle-class family at Kirkintilloch, just outside Glasgow, in 1881. While at Glasgow University he became a member of the Independent Labour Party and the Fabian Society then, in 1905, inherited a small printing firm and in a series of pioneering, if partisan, histories, *Our Scots Noble*

Families (1909) and *A History of the Working Classes in Scotland* (1922), he began to reinterpret the myth-laden Scottish past. Aided by various veterans of the old Scottish Labour Party and west of Scotland radicals, he founded *Forward* in 1906 and made it the leading periodical of the ILP. Much more influential than the Marxist dialectics of John MacLean, *Forward* preached the pacifistic, humanitarian radicalism which the Clydeside MPs took south in 1922. Yet Johnston did not follow them in their disillusion with the parliamentary process, nor did he break his links with Scottish home rule and local government politics. As a junior member of the minority Labour government of 1929–31 and a director of the Empire Marketing Board, he shifted towards the political centre. While the ILP walked into the political wilderness he made close contact with 'middle opinion' groups which sought social reconstruction through bipartisan policies of physical planning and economic growth. As a sponsor of the Saltire Society and a leader of self-government pressure groups within the Labour Party, he gave such developments a specifically Scottish context.

Churchill gave Johnston his chance in February 1941. Johnston was able to name his terms and got what amounted to a promise of *de facto* home rule for the duration of the war. He was to have a Scottish Council of State, consisting of all the ex-Secretaries of State, who would vet legislation proposed for Scotland. If it received their approval, it was to go through Parliament without delay. The Scottish Grand Committee of MPs was to meet, experimentally, in Edinburgh. A Scottish Council on Industry was to be set up to involve businessmen, bankers, trade unionists and local government leaders in planning industrial development – virtually taking over the role of the Board of Trade in Scotland. The prospect was one which suited the convenience of Westminster as well as of the Scottish administration. Parliament did not have to absorb itself with Scottish legislation; the need for frequent communication with the south was obviated. Not all of Johnston's proposals worked.

The Scottish MPs – most of them still Tories – showed little interest in meeting in Edinburgh and after a couple of attempts the meetings lapsed, being effectively replaced by the activities of the Scottish Council. But the commitment to act on the wishes of Scottish opinion, where that opinion was manifest, was adhered to by the Westminster government. During the war Johnston was able to get sanction for the North of Scotland Hydro-Electric Board, for the transfer of planning powers to the Scottish Office, for the extension of agricultural intervention and forestry development, for the imaginative management of health and welfare schemes. 'We had got Scotland's wishes and opinions respected and listened to', he wrote later, 'as they had not been respected or listened to since the Union.'[41]

Johnston left office and Parliament in 1945. His achievement was ambiguous. Home rule was not gained after the war, though a Labour majority in Scotland during the war might have brought it close. Despite his own formal commitment to it, Johnston himself probably contributed to its deferment. Always a 'doer' rather than a 'talker', his absorption in boards, committees and *ad hoc* authorities as instruments of government meant, effectively, that he preferred the consensus that such bodies could achieve to the divisiveness of elected assemblies. The Jacobin who had assaulted 'Our Noble Families' became something of a territorial magnate himself, as chairman of the Hydro Board and the Scottish Forestry Commission. Rather than fight for further devolution in Attlee's Cabinet he preferred to consolidate the institutions he had set up.

In the short run Johnston's success in devising *ad hoc* authorities for Scottish government was to legitimise such bodies as alternatives to legislative devolution. If the quarter-century after 1940 was the age of enlightened, apolitical, 'Butskellite' administration, then he had at least assured that such executive authority was not concentrated in Whitehall, but was at least shadowed in Scotland. In 1940–1, according to Paul Addison, 'middle opinion' took power in England;[42] Johnston ensured that a specifically Scottish 'middle opinion' – his colleagues on the Saltire Society, the Scottish Council for Social Service, and the various Labour self-government groups – gained influence during the war years.

In the long run a much more drastic shift had been achieved. The concentration of authority in the hands of the Secretary of State was now such that the preoccupations of Scottish politicians were increasingly contained within the country. The age of the carpet-bagger was nearly at an end, although this might be reflected only in the mediocrity – if *native* mediocrity – of Scottish MPs.[43] After almost two hundred and fifty years, during which the central concerns of economic life had eluded nationalist politics, the traditional components of European nationalism were at last beginning to be perceptible in Scotland. As the country, its industrial base still as lopsided as ever, lurched into the post-war world, its future was, as never before, linked to the performance of its devolved executive government.

Chapter 2

An Achieving Society: Unionist Scotland, 1707-1945

Scotland is unique among European nations in its failure to develop a nationalist sentiment strong enough to be a vital factor in its affairs – a failure inconsistent alike with our traditional love of country and reputation for practicality. The reason probably lies in the fact that no comprehensive-enough agency has emerged; and the common-sense of our people has rejected one-sided expedients incapable of addressing the organic complexity of our national life. For it must be recognised that the absence of Scottish nationalism is, paradoxically enough, a form of Scottish self-determination.[1]

C. M. Grieve, *Albyn, or Scotland and the Future*, 1927

I

Out of step with nationalist movements elsewhere in the world, Scottish nationalism was judged by their criteria and found negligible. Yet a sense of 'Scottishness' still persisted, preserving the rudiments of a political nationalist movement. Traditional nationalists rarely appreciate the nuances of this. In their Manichean world a national community ought to face continual threats from external enemies and internal traitors, and, as this was not the case in Scotland after 1707, they have been as unforthcoming about it as their Anglicising opponents. With reason. Nationalist history has to idealise the State as moral community. It cannot digest a nationality, which, even if apparent, is part of a complex and less morally commendable political situation. It does not wish to be reminded that post-Union Scotland experienced industrialisation and imperialism in markedly different ways from England, if what emerges is ethically less presentable. The conviction that, in Professor H. J. Paton's words, 'the passion for liberty runs right through Scottish literature and political thinking'[2] is comforting, however far from the truth. The rise of nationalist support may prove that such myths are important, but myths they remain. A diet consisting of them can be dangerous, as Yeats regretted when an Irish nationalism which exalted feeling over fact plunged his country into civil war in 1922–3:

> We had fed the heart on fantasies,
> The heart's grown brutal with the fare;
> More substance in our enmities
> Than in our love; O honey-bees,
> Come build in the empty house of the stare.

Ireland's diet was enforced by continuous resentment at the Union of 1801 and the denial of home rule after 1886. But in Scotland, for most of the two and a half centuries after 1707, the myth of a stolen parliament merely masked the fact that the Union functioned with the consent, co-operation and enthusiasm of the Scottish people. The problem is to discover the terms on which this consent was given, a task not made any easier by the competing myth – fashionable until very recently – of 'assimilationist history' which, marching in step with the growing authority of Whitehall, has assumed that within a United Kingdom dominated by a sovereign parliament, Scottish affairs are merely minor variations on British themes.

The two myths are complementary. The assumption of political homogeneity which has underlain post-war British politics – and the resulting political insensitivity – has reinforced Scottish nationalism and such historical traditions as its supporters choose to remember. In order to find concepts which fit the facts of Anglo-Scottish politics since the Union, we have to retreat to a period when confidence in central government was less wholehearted: to the assault on the sovereign state – 'a kind of modern Baal to which the citizen must bow a heedless knee'[3] – in the years before, during and after the First World War. 'Pluralist' political thinkers, who wished to substitute a range of near-autonomous authorities for the state, drew attention to the 'semi-independence' Scottish institutions had enjoyed since the Union, precisely at the time when the last vestiges of that unique status were being destroyed by the centralising impulse of the war.

Given his involvement with groups like the Guild Socialists which advocated the reconstruction of society on pluralist lines, it is not surprising that MacDiarmid, in *Albyn*, considered that the Scots – or at least the ruling groups in Scottish society – had secured their own national settlement *within* the Union. In this he echoed Harold Laski who, in *Studies in the Problems of Sovereignty* (Yale, 1917), had discovered, on the part of the presbyterians who had in 1843 withdrawn from the Kirk to found the Free Church, a recognition of the Union as purely a contractual agreement:[4]

> They were fighting a State which had taken over bodily the principles and ideals of the medieval theocracy. They urged the essential federalism of society, the impossibility of confining sovereignty to any one of its constituent parts.

Arch-unionists and ideologues of parliamentary sovereignty that they were, even A. V. Dicey and R. S. Rait, in their *Thoughts on the Union*, stressed the way in which the Act of 1707 had, through constitutional conventions, been interpreted in such a way as to preserve Scottish nationalism. A distinctive legal, educational and religious system had remained remarkably free from southern interference, and this had, in its turn, affected the elements in Scottish society which benefited from the opportunities provided by the Union.

The fact that such studies were the work of English scholars, or scholars trained in England, emphasised a deficiency in Scottish consciousness which even Grieve was unfitted to remedy. Laski found that the nation which in the eighteenth century had produced Burnet, Hume and Robertson did not even possess by 1916 an adequate history of the central event of nineteenth-century Scottish history, the Disruption of 1843. The weakness in other aspects of history – economic, political and intellectual – was even more profound. On the continent historians were the pedagogues of the new nations. In Scotland their absence both contributed to the poverty of political nationalism and stemmed directly from the nature of the 'Scottishness' which the Union guaranteed.

Post-Union Scotland was pervaded by a cultural dialectic which gradually gave its society a character of baffling complexity. At one pole were the formal national institutions – a civil society which was geographically and recognisably Scottish. At the other was the shared experience of industrial and imperial development. The outcome was, however, not a 'British' experience. In contrast to the stability of the 'Scottish' pole, it was protean; after about a century of the Union it ceased to be geographically centred in Scotland, and could no longer be comprehended within the terms of national historiography. The dynamic part of the dialectic had overwhelmed the traditional institutions, without destroying them. Before about 1830 a powerful Scottish literary-historical tradition could treat of a society which was both lived-in and 'improving'; after 1830 a weakening tradition had to deal with a 'provincial' Scotland, or something which wasn't Scotland at all.

The main historical phases of Unionist Scotland were governed by intellectual perceptions of the state of Scottish society. Between 1707 and 1830 – the age of 'semi-independence' – these were reasonably precise. Likewise after about 1920, when economic reversal and the literary revival introduced, for the first time, the categories of orthodox nationalism. The problem is the near-century during which industrialisation and liberalism, unassisted by any adequate historical interpretation, let alone a nationalist one, created the social structure and the functional politics of modern Scotland. But of all three periods it could be said that, for a complex and variable range of reasons, Unionist Scotland remained as distant from assimilation as it did from nationalism.

II

Professor K. W. Deutsch, the American sociologist, has defined nation-states as 'diffuse, particularistic and ascriptive'. *Diffuse* means that their key institutions are not specialised but generally competent; *particularistic* means that only their citizens are entitled to use them; and *ascriptive* 'says that because you are who you are, you will be presumed to have certain qualities'. Such a national society[5]

> offers few choices to the individual, but it also imposes few burdens. The member does not have to worry about how to choose his course; most things and relationships are more or less given.

Its opposite is a society in which institutions are functional, with open access and universal validity, and status is determined by achievement.

It is difficult to recognise post-Union Scotland in either scenario. The compromises of Unionism complicate matters for a start, but even the specifically Scottish context is scarcely more straightforward. Because of the lack of parliament the nation was not omnicompetent, yet the distinctive institutions which survived claimed to exercise authority beyond their specific functions. The Union theoretically created a common citizenship, yet the Scots continued to enjoy privileges in Scotland denied to the English. The Union enhanced aristocratic control of politics, yet accelerated the social mobility of the ambitious and talented from the lower classes. It created a society in which nationalist and universalist elements were uniquely combined.

Its later supporters argued that this balance had been anticipated in the measure itself. They credited the politicians of 1707 with a prescience that that 'parcel of rogues in a nation' would scarcely have claimed for themselves. Burns's jibe is fair enough. The motives of the men who ended Scotland's parliamentary independence were for the most part as short-term and selfish as later nationalists were to claim. Even Daniel Defoe, who had worked hard to promote the Union, was appalled at the outcome:[6]

> The great men are posting to London for places and honours, every man full of his own merit and afraid of everyone near him: I never saw so much trick, sham, pride, jealousy and cutting of friends' throats as there is among the noblemen.

Principle played little part in the forging of the Union, and would have played even less in its repeal, which was nearly carried in the Westminster parliament six years later. The incorporation of the Scottish parliament involved a drama of Byzantine manoeuvre acted out by the great territorial magnates of Scotland, the Dukes of Argyll, Hamilton, Atholl and Queensberry, and the leaders of the English parties, anxious to secure their northern flank and the protestant succession against the French and the Stuart pretender. Political parties in Scotland, if they can be dignified with the name, were tools of aristocratic intrigue, or responses to it. The traditional institutions, Kirk, law, burghs, were treated at best as clients, or at worst had their representations altogether ignored.

Yet, although short-term calculation prevailed, most responsible Scots believed that some form of lasting union was inevitable. Even Lord Belhaven, whose 'Vision' speech – 'I think I see our ancient mother Caledonia, like Caesar, sitting in the midst of our senate . . . attending the final blow' – was the only memorable oratorical performance of the whole affair, and has frequently been quoted by nationalists ever since, mourned the dire straits into which the country had plunged. Against the opulence of England, he admitted:[7]

> We are an obscure, poor people, though formerly of better account, removed to a remote corner of the world, without name and without alliances, our ports mean and precarious so that I profess I do not think any one port of the kingdom worth the bringing after.

The experience of the 1690s bore witness to this. Four bad harvests brought the last and possibly the worst famine in the country's history. Her one attempt through the Company of Scotland at colonisation in Central America perished in 1699 in the swamps of Darien. In Europe the terms of trade were shifting against traditional Scottish activities. The ideal of austere independence had few takers; aristocrat and merchant alike looked south, the first attracted by political power and patronage, the second by an expanding English market and the possibility of liquidating his Darien losses. 'The motives will be, Trade with most, Hanover with some, ease and security with others,[8] wrote the Earl of Roxburghe in 1705. He and his party, the Squadrone Volante, had opposed earlier Union negotiations. Foreseeing English determination and Scots acquiescence, he now switched sides and worked to expedite the business. His reward was a Dukedom.

This mixture of opportunism and fatalism was predictable. Before 1688 the King managed the Scots parliament through the 'Committee of the Articles'. This not only maintained royal authority but minimised conflict with Westminster, although it aggravated internal strife in Scotland. Thereafter, freed from this constraint, the two legislatures became locked in conflict. The aristocratic rulers of both countries had to find a substitute for royal authority as arbiter between the two parliaments, and in this conflict the weaker legislature could not hope to win.

For the groups which wielded power in Scotland, there were worse alternatives than an incorporating Union. Presbyterians and Whigs could never regard independence offered by the Stuarts as anything other than a poisoned chalice, while aristocrats could remind themselves that failure to come to terms could, in the event of rebellion or civil war, lead to an English-imposed settlement infinitely more drastic than anything considered by the commissioners of 1706. Elderly Scotsmen could still recall the nine years during which they had been ruled – on the whole efficiently and equitably – by eight commissioners 'of the parliament of England for ordering and managing the affairs of Scotland'.[9] Cromwell's officers had felt no inhibitions about interfering with Scots religion and Scots law, enforcing toleration and breaking the authority of ministers and lairds. Mixing social revolution and assimilation, one of them, the Welsh regicide Colonel John Jones, wrote:[10]

> It is the interest of the Commonwealth of England to break the interest of the great men in Scotland, and to settle the interest of the common people upon a different foot from that of their lords and masters. . . . The great men will never be faithful to you so long as you propound freedom to the people and relief against their tyranny.

Given a few more years of their rule, the power of traditional institutions might have been overthrown completely, and the movement towards total assimilation become irresistible. There remained the option of federalism, popular among the mass of the people and forcefully advocated in Parliament by Fletcher of Saltoun. Popular sanction, however, did not count among the interests which disposed of power in Scotland; if the Union settlement recognised the rights of Church, law and nobility, these had no wish to share them with a legislature.

III

The Union won few friends in its early days. Even if the Scots regarded the Treaty as fundamental, it was not, of course, immune from the activities of a sovereign parliament. The abolition of the Scottish Privy Council in 1708, the assimilation of the law on treason to that of England in 1709, the re-establishment of ecclesiastical patronage in 1712: all were seen as instances of English perfidy and arrogance. In fact the first and third were the result of intrigues by Scots politicians: the Squadrone wanted the Privy Council suppressed before it could become a platform for Jacobite agitation; the Jacobites, headed by Lockhart of Carnwath, a fierce opponent of the Union, used a Tory victory to re-establish patronage as a stepping-stone to the return of episcopacy. The change in the treason law was an understandable over-reaction to the Jacobite menace. Party contests caused these breaches in the Union settlement; they could also have overthrown it completely. What endured was aristocratic involvement in United Kingdom politics and presbyterian hostility to the Stuarts. Matters might have been different had the pretenders been diplomatic enough to conciliate Scots religious sentiments. But had they been diplomats they would not have been pretenders in the first place. Until 1715 the margin may have been narrow, but it was decisive: Hanover and the Kirk was a better option than Stuart and the parliament. After 1715 the Union was strengthened by the evolving capacities of a new system of government. Political management, Kirk, law and education became the cornerstones of Scottish 'semi-independence', the structure within which there developed the economic and social forces which were ultimately to overwhelm it.

'Semi-independence' was pivoted on a political system which differed from that of England not in degree but in principle. Even though English parliamentary constituencies were far from symmetrical, the ideal of representation was cherished, and in some places was a reality. But if in 1831 one Englishman in thirty could vote, the equivalent figure for Scotland was one in six hundred. Scarcely three thousand 'county freeholders' voted for the thirty county Members; the fifteen burgh Members were elected by town councils, a self-selecting oligarchy. With a total smaller than many English borough or county electorates, the Scottish Members of Parliament represented no one but their paymaster, usually the confidant of the government who managed Scottish affairs.

But the Scots electoral system had never claimed to be representative. The Scots MPs were there to be bought, and, in return for this amenability, the 'Scotch manager' would see that government demands were squared with Scottish interests and that patronage was appropriately distributed. In Scotland the manager presided over an informal, but complex and subtle, system of institutional consultation. Before the Union was a score or so years old, Scots legislation was being discussed in Edinburgh between the manager, the Scots law officers, the Faculty of Advocates, the Convention of Royal Burghs, the county freeholders, and the Church. When agreed, such legislation could be carried at Westminster and enforced in Scotland.[11]

'Semi-independence' depended on an institutional federalism which was essentially pluralistic. Although Westminster was theoretically sovereign, the failure of its attempts to enforce its will persuaded it to acquiesce in Scottish autonomy. Law had to be enforced, and enforcement had to be devolved to Edinburgh, even if the result was that the Scots to a great extent legislated for themselves. This spirit even survived the decline of 'semi-independence' after 1830: the Scots seemed to make up their own public health legislation later in the nineteenth century, applying their own variations to United Kingdom enactments.[12]

This flexibility helps to explain the paradox of Scotland in the 'age of improvement': the co-existence of intellectual and social vitality and apparent political servility. By Deutsch's definition the 'diffuse' nation-state was moribund where it wasn't corrupt, and local government was little better. But these did not retard the rest of the political system, as they played little part in it. Instead a range of institutions which were both 'Scottish' and functional created a healthy and unobtrusive politics and encouraged a scale of values, in social and intellectual life, which extended beyond the nation. These were the vertebrae of an achieving society.

The practical politics of eighteenth-century Scotland revolved round the law and the Kirk, two institutions which mediated between authority and the potential anarchy of popular feeling in a way the formal electoral system was incapable of doing. A preoccupation with the affairs of the parliament between 1688 and 1707 has tended to draw attention from the way in which its competitors were consolidating their doctrines and power, almost in anticipation of its extinction. The theory of Scots Law, with its roots in Roman Law and its distinctiveness from English Common Law, was made explicit by Viscount Stair in his *Institutions of the Law of Scotland*, published in 1681; the autonomy of the Faculty of Advocates was recognised after energetic internal politics among Scots lawyers in the 1670s and 1680s. Law was to provide the skills for management as well as, in the Faculty, a forum for the discussion of legislation. As the eighteenth century wore on, legal families like the Forbeses, Dundases and Erskines took over from the aristocrats as the directors of Scottish politics. The hegemony of the lawyers survived reform in the 1830s. Until the creation of the Secretaryship in 1885 the Lord Advocate, the head of the Scottish legal profession, remained the chief government agent in the north.

Stair advocated a limited monarchy. He wrote in 1660:[13]

> I have been persuaded that it was both against the interest and duty of kings to use arbitrary government; that both kings and subjects had their title and rights by law, and that an equal balance of prerogative and liberty was necessary for the happiness of a commonwealth.

This balance was reflected in the eighteenth-century partnership between Westminster, Scottish institutions and Scottish society which the manager had to keep in being by continual adjustments. Sir Walter Scott dramatised the process in *The Heart of Midlothian* (1818), that brilliant documentary of politics and society in the early years of the Union, which centres on the Porteous Riot of 1736. Porteous, the captain of Edinburgh's town guard, was sentenced to death for ordering his men to fire on a crowd at a smuggler's execution. His reprieve by royal prerogative was regarded as an infringement of Scottish liberties, and in the course of a well-organised uprising he was taken from the Tolbooth and hanged. Parliament enacted severe penalties for Edinburgh, but these were mitigated after intervention by the Duke of Argyll, whose brother, the Earl of Islay, was the Scottish manager. The reality was far less symmetrical, and Argyll's policy was far from consistent, although his power was such that his defection cost Walpole his prime-ministership in 1742. Scott, the high Tory, realised that Scottish identity depended on a sort of contract, in which the informal pressures of mob violence and patronage played as active a role as that of the great institutions of state.

The politics of 'semi-independence' were patrician – concerned with consultation and control. They became popular only when the mob intervened, and the problem was to ensure that such interventions never gained an independent momentum. A similar course of action was necessary in religion, where authority had likewise to coexist with a popular claim, only this time a more articulate and persistent one. The Kirk, under the rule of the Moderates – ministers who were liberal in theology and philosophy, but prudently conservative in politics – exercised a major role in Scottish government. Its parishes controlled education and poor relief; its ministers and laymen debated politics as well as religion at the annual General Assembly in Edinburgh. Yet its articulation with landed power and enlightened philosophy was secured to it by a breach of presbyterian principle: the restoration of patronage in 1712. In *The Wealth of Nations* Adam Smith, a Moderate and deist, commended the non-hierarchical organisation of presbyterianism as giving its clergy 'more influence over the minds of the common people than perhaps the clergy of any other established church[14] but he also upheld patronage as a security against fundamentalist zealots; Whig rationalism applauded the offspring of a Jacobite intrigue. Yet this betrayal of the Covenant was to agitate the religious establishment for over a century until, in 1843, it split it down the middle.

Religious politics and divisions were quite different from the south. English dissent dated from the time of the Commonwealth, and meant a clean break with state-sponsored religion. After the Restoration, and the exclusion of nonconformists from government, the ideal of the self-governing congregation holding to its own variety of religious belief became, in time, linked with the encouragement of manufacture and entrepreneurship, notably in the cases of the Unitarians and the Congregationalists. In Wales the impact of nonconformity, later but even more dramatic, underlay the democratic nationalism of the latter years of the nineteenth century. In all these cases, the road from religion to politics was indirect. Sects decided for themselves whether they would ignore the Establishment, try to get concessions from it, or attack its very existence, and their political affiliations resulted from these decisions. But in Scotland religious disputes centred on the directly political point of who controlled the Establishment, on whose legitimacy all but a tiny minority were agreed. The various secessionist groups did not retreat into their own private theologies. Each was convinced that it was the true legatee of the Covenanters of 1639.

The values of English dissent, transferred from politics to commerce, posited new goals and provided networks of family connections. In Scotland this relationship was inverted: the tranquillity that Adam Smith commended existed because dissenters did *not* withdraw from politics. They abused the Establishment but they never challenged the principle. Yet the world of the Calvinist Zealot Davie Deans, in *The Heart of Midlothian*, peopled with worthies who had been martyred for their fidelity to the Covenant, was as valid to him as the songs of the patriot dead are to the IRA gunman: a surrogate politics which fulfilled the excluded while leaving the security of the settlement intact. Brawling over Church patronage was a major source of disorder in the eighteenth century, but the discontent was never more than symbolic and left the modernisation of society, eagerly encouraged by the Kirk, unchecked. The Reverend Micah Balwhidder, the worldly Moderate minister of Dalmailing in John Galt's *Annals of the Parish*, is 'intruded' on his charge in 1760, to the accompaniment of a riot. When he quits it fifty years later, after having played no small part in its evolution into an industrial town, the dissenters turn up to his final service, out of respect.

IV

Both managed politics and Moderate religion had latent weaknesses which later developments were to aggravate to breaking point, but they provided security for the economic growth of

Lowland Scotland. After 1746 they were unchallenged: the last assertion of the alternative politics – independence, a French alliance, a Catholic or Episcopalian church – perished at Culloden. Although Webster's census in 1750 found that about 30 per cent of the population still lived beyond the Highland line, the relationships which bound Highland society together rapidly disintegrated. The judicial powers of the chiefs were abolished, the missionary activities of the Kirk were increased. Where Highland society prospered – and kelp burning (which produced agricultural fertiliser), cattle raising and herring fishing helped sustain a growing population for another century – it did so through Lowland finance and a Lowland market. But more often its surplus population, accumulating on sub-divided crofts and feeding itself on potatoes (which increased the nutritive yield of the land by 300 per cent, compared with oats), simply supplied the new industrial areas with the manpower they required.

In the course of his magnificently wrong-headed analysis of 'the Celtic fringe in British national development', the American sociologist Michael Hechter has discovered a process of 'internal colonisation' in which:[15]

> The movement of peripheral labour is determined largely by forces exogeneous to the periphery. . . . Economic dependence is reinforced through juridical, political and military measures. There is a relative lack of services, lower standard of living, and higher level of frustration . . . (and) national discrimination on the basis of language, religion, or other cultural forms.

Something like this certainly happened in the highlands after 1746, but the internal colonisers were Scots. More Scots had fought for Cumberland than for Charles Edward; more Scots than English soldiers thereafter wasted the glens; it was Scots landlords and factors, not Englishmen, who forced the Highlanders on to the emigrant ships. It was not until much later that the Highlanders could look south for pity, and their bards could only commemorate them, with dignity and rare beauty, in the last flowering of a dying tongue. The Canadian Boat Song of 1829 had both:

> When the bold kindred, in time long vanished,
> Conquered the soil and fortified the keep,
> No seer foretold the children might be banished
> That a degenerate lord might boast his sheep.

But the bitterness and eloquence were those of an Irishman, Tom Moore.[16]

The lairds and bailies of the Lowlands who had done their best to ignore Charles Edward, were, even at that date, preoccupied with the economy, and once it really started to expand, in the 1780s, political union was rapidly transformed into economic integration. The industrial revolution, until 1914 the greatest discontinuity Britain experienced, seemed to create a common history for England and Scotland, separating them from Ireland and their continental neighbours. But how much was this identity due to the common institutions created by the Union?

Economic historians have generally stressed this, and have treated the Scottish experience, by extrapolating from British statistics of economic growth, as a marginal variation, qualitatively different in certain aspects but broadly similar in its overall tendencies. Since accurate figures for production and employment only became available when integration had been achieved, this is understandable, but a profession increasingly preoccupied with quantification may have neglected the other routes that the Scottish economy could follow to attain this end. On the other hand, the undoubted success of economic integration meant that the nationalists steered clear of it, limiting themselves to a few condemnations of its social shortcomings. But the assumption that Scotland was pulled along by innovations and market forces generated in England may be rather too facile. Given the problems her society had to contend with, and the distinctive nature of the Scottish governing elite, was it not possible that the expansion of her economy, and the benefits and evils that followed from it, had a history similar to that of the semi-independent state, and owed much to the institutions and relationships which it promoted?

Before 1830 the manufacturing sections of both Scottish and English economies were dominated by textiles; thereafter Scottish distinctiveness was treated as an aspect of regional product specialisation. Yet there were significant differences, even in the ultimate integration. Scotland sustained, throughout her industrialisation, a far higher rate of emigration than England. Had natural increase taken its course, as by and large it did in the south, the Scottish population in 1900 would have been 6 million instead of 4·5; partly as a result of this, she did not build up a market for the increasingly consumer-oriented industry of the early twentieth century; although average wages were comparable, per capita income fell as the wealthy moved south; and the physical state, accommodation and health of her working classes was significantly poorer than in England. Further, Scottish economic development was relatively lacking in continuity. The economy lurched from crisis to crisis, from one industry to another. Linen and the banks were in trouble in the late 1760s, the American trade collapsed in 1776, the cotton industry stagnated after 1815. To the inevitable instabilities of the international economy the Scots added variations of their own.

It would be easy to see this as an aspect of internal colonisation – English entrepreneurs building up marginal capacity which could be discarded in times of recession – but this would be misleading. Although there was a tradition of English enterprise in Scotland, at each crisis it was the Scots who seized on new options and took the initiative: cotton in the 1780s, iron in the 1820s, ships in the 1860s, steel in the 1880s. This adaptability was only possible within a society which commended it as a social and educational goal, and provided the sort of economic infrastructure which made it possible.

One hypothesis about the ingredients of industrial progress may be relevant to the Scottish context. The French economic historian Francois Crouzet has attributed the structural changes which underlay the British industrial revolution in the eighteenth century to difficulties in attaining economic growth which were present in Britain but not in France.[17] These difficulties stimulated the research and innovation which was neglected by the French entrepreneurs, who lived off the relative bounty of a country which had enjoyed for most of the century an equivalent growth-rate. If Crouzet's generalisation works for Britain as a whole then it is even more appropriate when applied to Scotland, where per capita income as late as 1867 was much lower than south of the border – £23 10s. compared with £32 – an indication that supplies of capital and the home market would be correspondingly restricted.[18] The road to integration was therefore likely to be a matter more of conscious planning than of the arbitrary operation of market forces.

Because it culminated in *The Wealth of Nations* (1776) the economic philosophy of the Scottish enlightenment is often assumed to have epitomised the ideals of individualism and free competition, and the distrust of collective intervention, which Adam Smith expounded. Yet the organisation of the Scottish economy in the eighteenth century seems rather to have emphasised the governing principle of Smith's moral philosophy, the importance of 'sympathy' – the capacity of men for altruistic conduct and for promoting the general good. The institutions of Scottish economic life represented not so much the triumph of individualism as the determination of public bodies to promote it. Smith was certainly aware of this: he admitted that Scotland was backward compared with England, yet attributed her discernible advance to distinctive factors like the absence of party politics and a court, which checked strife and luxury; the flexibility of poor relief, which meant that labour was mobile; and the system of public education, which gave a docile and adaptable work-force. The sort of road-mending and school-building government he envisaged was a 'local or provincial administration' not at all dissimilar to the one he lived under.[19]

In eighteenth-century England industrial development proceeded despite government, or at best through its abstention from involvement. Even the merchant and banking society of London was only marginally interested in economic growth. In Scotland, by contrast, much influence was wielded by organisations which were corporate rather than competitive, which depended on close links with the Scottish administration and distinctive Scottish institutions. Despite its failure, the Company of Scotland had provided a precedent for this sort of venture, proof that economic advance was a conscious concern of the Scottish governing elite. This concern subsequently expressed itself in statutory bodies like the Board of Trustees for Manufactures and Fisheries, set up in 1727, which played a vital role in expanding the linen industry, in government funding of roads, harbours and waterways, in the administration of forfeited Jacobite estates in the Highlands, and in the encouragement of the fishing industry through bounties. Whether or not these measures were successful in their immediate objectives – and admitting that the real take-off came after the establishment of southern technology in the textile industry in the 1780s – they concentrated public attention on problems of national development and the acquisition of appropriate technology and trained manpower.

The efforts of government were supplemented by numerous voluntary bodies, some ephemeral, some long-lived, of which the Society for Propagating Christian Knowledge in Scotland (1708), the spearhead of the attack on Gaelic culture, was as important in its way as the Society for Improving the Knowledge of Agriculture (1723–45); and by joint-stock bodies concerned to provide the infrastructure for enterprise, like the banks, insurance companies and canal companies. The frontiers between these and government were fluid, and their efforts also overlapped with those of individual lawyers, academics, merchants and landowners, always eager to offer instruction to their contemporaries through pamphlets and patronage. Even the entail, the hereditary mortgage on an estate, which south of the border was usually seen as a fund for aristocratic high living, became in Scotland the means towards investment whose benefits might only be realised by future generations. 'Be ay sticking in a tree; it will be growing, Jock, when ye're sleeping.' Scott's Laird of Dumbiedykes may have been uncouth, but his advice typified the attitude of the men who, over a century, transformed the Scottish landscape.

Industrialisation, in fact, had its roots in the land. Between 1745 and 1845 Scottish lairds pursued a conscious strategy of creating new villages – some 150 in all – which would provide hand-work or even factory industrial employment for a rising population while also allowing agricultural modernisation. In other words, the early stages of economic growth were a 'controlled' process of what has been called 'proto-industrialisation' in which the productivity of society was increased while traditional, social relationships remained. Hence the popularity of Robert Owen's super-paternalist New Lanark. So absolute was the control of the lairds that even the serfs of Russia – who could at least elect their head-man – seem to have had more freedom than the countrymen of Burns. And it was not until six years after his death that Scotland lost its own hereditary serfs, the colliers, bound to their masters by an Act of the old Scottish parliament.[20]

Investment in the future was not limited to land. When Thomas Telford was at work on his great programme of Highland road, canal and harbour building in the 1800s he wrote that he regarded it 'in the light of a working academy from which eight hundred men have annually gone forth improved workmen'.[21] The idea of education as a suture which bound industry to the traditional Scottish institutions was shared by academics, and bore fruit both in the application of theory to industrial problems and in the movement for educational extension. The collaboration between Joseph Black and James Watt at Glasgow provided a precedent for a connection which, in later years when the intellectual pre-eminence of the country had passed, was to be a continuing strength of the Scottish universities. The bequest of their friend and contemporary John Anderson was to give Glasgow one of Europe's first and most successful technical colleges. Scottish secondary and higher education may not always have reached its own high claims, but it was, in terms of public access, much superior to the system south of the border. A Royal Commission on secondary education reported in 1868 that one Scot in every 140 was attending a secondary school, and one in every 1,000 a university; the equivalent proportions in England were 1 in 1300 and 1 in 5,800.[22] The subjects taught were, moreover, more relevant to the needs of a changing society. Lyon Playfair, scientific adviser to several Victorian governments and a member of an important Scots academic dynasty, observed in 1889:[23]

> The old English universities have not the same function as the Scottish and Irish universities. The former teach men how to spend a thousand a year with dignity and intelligence, while the latter aim at showing men how to make a thousand a year under the same conditions.

Men trained through universities, technical colleges and apprenticeships sustained Scottish industrialisation through its numerous crises. During a long tenure of the chair of natura philosophy at Glasgow Lord Kelvin proved, not for the last time, that it was possible to combine the roles of academic and industrial magnate. Anderson's foundation, later to become the

Royal Technical College and finally Strathclyde University, employed George Birkbeck, the founder of mechanics' institutes, and Andrew Ure, one of the most famous, or notorious, apologists for the industrial revolution, and produced, besides several generations of engineers and metallurgists, James Beaumont Neilson, 'the Arkwright of the iron industry', David Livingstone, and Lyon Playfair himself. But industry itself remained the great 'working academy' in which the mass of skilled workmen, and many future managers and engineers, received their training. As well as the universities and colleges, the works which, in the early nineteenth century, supplied the mines and cotton mills, produced the pioneers of the marine engineering and locomotive building industries.

Watt's condensing steam engine had been pioneered in Scotland, but could only be developed where capital and a market existed, in the west Midlands. The steamship, on the other hand, was a native achievement. Scots engineers like the Napier brothers dominated the paddle-steamer era when the narrow seas and the mail routes were conquered, and it was the Clyde again, in the 1850s and 1860s, which made the technical breakthroughs – the compound engine and the surface condenser – that enabled the long-distance freight steamer to oust the sailing ship. Initially the growth of the Lanarkshire iron industry aided this. The town chamberlain of Greenock commented in 1852 that:[24]

> Our superiority in producing engines has hitherto been the cause of these potentates preferring the work of our artisans to that of any others. But, now that iron is superseding timber and becoming the principal component, not of the engine only, but also of the hull, our power to excel is vastly increased.

By the 1880s, however, matters were the other way around. The survival of the Scottish iron industry, and its conversion to steel production, depended on the market provided by the heavy industries of the Clyde, where shipbuilding had been joined by locomotive building and structural engineering. Resources and markets were now finite: the economy had evolved in such a way that it had created a dictatorship as rigid as that of the Tory managers in Scottish politics at the beginning of the century.

William Cobbett anathematised 'improved' Scotland, as he rode through it in the 1830s. The great farms of the Lothians were 'factories for making corn and meat chiefly by means of horses and machinery'.[25] Their workers were housed in barrack-like rows of steadings or, if unmarried, in the squalor of shared bothies. The agricultural villages had the harsh symmetry of little industrial towns. Cobbett was never a man for the measured judgement, but he had recognised the other face of the Scots enlightenment. A society dedicated to extending equality of opportunity and easing recruitment into the elite was unlikely to be merciful to those who could not, or would not, take advantage of the opportunities it provided. The elite creamed off the potential leaders of the working class, and imposed its will on those that they might have led. In eighteenth-century Scotland there was, as Professor T. C. Smout has observed, no tradition of popular, secular, radical literature like that provided by Wilkes, Cartwright, Spence and Cobbett. The only possible candidates, Burns and James Mackintosh, were as famous for their politic recantations.[26] Reform agitation there was, but it was largely controlled by Whigs, by English or French missionaries, or even fomented by *agents provocateurs*. Edward Thompson has written that 'it is possible, at least until the 1820s, to regard the English and Scottish experiences as distinct'[27] but what made them so was not the presence in the north of a national issue and the pressure of organised labour, but the weakness of both.

In 1841 a government report on distress among the hand-loom weavers commented on the situation of the poor in Glasgow:[28]

> A very extensive inspection of the lowest districts of other places, both here and on the continent, never presented anything half so bad, either in intensity of pestilence, physical and moral, or in extent proportioned to the population.

Even at the end of the century, after fifty years of energetic and expensive public health reform, over 60 per cent of the city's population was living in one- and two-roomed houses, overcrowding was five times worse than in England, and the urban death-rate very high. 'If the mid-Victorian years were a gloomy age in the social life of the English poor,' according to Eric Hobsbawm, 'they were a black one in Scotland.'[29] Throughout this period, however, Scottish working-class activity was mild, conciliatory, and on the whole acquiescent in a deal which was very raw indeed. Why?

The reasons are, again, distinctively Scottish. Political radicalism lacked even the slight degree of constitutional representation it had in English 'popular' constituencies like Westminster. Working-class leaders could be co-opted into the elite or bought by it, like the weavers' leader Alexander Richmond. Religion, now reinforced by the evangelical movement, still provided a powerful and satisfying form of surrogate politics. Where expectations were high, emigration was always a possibility; where life was already miserable, in a hovel on Skye or in Donegal, the city, slums and all, offered a way out. In Europe, even in Cobbett's England, nationalism, the memory of a *volkish* golden age, acted as a focus for the resentments of the new industrial population, a means of creating expectations of what the new social order ought to be. Both right and left could subsequently draw on it. In Scotland, on the other hand, industrialisation had been carried through with such swiftness and ruthlessness *because* of the distinctiveness of the state. The alliance between a resourceful middle class and a flexible aristocracy which had exploited to the full its unchallenged control over Kirk, law, education and poor relief was undeniably Scottish. As it began to run into trouble in the early years of the nineteenth century, both its opponents and those of its beneficiaries who wanted security for their gains could not look to a national ideal for relief. Instead they looked to the south.

V

In the half-century after 1789, 'semi-independent' Scotland destroyed itself. Economic tendencies were towards integration anyway, but the failure of Scottish politics to sustain the conventions it had built up since the Union steadily forced Scots of both parties to look to Westminster, first for support, ultimately for survival. The power of the Dundas family as managers, linked after 1789 with pervasive anti-Jacobin repression, led to a despotism conducted on behalf of the Tory Party. In the Kirk the Moderates recoiled from their liberal past and became apologists for the status quo, as deferential as the episcopalians of the seventeenth century. Public docility was enforced by the police spy and the state trial, and, more alarming to the professional middle class, by patronage and favour. As totalitarian regimes went, the 'Dundas despotism' was more clumsy than savage, and its increasing unpopularity stemmed more from its incompetence, shown up by smart young Whig lawyers in the Edinburgh courts, than from its viciousness. But politics had at last become polarised on lines similar to those in the south, and Scots Whigs and Tories realised that their struggle could only be resolved by backing their southern counterparts. While the Tories remained in power they preserved the old Scottish political system, though in poor repair. When the Whigs took over in 1832 they dismantled it, rapidly and without regret. Their leader in Scotland, Francis Jeffrey, former editor of the *Edinburgh Review* and now Lord Advocate, told the Commons: 'I glory in making the avowal that no shred or rag, no jot or tittle, of the old system will be left.'[30]

Jeffrey's lieutenant, Henry Cockburn, subsequently the historian of early nineteenth-century Scotland, enthusiastically concurred. 'The Reform Bill', he announced, 'is giving us a political constitution for the first time'. Indeed, the years from 1832 to 1835 saw a formal extension of political rights in Scotland far more drastic than the results of the French Revolution of 1830, which had sent a bemused Charles X to exile at Holyroodhouse. The French electorate had increased from 90,000 to 166,000; the Scottish electorate from about 4,500 to 65,000. In 1833 the Scottish Burgh Reform Act, which preceded the equivalent English measure by two years, vested the control of the towns in the £10 ratepayers. The millenium of the Whig intellectuals was ushered in.

Yet it was a flawed paradise. Jeffrey blundered badly in his drafting. His ignorance of Scots feudal law meant that he left loopholes that landowners could exploit to create – as they had done in the past – 'faggot votes'. This, and the coercion of tenants, was to continue for another half-century, accounting for much of the torpor of Scottish politics. It reflected the deracination of the Whigs, the extent to which their absorption in the political struggle had distanced them from the actual problems of Scottish government. 'It is strange', one of them observed, 'how little one knows of the real condition of the society about one till something leads one to examine it.[31] Henry Cockburn was more aware than the others of the opportunity which had been missed. He regarded a Scottish minister as an '*absolute necessity*', yet thought that the assimilationist tide was now too strong to turn back: 'Our associations and experience make us jealous of anything resembling provincial government.'[32]

It was under the eyes of a weak Scottish administration that the drama of the 'ten years' conflict' about who should control the Kirk was played out. It would be easy to think of the

Disruption as the religious equivalent of the political revolution, but this would be misleading. In 1832 middle-class and professional society consciously opted for assimilation. In 1843 it admitted that it had failed to secure, modernise and extend the influence of the most important *national* institution. The ultimate result was the same: the founding of the Free Church accelerated assimilation. But this had not been the intention of the men involved.

At issue was the same question of patronage which had obsessed Davie Deans and the eighteenth-century seceders, but it now appeared in a new context. Like the Church of England, the Kirk had been profoundly affected by the evangelical revival, which made a particularly strong appeal to the growing urban middle class, not least because it endorsed the virtues of thrift and self-sufficiency. Ironically, the lay patronage which Adam Smith had commended as encouraging liberal thought and market economics was to be attacked under the leadership of a divine whose belief in *laissez-faire* was total.

Thomas Chalmers was the most formidable Scottish churchman since Knox, sharing his gifts as a preacher, ideologist and politician. As a young minister he had almost fallen, like many Moderates, into the pit of deism, but in 1810 he experienced conversion and became probably the greatest evangelical orator of his age, capable of reducing someone as unpromising as George Canning to tears. In the course of seven years' ministry in central Glasgow, he set himself to bring the Kirk abreast of new developments in science and economics while restating its claims, as an established church, to superintend, in Cockburn's words, 'the whole Christian and civic economy of our population'.[33] The Kirk still controlled education and poor relief. He believed passionately that, even in the industrial towns, this control should remain and, in the case of poor relief, be tightened. In Glasgow he set out to prove that the Kirk could relieve poverty through its own collections, without the need for a poor state, and succeeded. In fact, what he claimed for the

Kirk was the status of a sovereign state. When, in 1834, the evangelicals at last ousted the Moderates from the control of the General Assembly, the stage seemed to be set for a revival of the theocratic nationalism of the reformation.

The language of the conflict which divided Scotland for the next decade seems so alien from our own day that it is difficult to appreciate the importance the participants placed on the issues at stake. Yet the evangelicals' contention that, despite the Patronage Act of 1712, a congregation had the right to veto a patron's nominee raised a national issue. Was the Kirk, as a corporation, in partnership with Parliament or subordinate to it?

By passing the Veto Act of 1834, the General Assembly insisted on the Kirk's autonomy. By upholding the right of a patron to appoint, the Court of Session and Parliament insisted on its subordination. Only Parliament could break the constraints imposed on the presbyteries, but the two parties were unwilling to move, the Whigs because anti-Catholic Scottish evangelicals had been campaigning against their conciliatory Irish policy, the Tories because of their class ties with the patrons, and their own interest in nominating to the 30 per cent of Scottish parishes where the patron was the government. The Tories came into office in 1841, and, with little representation in Scotland, their attitude to the Kirk was more robust than diplomatic. In 1841 a campaign by Professor W. P. Alison, the brother of a leading Scots Tory, Sheriff Archibald Alison, resulted in a Royal Commission being launched on Scottish poor relief, which lay at the heart of Chalmers's theocratic ideal. The following year the Kirk's 'Claim of Right' was brusquely dismissed, in the expectation that a hard line would force waverers back to the Moderate side. The evangelical remedy was desperate. At the General Assembly of 1843 over a third of the Kirk's ministers withdrew, processed to a neighbouring hall, and constituted themselves the Free Church of Scotland, under Chalmers's leadership. Within a year they took about 40 per cent of the Kirk's communicants with them mainly from the Highlands and the growing industrial towns.

In the short term the Disruption abated conflict between the Free Churchmen, who were still pledged to the principle of establishment, and the earlier secessionist bodies. Politically, it greatly enhanced the powers of the Liberal Party, especially in urban constituencies. Between 1832 and 1885 the Tories won only seven burgh contests. But it also meant that the process of assimilation was now out of control. However much compromised by patronage, the Kirk had overseen a substantial part of Scottish government. Now that it only represented a minority, its power and influence rapidly diminished, to be replaced by conflicts between the Kirk and its opponents which destroyed the possibility of any Scottish consensus and placed the initiative in legislation securely in the hands of Westminster politicians who, without any particular animus, simply did not *care* about Scottish affairs. English precedents were followed not out of conviction, but simply because there was no unified countervailing force.

In 1845, after the report of the Royal Commission, poor relief was transferred to ratepayer-elected parochial boards under a Board of Supervision in Edinburgh; in 1855 religious tests were abolished at the Scottish universities; in 1861 school inspection powers were transferred to the universities; and in 1872 elected school boards were set up in every parish, under the supervision of the Scotch Education Department, based in London. In 1874 a Tory government abolished patronage, but by that time the gesture was meaningless, as in 1887 the Free Church reversed its position and joined the secessionists in getting the Liberal Party to back disestablishment. The terms of religious politics had shifted from the context of the unique role of the Kirk in Scottish social and cultural life to a campaign similar to that of the dissenters in England, a campaign which gained in acrimony what it steadily lost in relevance.

Chalmers did not long survive the split in the Kirk and the

end of the old poor law. He died in 1847, leaving a thriving church but an altogether narrower religious ideal. His successor as chief spokesman for dissent in Scotland, the Liberal MP Duncan McLaren, did nothing to broaden it. A draper, provost of Edinburgh and brother-in-law of John Bright, McLaren represented sectarian individualism at its narrowest. His domination of Scottish Liberal politics began with the Anti-Corn Law League in the 1840s and for backsliding on this issue he had Macaulay ejected from his Edinburgh seat in 1847 'notwithstanding the charm of his oratory and his world-wide reputation as a man of letters'.[34] For a further thirty years the 'member for Scotland' imposed his definition of Liberalism as a narrow, rancorous pietism, devoid of imagination, personality or social sympathy. Scottish politicians, Dicey noted in 1867, were the delegates of the aristocracy and middle class. They did not ameliorate, merely reflected, the prejudices of their masters. When the standard of Liberal MPs rose, as it did after 1880, it was as a result of an influx of carpet-bagging Englishmen and Anglo-Scots, of whom Gladstone was the most famous. Despite the concessions Liberal governments made to Scottish nationalism, nationalism was not, as in Wales after 1868, reflected in the choice of candidates.

On top of the ending of the old governmental system and the collapse of the Kirk came the communications revolution of the 1840s. By 1848 central Scotland was connected to London by two main railways, and within a couple of years the tracks reached as far north as Aberdeen. At the time of the Union an overland journey to London could take a fortnight; road improvements had reduced this to forty-three hours by 1836, and a similar time could be achieved by steamer. But by rail this time was cut to seventeen hours, and by 1876 almost halved to nine. Almost as important, the electric telegraph arrived only months after the railway. Instantaneous communication now meant that government or private business in Scotland could frequently be conducted from London and, in an age of minimal government, the maintenance or expansion of regional agencies was deprecated. The technological basis of assimilation was now virtually complete. Moreover, the financing of these new utilities was largely the work of the London money market. Up to the early 1840s most cash for Scottish railways had come from Scotland (several lines had actually been built to a distinct 'Scotch Gauge' of 4 feet 6 inches) but those promoted during the Railway Mania drew on English capital and used (fortunately) the English standard gauge of 4 feet 8½ inches. Although in practice the character of the five separate Scottish railway companies which survived until 1923 was almost aggressively Scottish, and the long-suffering English shareholders usually deferred to their Scottish managers, this cash situation was always to inhibit rationalisation of an unsatisfactory system and ultimately, in the 1920s, prevent the formation of a unified Scottish railway authority.

Improvements in communication completed the creation of a new, and appropriately commercial kind of Scottishness. As well as cutting journey times, the railway reduced travelling costs by up to 80 per cent and enabled the scenery, sporting facilities and romantic historical associations of Scotland to be marketed to the middle classes of industrial Britain. Thomas Cook and David MacBrayne completed the work that Scott, Mendelssohn and George IV had begun. Hotels, hydropathic establishments, houses for summer letting and golf-links followed the railway and the steamer into the Highlands. In counties where eviction and emigration were decimating the landward population, towns like Inverness doubled in size between 1851 and 1891 while Oban on the west coast had a threefold increase. Tourism detracted from political nationalism in two ways: it enhanced the sentimental, tartan and Kailyard image that twentieth-century nationalists were to spend so much time denouncing; and by making Scottish holidays a part of British upper-class life it fostered the illusion that assimilation was a two-way process. Queen Victoria visited

Ireland only four times in her reign, but after 1848 spent the autumn of each year at Balmoral, dragging attendant politicians northwards with her. (Disraeli counted himself fortunate to escape with two visits.) Gladstone, who talked about the place practically without interruption for the last fifteen years of his life, visited Ireland only once but was in Scotland fairly regularly, even before Midlothian. In the early twentieth century government was virtually conducted each summer from the country houses of Balfour, Campbell-Bannerman and Asquith, from the grouse moors and salmon rivers of Relugas or Strathconan, or the links of St Andrews or North Berwick.

Eccentric and ephemeral though it was, the Scottish Rights Society of the 1850s was an understandable reaction to this headlong anglicisation. Even its opponents like Cockburn or *The Scotsman* acknowledged that Scottish affairs were ineptly handled at Westminster. Yet, however legitimate, it could never agitate from strength. Nationalism had been identified with Toryism before 1832. It had been defeated. It had been identified with the liberties of the Kirk before 1843. It had been defeated. In respectable society it had been weakened, right and left and it lacked the leadership and the ideology which could fuse it with popular demands. Terrified of the new working class, the Scottish Whigs had no O'Connell bold and generous-spirited enough to use nationalism to unite the classes that 'improvement' and industrialisation had separated. And in this vacuum the Chartist movement, which did produce prudent and energetic working-class leaders, remained, like earlier working-class movements, oriented towards a British reform. Lacking the political organisation to demand devolution, and the backing of a class which identified devolution with its own interests, even assimilationists realised that events had forced the Scottish cause from the scene. The irony was that this coincided with the adoption of radical nationalism by the confraternity of European liberal exiles. Mazzini may have misunderstood Irish nationalism; he was totally ignorant of Scottish nationalism.

Yet assimilation was never more than partial. Scots Law was still distinct, so there were always delays in applying British reforms to Scotland. Religious conflict continued, creating its own obsessive politics. Industrial development, flawed, perhaps, by the preoccupation of Scottish entrepreneurs with voluntary local government work and Westminster politics, added dangerous dependence on the heavy industries to bad living conditions and high emigration. Thus, even when integration was at its zenith, there was a good case for legislative devolution. A local parliament could have provided a forum where such problems could be articulated and rationalised, if not solved. It might have helped to mitigate the antipathies of the churches, and to make industry consider its long-term future. It might have pioneered social and regional planning – there were certainly enough problems and experts to hand. It might even have created the literary class that nineteenth-century Scotland lacked, just as Scandinavian nationalism patronised, and was savaged by, Kierkegaard, Ibsen, Brandes, Bjornson and Strindberg. At any rate, in hindsight, the cause of devolution appears too important to have been left to the clutch of eccentrics who were almost alone in consistently advocating it.

VI

> Offensiveness in the manner, or in the extent of the swamping ought to be blamed or checked, but it is vain, and though practicable would be absurd, to proclaim anything hurtful to the good interest of the Empire, merely because it is either Scotch, or Irish, or English.[35]

Henry Cockburn, dismissing the Scottish Rights agitation, admitted that nationalism had a rival, whose attractions effectively inhibited the discussion of the 'condition of Scotland question'. For opportunities were no longer constrained by the geography of Scotland: her partnership with the empire was reaching its zenith. To ask a middle-class Scotsman to immerse himself in Scottish affairs was like urging him to attend to his house and neglect his business. For the chairman of the Scottish National Party, Andrew Dewar Gibb, writing in the 1930s, Union and Empire were virtually synonymous:[36]

> The existence of the Empire has been the most important factor in deciding the relationship of Scotland and England in the last three centuries . . . a share in the trade of the nascent English Empire was offered to the Scottish Commissioners for the Union of the Parliaments. The bait was taken and the partnership began. For its beginning and for its duration the Empire is largely responsible.

But for every Scot like Gibb who might feel doubtful about the whole episode there were, by the time he wrote, four emigrants, or descendants of emigrants, in the empire and the United States – a nation of twenty millions, as Tom Johnston called it. And by and large, as those who met him admitted, the Wandering Scot had done well. 'He was in the habit of alluding to his Scotch connections,' says Marlow of the crooked financier de Barral in Joseph Conrad's *Chance*, 'but every great man has done that.' Sir Charles Dilke, in his apotheosis of British colonisation, *Greater Britain* (1868), was more explicit:[37]

> The Scotch are not more successful in Adelaide than everywhere in the known world. Half the most prominent among the statesmen of the Canadian Confederation, of Victoria, and of Queensland, are born Scots, and all the great merchants of India are of the same nation. Whether it be that the Scotch emigrants are for the most part men of better education than those of other nationalities, of whose citizens only the poorest and most ignorant are known to emigrate, or

> whether the Scotchman owes his uniform success in every climate to his perseverance or his shrewdness, the fact remains, that wherever abroad you come across a Scotchman, you usually find him prosperous and respected.
>
> The Scotch emigrant is a man who leaves Scotland because he wishes to rise faster and higher than he can at home, whereas the emigrant Irishman quits Galway or County Cork only because there is no longer food or shelter for him there. The Scotchman crosses the seas in calculating contentment; the Irishman in sorrow and despair.

Dilke may have exaggerated, but his picture was more accurate than that of the emigrant as homeless crofter, driven by factor and shepherd to the Canadian boat. The Scots who went abroad were mainly from the Lowlands, craftsmen with their certificates, clerks, weavers with their savings taken from the penny bank. They were concerned to get on, and they created an emigration ideology to justify their move.

> Mark you what the proverb says
> Of Scotsmen, rats and lice;
> The whole world over take your ways
> You'll find them still, I guess.[38]

The Wandering Scot, merchant, cleric, mercenary soldier or scholar, was already familiar in Europe when that scurrilous verse was written in fourteenth-century France. The Auld Alliance, the Church and the universities provided the men of a poor country with the prospect of success in the traditional professions of Christendom. If the Reformation curtailed this internationalism, the wars it provoked offered even greater prospects for warlike men from the north, whose compatriots were only too anxious to see them employed elsewhere. At one time or another during the seventeenth century there may have been as many as 100,000 Scotsmen in Europe, usually fighting. In addition, the Stuarts began the process of planting Ulster with Scots presbyterians. This Irish province, hitherto Gaelic-speaking and Catholic, had acted as a bridge between the troublesome Irish and the troublesome Highlanders. After 1609 the equally troublesome zealots of the Lowlands and Borders moved in, removing an endemic cause of friction between England and Scotland. By 1650 some 50,000 Scots had taken so enthusiastically to colonisation that government had to curb their expansion. During the next two centuries the Scots-Irish were to be equally adept at colonising the New World. By 1772 there were 150,000 of them in America, compared with only 50,000 from Scotland itself. It was the Scots-Irish, not the more recent immigrants from the mainland, who provided much of the manpower for the revolutionary armies in the war with Britain.[39]

Until the 1780s government and the landed classes were hostile to emigration from Scotland, but in the early nineteenth century government opinion changed. Population expansion and economic uncertainty made the Highland problem intractable; in the aftermath of war a restless new industrial population posed a constant threat to social stability; wages-fund economics and Malthusian theories of population asserted that only by reducing their numbers would working people improve their living standards. Emigration rapidly gained intellectual and imaginative sanction. The Earl of Selkirk, whose grasp of Scottish social development was commended by his friend Scott in *Waverley*, advocated and practised the systematic settlement of Canada, where many Scots 'Loyalists' had ended up after the American War of Independence. John Galt was similarly active as a government agent and publicist. Before long, Carlyle had elevated emigration into a philosophy of life, a new world where:[40]

> Canadian forests stand unfelled, boundless plains and prairies unbroken with the plough; and on the west and on the east green desert spaces never yet made white with corn:

> and to the overcrowded little western nook of Europe, our territorial planet, nine-tenths of it yet vacant or tenanted by nomads, is still crying – come and till me, come and reap me!

Between 1815 and 1905 some thirteen million emigrants left British ports. 8·2 million sailed for the United States, 2·1 million for Canada, 1·7 million for Australia and 0·7 million for New Zealand and South Africa. Records of country of origin were not kept until late in the century, so arriving at ratios of settlers from Scotland, England and Ireland involves some back-projection from early twentieth-century statistics. Using those in Gordon Donaldson's *The Scots Overseas* (1966) we find that, at a rough estimate, for every 10 Americans of Scots birth or descent, there were 30 of English and 50 of Irish birth or descent. The ratios for other settlement areas were:

	Scots	*English*	*Irish*
Canada	10	12	13
Australia	10	35	14
New Zealand	10	22	9
South Africa	10	30	5

Although, numerically, English and Irish emigrants predominated over the Scots, as the proportion of Scots to English in Britain was never greater than 1 : 7, the contribution of the Scots to overseas settlement was disproportionate everywhere, particularly so in the Empire, and almost equal to that of England in Canada.[41] The political and commercial success they enjoyed was thus based on numerical advantages: a calculation which would promote contentment, especially as the Scottish emigrants were as a whole of higher status than those from England and Ireland.*

Scotland was unique among European nations in combining

* G. R. Porter's *Progress of the Nation* (Murray, 1851) gives numbers for cabin and steerage emigrants from Britain in 1844 (pp. 130–1). The ratios work out at: England: cabin 1: steerage 11; Ireland 1:102; Scotland 1:6.

an emigration rate of about 4 per cent per decade with an industrial economy. In some ways her situation was closer to that of the seaboard industrialised regions of the new world, from which emigrants moved to a steadily advancing frontier. When Frederick Jackson Turner wrote in the 1890s of the values of American society being shaped on the frontier and then transmitted back to the east coast, his words had relevance also to the Scottish experience.[42] Eighteenth-century Scotland had been a frontier society. Its intellectuals and practical men, with their stress on 'improvement', had created the values and techniques appropriate to overseas settlement, and reserves of technical competence, skilled labour and professional (notably medical) training which could realise them. There was always a pull as well as a push: the promise of high pay, of support from friends and kindred already established. This owed something to the clan tradition and Highland habits of interdependence which had migrated to the Lowlands; it was enhanced by university and apprenticeship relations, Masonic membership, commercial partnerships and religious affiliations, many of which had been forged in the new industrial society. The 'emigration ideology' was never as powerful as the Turner thesis. It lacked the official sanction which made the latter virtually an article of faith in early twentieth-century America. But it altered the Scots' idea of what their country was or ought to be. It drew on and reinforced traditions which lessened their attachment to their native soil, some of which had a history almost as long as that of the nation.

Middle-class emigration and the maintenance of links with the mother country were common enough in the nineteenth century. Many European emigrants were talented professional men, frequently driven abroad by political persecution; the resentment of the Irish exiles was channelled into a political movement for resistance to British rule at home. But the Scots conformed to neither pattern. Instead they established themselves in several activities which provided two-way linkages with the home country, which had the result of inhibiting nationalism while restricting Anglicisation. The most important of these, in myth and reality, were government service, missions, trade and investment.

The government could draw on a tradition of Scottish militarism which conferred on the soldier a status he did not enjoy in England, where 'going for a soldier' implied a sort of social suicide. Kipling, for instance, who did so much to rehabilitate the downtrodden 'Tommy Atkins', rarely mentions a Scottish soldier, although he was partly Scots himself. The myth was different. The veterans who bragged to the young Alexander Somerville of the heroics of the Scottish regiments in the Napoleonic Wars were in line of descent from the old mercenaries who would have earlier have talked of Gustavus Adolphus and the battlefields of Germany. Most Scottish soldiers could write and count, and they put these gifts to good effect to create a martial literature which was a persuasive recruiting sergeant. 'It was the *writing*', wrote Somerville, 'quite as much as the *fighting* of the Scottish regiments that distinguished them.'[43] The raising of twenty-seven Highland regiments after the Forty-five brought the further glamour of claymore, pipes and kilt, and stories of settlement in the New World to set beside the booty of Frankfurt and Mainz.

Scots militarism may appear very close to that of the Croats and Cossacks on the continent – a primitive, peripheral society of fighting men supporting a conservative empire – which Marx saw as a menace to bourgeois nationalism.[44] In fact, it was all myth. The proportion of Scots in the Victorian army was never higher than 1 : 7 and steadily dropped until it was about 1 : 14. In half the Scots regiments officers and men were predominantly English or Irish.[45] But the myth was persuasive: militarism, if not military service, was real. When the Volunteers were founded by the government in 1859, Scotland's recruitment was twice the national average, and it was out of the Volunteer movement and the Free Church that the Boys' Brigade emerged in the

1880s, with its fusing of the military ideal and evangelical religion in what Hanham has called 'liberal militarism'[46] Such developments reflected a society which revelled in military prowess, usually from a safe distance. Over two centuries, from Quebec in 1759 to Aden in 1967, the Scottish infantry, 'the ladies from hell', personified the nation at its most aggressive. Each war produced its heroes: Moore at Corunna, Ensign Ewart at Waterloo, the 'Thin Red Line' of the 93rd Highlanders at Balaclava, Sir Colin Campbell in the Indian Mutiny, the 9th Highland Division at Loos, the 51st Highland Division in North Africa and Italy. And the reputation that usually lodged in bar-room memories was of Scottish bravery compensating for the incompetence or cowardice of Englishmen, usually English officers. In this way the common opportunities of the Empire were used to restate both a class and a national loyalty.

The success of Scots in imperial administration owed much to an equivalent combination of boldness, competence and a relative lack of caste, but its motive power was less inspirational – patronage. The Nabob, the Indian official who had done himself well, was a familiar feature of eighteenth-century Scots society. The East India Company in the aftermath of the Union had been anxious to mollify the Scots who were still smarting over the collapse of their own colonial venture. The old mercenary spirit adapted well to the rough-house of Clive's conquest of French India, although its less savoury side later emerged. The governorship of the Skye minister's son Sir John MacPherson was described in 1784 by his successor Cornwallis as 'a system of the dirtiest jobbery.'[47] It was to be Cornwallis's reforms, separating political from commercial control and Europeanising the services, that really opened India to the Scots, especially as the ruling power on the new Board of Control in London was none other than Henry Dundas. The twenty years of Dundas's reign meant that tranquillity in Scotland was assisted by transferring much of the country's talent to India, both to the army and to the administration. For almost a century British India was to be dominated by a disproportionate number of Scots administrators like Mountstuart Elphinstone, Sir John Malcolm, Jonathan Duncan and Lord Dalhousie. These men presided over the great epoch of utilitarian reform, in which the sub-continent was treated as a laboratory for financial, legal and educational experiment.[48] Through them, and through the direction of the London office of the Company after 1818 by James Mill, the disciple of Bentham and Dugald Stewart and historian of British India, this process became a practical demonstration of the social speculations of the Scots enlightenment.

Ironically, it was to be the full working-out of this policy, with the introduction of competitive competition for the new Indian Civil Service in 1852, that penalised the Scots. This gave advantages to the two old English universities, where examinations had been the arbiters of excellence since the beginning of the century, and reform was rapidly making progress. The attempts of the Scottish universities to produce suitable candidates were to lead to their steady approximation to the English norm.[49] Although many notable reputations were subsequently to be made in Indian administration, right up to 1947 (the great regret of Lord Reith was that he was never 'fully stretched' by being made Viceroy) the age of Scots domination had passed.

By the time the scramble for 'underdeveloped' territories got under way in the last three decades of the nineteenth century the colonial service reflected the ethos of English public school and university reform. But the Scots contribution to the more aggressive and racialistic ideology associated with Alfred Milner and the 'Kindergarten' was considerable. About half of Milner's close associates – John Buchan, Philip Kerr, Patrick Duncan, Starr Jameson, F. S. Oliver – were Scots, and their attitudes were moulded in part by the conservative re-interpretation of utilitarianism articulated by James Fitzjames Stephen and Henry Maine, also of Scots descent. But to read John Buchan's *Prester John* is to realise the moral and intellectual decline since James Mill wrote his *History of India.* Power had corrupted. Mill's dogmatism, the assumption that the Indians could only govern themselves if they became good utilitarians, has been replaced with a pervasive and vulgar racialism, in which the enemy is the educated native, the very man whom Mill strove to create.

Should Prester John really only be taken as fantasy, its Africa a science-fiction world whose inhabitants bore no relationship to reality? There might be truth in this. Kipling, politically a much nastier animal than Buchan, wrote sympathetically about real Indians whom he knew; Buchan wrote nastily about imaginary Africans but comes alive when he describes his settler David Craufurd 'getting on'. In doing this he was retailing, in a form then acceptable, the great Scottish myth of the nineteenth century.

Buchan, although he persuaded himself otherwise, celebrated the settler, with his indifference to the native population, not the trustee. Fittingly, he ended his career as Governor-General of Canada, whose very identity was the triumph of its nineteenth-century Scots settlers. The Dundee-born radical William Lyon Mackenzie in 1836 started the disturbances which brought about the report of Lord Durham's Commission and the concession of representative government; the Glasgow-born Conservative Sir John A. Macdonald accomplished the diplomacy which led to the founding of the federal Dominion in 1867. From then until his death in 1891 he dominated Canadian politics and carried through, with the aid of the Banffshire cousins John A. Smith and George Stephen, later Lords Strathcona and Mountstephen, the construction of the Canadian Pacific Railway, which gave the Dominion a physical unity. Given their numbers, the influence of the Scots was predictable enough, without having to look for national characteristics which would explain it – although one of Macdonald's Liberal opponents, the former Oxford professor Goldwin Smith, a notorious anti-Semite, got worried about the Hebraic appearance of the Highlanders.[50] But they could always call on a relatively homogenous community, focused on church and school, and capable of producing the degree of organisation and literacy that politics in a new country required. The same sort of situation obtained in Australia and New Zealand, which had by the end of the century produced a dozen or so Scots-born colonial premiers. The classes which had in Scotland been denied political authority, first by the aristocracy, then by the plutocracy, now had the chance of power. Alexander Mackenzie, a Perthshire stonemason, beat Macdonald to become prime minister of Canada in 1873 (the trouble was, Goldwin Smith observed, that he didn't stop being a stonemason); in 1884 Robert Stout, an Orkney teacher and freethinker, became prime minister of New Zealand; in 1908 in Australia Andrew Fisher, an Ayrshire miner, became the first Labour prime minister in the world.

For the Scots working man emigration was the road to freedom, the realisation of the libertarian impulses of Burns, himself a near-emigrant. Emigration led away from the rule of government, laird and kirk session, from the supervised poverty of the villages and the unsupervised squalor of the towns. It was in the settlements, not in Scotland, that the aggressive individualism of Burns's 'Jolly Beggars' was celebrated, for example by the Renfrewshire weaver John Barr, who went to New Zealand in the 1850s:[51]

Nae mair the laird comes for his rent,
  When I hae nocht to pay, sirs.
Nae mair he'll tak me aff the loom,
Wi hanging lip and pooches toom,
To touch my hat, and boo to him,
  The like was never kent, sirs.

At my door-cheeks there's bread and cheese,
I work or no', just as I please,
I'm fairly settled at my ease,
  And that's the way o't noo, sirs.

The Maoris who were, in the same colony, ruthlessly dispossessed by Sir Donald McLean, the Tiree tacksman's son who ran the Land Purchase Department, could reflect ruefully on the consequences of the belief that 'courts for cowards were erected'. In other colonies other native groups and less astute settlers suffered similarly. 'Ten times Scotch are the highlanders,' wrote an anguished prospector from the Australian diggings in 1839. 'Poor as rats at home they are as rapacious as rats abroad.'[52]

Settler patriotism was as ambiguous as settler liberty. Wherever the Scots went in any numbers they were quick to establish a cultural presence. They set up Caledonian Societies and Burns Clubs and held Highland Gatherings, in many cases anticipating the foundation of such institutions in Scotland. They also sent back to Scotland a lively if rather eccentric succession of nationalist agitators, from the Australians T. D. Wanliss and Theodore Napier to the New Zealander Sidney Goodsir Smith and the South African Wendy Wood. Yet, despite the number of emigrants, their support of the nationalist cause was rarely significant. They tended to produce either a bizarre nostalgia, like the Jacobitism which continued to flourish in Australia and America until the end of the nineteenth century, or else a straightforward radicalism which had little time for the traditions which native nationalists were trying to conserve. Andrew Carnegie, as ambivalent a practitioner of 'triumphant democracy' as can be found, brusquely rejected an appeal to subscribe to a monument to Robert the Bruce: 'A King is an insult to every other man in the land.'[53] The settler was as patriotic as it suited him to be. He could integrate with his adopted country at whatever level his talents could carry him to, and thereafter he adopted its social mores and class distinctions. The National Party of Scotland found out the hard way in the 1930s that the streets of Detroit and Toronto were not paved with emigrant gold. Arthur Donaldson, later Chairman of the Scottish National Party, attempting to raise funds for the party, wrote back, disillusioned, to Roland Muirhead:[54]

> Trade has been bad here and still is. It has hit our people hard because so many of them are wage-earners and many of them were not provident during their prosperity. The Scots who do have money are either of the second generation or else have been here for very long periods and they are not interested in our movement – will not be, I am afraid, until it becomes internationally interesting. . . . I have come to the conclusion that we should not appeal further for members in the United States and the Dominions.

If the 'nation of twenty millions' was a myth, it was an important one. It preserved, within the imperial experience, a degree of cultural continuity that ultimately survived it. At one level it endorsed the Union, which had made such colonisation possible; at another it called the Union into question: if the Scots could govern colonies, why couldn't they govern Scotland? Between the wars these reactions were joined, not altogether consistently, by the view that without the Union emigration might not have been necessary anyway. Few questioned the ethics of colonisation. Scotsmen who swelled in pride at Dilke's commendation of their achievements rarely disputed his assumption that they, as a superior race, were bound in time to extinguish the 'lower races' whose land they occupied. Yet paradoxically, when in the second half of the nineteenth century colonisation was joined by the scramble for 'underdeveloped' territory, a new and even more potent myth emerged which sanctioned the Scots' role in that – the myth of the missionary. Even today, for every Scots schoolchild who knows who Sir John MacDonald was, ten know about Mary Slessor – the Dundee mill-girl who became a missionary in Calabar – and a hundred about David Livingstone.

Missionary activity reached a peak between 1874 and 1914

when no Scots congregation could fail to be aware of the hundreds of clergymen and evangelists sustained by the three main Scottish Churches throughout the world. Yet the reality was more complex. The Church of Scotland's main mission at Blantyre in the Shire highlands of Nyasaland had a long struggle to survive against indifference at home and much the same was true of the Free Church Missions.[55]

Missions in fact came late to the Kirk, and gained their greatest successes when working in close collaboration with imperial government. It was not until 1829, nearly forty years after the first foreign mission societies had been formed in England, that the Church of Scotland sent its first missionary, Alexander Duff, to India. When the idea had been mooted in 1796, it had not commended itself to the Moderate majority, who drew parallels between missionaries and Jacobin agitators. One supporter of the majority remarked that[56]

> to spread abroad the knowledge of the Gospel among barbarous and heathen nations seems highly preposterous, in so far as it anticipates, it even reverses, the law of nature.

The law of nature, which, in the estimation of Lord Monboddo, a Moderate judge with anthropological leanings, placed the negro close to the orang-utang, won out over the word of God. When Scots missionaries went abroad, they went, like Robert Moffat and his future son-in-law David Livingstone, as agents of the London Missionary Society. The decision to commence activity on the part of the Church was the work of Chalmers and the Evangelicals, but it was far from being an emotional response. Duff's intentions in India were for a comprehensive plan of educational extension for the Indian upper classes, undertaken in collaboration with government.[57] Macaulay's Minute on Education in 1835, which prescribed the reconstruction of Indian education on Western lines, suited the purposes of the Scots missionaries exactly, and the Church's colleges became a recognised part of the government system. Despite a setback in 1843, when the missionaries to a man left the Kirk for the Free Church, the momentum was not lost.

The Free Church had missionaries but no missions; the Kirk missions but no missionaries. In some ways the financial problems of both stemmed from this enforced doubling of effort, as the Kirk, through a lay association, set out to recover the ground it had lost. The Free Church was imperially conscious, and joined Edward Gibbon Wakefield in promoting planned colonisation in Otago in New Zealand in 1848. Leaving his Indian educational colleges to the Kirk, Duff established new ones under Free Church auspices, and the Free Church also expanded black education in Southern Africa through patronage of the Lovedale seminary established by the Glasgow Missionary Society in 1824. With the contribution of medical missions, in which the university of Edinburgh took a leading role, missionary activity was largely a broadening of the 'stream of social education'. But the personality that was stamped on it after the middle of the nineteenth century was that of Livingstone, and the combination of exploration and evangelicalism that he represented. As a dissenter, Livingstone stood on the fringes of Scottish religious life, and it was the congregationalist London Missionary Society and the Anglican Universities' Mission which involved themselves most in his explorations. But his memory provided the impulse which established the Central African Missions of the two Churches in the 1870s, and involved them directly in the scramble for Africa.

The Free Church established its mission station at Livingstonia on Lake Nyasa in 1874, followed by the Kirk's Blantyre in 1876. Several hundred Scots settlers followed, and shortly found themselves in conflict with the slavers and the Portuguese whom Livingstone had fought. Following the settlers came the African Lakes Trading Corporation, largely promoted in Scotland, which turned the conflict into a small but persistent war which lasted from 1885 to 1896. It was almost like a replay of Darien, with the difference that imperial support, in the shape of Cecil Rhodes, Frederick Lugard and Harry Johnston, was thrown behind the Scots, and success ultimately guaranteed.[58] For the next eighty years Nyasaland was effectively a sort of Scots colony, whose internal affairs remained, at successive General Assemblies, a concern of Scottish politics until the mid-1960s.

Almost in antithesis of the settler ideology, the missionaries favoured, and attempted to protect and co-operate with, the native population. Attitudes could vary from the respect and equality with which Livingstone treated his African allies to the insensitive condescension rather more frequently associated with the concept of trusteeship. But the Livingstone tradition helped counter the latter: no working-class missionary coming from a Lanarkshire mill village – or, for that matter, from the Highlands – could have many illusions about the superiority of European society. The fight against slavery and disease counterbalanced the insensitivity of 'banjo Christianity' and enabled the Scots to exploit the moral and material advantages of their relative lack of involvement in the slave trade and their excellent facilities for medical education. Fundamentalism, however, had its part to play. Missionary activity owed a great deal to the coincidence of Livingstone's death in 1873 and the great Scottish revival conducted by the American evangelists Dwight L. Moody and Ira D. Sankey between 1873 and 1875, in which a leading role was taken by a young Scots scientist, Henry Drummond, who subsequently became a fervent promoter of missions, settlement and colonial trade, and the sort of domestic welfare policies which would facilitate them. Drummond's equation of industrial and scientific advance with world-wide evangelism provided a popular ideology for the Liberal Imperialism which, advocated by politicians like Rosebery and R. B. Haldane (whose grandfather had pioneered Scottish foreign missions), became politically significant in late nineteenth-century Scotland.

Running in harness with imperial involvement, moral or otherwise, was trade. As the Earl of Roxburghe had observed in 1705, trade was one of the main Scots motives for Union. The traditional commerce with France and north Europe was declining; legal and illegal trading with England and her possessions increasing; yet the Darien disaster showed the impossibility of a small and weak nation trying to compete with the great European powers. The prospect of being lifted to prosperity on the backs of the English appealed. Success was not instantaneous, and when it came it owed something to good fortune. The seas west of Scotland were out of range of French privateers; the winds blew fair from Chesapeake to Clyde, and back again. A ship could make two voyages a year from Port Glasgow against one from the Thames. By 1770 Glasgow was rivalling Liverpool and Bristol as an entrepôt for American and West Indian goods, and was handling more than half the tobacco imported to Britain. Through the leaders of its commerce, the 'tobacco barons', Defoe's 'beautifullest little city' attempted to rival what Adam Smith considered the ceremonious vices of its scruffy gothic neighbour. But such men created commercially resilient institutions in the joint-stock banks, and along with the Board of Manufactures they stimulated the linen industry. A new trade and new manufacture – cotton – found a commercial environment ready to receive it when, after the American War of Independence, the tobacco trade collapsed.[59]

Scots traders looked across the Atlantic because they could scarcely look elsewhere. Apart from coastal traffic and the 'triangle' trade to West Africa and the Americas, the East India Company dominated external trade. The leading role that the Scots took in its administration was, in part, due to their official exclusion as independent traders from the half of the world that it controlled. Nevertheless, on the Atlantic trade the Scots perfected the combination of effective agencies, technological alertness, and commercial flexibility, allied to a shrewd realisation of the value of collaborating with government, that they were subsequently to apply elsewhere. The end of hostilities with France in 1815 might have meant a shift of trade to the south, but it resulted in the breaking of the East India monopoly by Kirkman Finlay, the great Glasgow cotton spinner and warehouseman, in 1816. Three years later Dr William Jardine left the East India Company to start trading, with another young Scot, at Canton. Within two decades Jardine, Matheson and Company, a conglomerate with interests in shipping, textiles, tea and – most important – opium, was the greatest European trader in China, on whose behalf Palmerston fought the Opium War. But most of Jardine, Matheson's home trade was with London or Liverpool. Important though the Clyde was during the nineteenth century, it never regained the significance it had enjoyed before the American revolt. Finlay died a wealthy man, but his friends and compatriots Sir John Gladstone and William Ewart, who traded from Liverpool, left fortunes three times as great. The Liverpool Scots – 'an alien group, prosperous and conspicuous' in S. G. Checkland's words – had their parallels in Melbourne and Calcutta. The coming of the steamer reinforced their distinctiveness, but if the Cunard packets were built on the Clyde they sailed from England, where their market lay.

Yet by the end of the nineteenth century the main stream of Scottish capital was flowing not into industry or trade, but into foreign investment. In October 1884 a writer in *Blackwoods Magazine* observed:[60]

> Whether this vast exportation of our surplus wealth be wise or unwise, Scotland is to a large extent responsible for it. In proportion to her size and the number of her population, she furnishes far more of it than either of the sister kingdoms. England gives sparingly and Ireland hardly any, but Scotland revels in foreign investment.

By 1914 the United Kingdom had about £4,000 million invested abroad, an average of about £90 per head of population. Scots investors accounted for £500 million, an average of nearly £110. In the 1870s they had pioneered investment trusts which poured money into land, mining and railway enterprises in the United States, Australasia and Asia, sometimes judiciously and sometimes disastrously. In the 1880s Scots investors were said to provide two-thirds of the capital for cattle ranching in the American West. You could not, a correspondent of the London *Statist* wrote in 1885, talk to any reasonably well-off man in the streets of Aberdeen, Edinburgh or Dundee, without railroads and prairies coming up. At precisely the time when the myth of the bawbee-minding Scot was becoming a stock turn on the boards of music halls north and south of the border, the Scots investor was throwing his money about with a flamboyance the Scots aristocracy had never managed.

This was the classic scenario of the economic interpretation of imperialism which J. A. Hobson was to advance at the time of the Boer War. The low wages of the industrial proletariat caused a perpetually depressed home market through under-consumption, and the surplus profits of the capitalist classes consequently had to be invested in colonial territories.[61] The impact of such economic calculations on imperial policy has not survived historical analysis, but in its time, as interpreted by Lenin, it was used very effectively to justify the Bolshevik's acceleration of the social evolution of Russia in 1917. In Scotland, too, it was peculiarly relevant. Wages and living standards were lower, the problems of creating new market-oriented industries considerable, while the contacts in administration, trade, settlement and professional services with the English-speaking world and the colonial empire were well developed. In the thirty years before 1914 the line of least resistance for Scottish enterprise was not to stay at home, nor even to migrate south, but to go abroad.

As in Turner's analysis of America, the frontier of Greater

Scotland transformed the attitudes of the core community. In particular it strengthened new loyalties within Scotland which were neither nationalist nor assimilationist: the identities of the cities in which about 40 per cent of the population lived by 1900, and in particular that of Glasgow, which accounted for 25 per cent. Urban life, rather than Scottish identity, was the central fact of late nineteenth-century Scotland. Yet, as Geoffrey Best has remarked, Scottish cities were socially and culturally distinct from English cities. Aberdeen and Edinburgh whose growth was modest, remained regional centres, reflecting traditional Scottish values in the statuses of their inhabitants and their civic culture. Dundee was tied to the empire through the jute industry and its enormous foreign investments. And Glasgow was already by the 1880s being called the Scottish Chicago.[62] It had its American counterpart's protean capacity for continual demolition and rebuilding. Its buildings were boldly experimental, steel-framed and concrete. Its artists and patrons took their taste from the Continent. It hosted the world at three lavish exhibitions. Its public utilities – tramways, electric and hydraulic power, water supply and sewage disposal – were internationally famous as examples of municipal socialism. The intractable problem of overcrowding remained, but the working class had been contained, disciplined, and provided with a standard of social welfare which was, in the circumstances, remarkable for being adequate. For the 20 per cent or so of its inhabitants who were middle-class, Glasgow provided collective opulence on an unprecedented scale: libraries, concert halls, clubs, elaborate suburban railways, tea-rooms which were the wonder of the age, orchestras, golf-courses and, above all, the huge playground of the Clyde, with its yachts and pleasure-steamers, its quiet resorts with their piers and Italianate villas. In its way, it was as symmetrical an 'improved' society as the late eighteenth century had seen: an independent city-state and its *contado*, closer to Europe or America than to England, or, for that matter, to Edinburgh.

But it was an improvement founded on the narrow base of the heavy industries. While trading by the 'Iron Ring' on the Glasgow Exchange set the world standard for pig iron prices, while Scottish marine and railway engineers in Singapore and Johannesburg offices sent orders back to the works in which they had served their time, Glasgow continued to flourish. But its competitors in Germany and America were already flexing their muscles.

In the early nineteenth century the semi-independence of Scotland had been absorbed effortlessly into the expansion of British political and economic influence. Scottish nationalism was pre-empted by British liberalism. Later on, as the second wave of 'peasant' nationalism was breaking on Europe, the distinctive role the Scots played in imperial expansion created a more elaborate identity which more than compensated for the rapid weakening of the remaining institutions of semi-independence. If some of the components of 'Greater Scotland' were mythic, myths, like that of military prowess, could still breed reality. And Greater Scotland was underwritten by the fact of success in settlement, administration, trade and investment: all in all, it seemed more substantial than the pretensions of nationalist eccentrics, and no less Scots. Defensive nationalism gained a presence only when difficulties in the balance which underlay Greater Scotland coincided with structural tensions in British politics. This happened in the 1850s, when the realisation of the weakness of the traditional institutions paralleled the Britain-wide attack on 'centralisation' which ended with the destruction of supervisory bodies like Chadwick's General Board of Health in 1858. It happened again in the 1880s, when the financial difficulties of Scottish investors, and the Highland land agitation, were matched by the Chamberlainite radicals' challenge to property and entrenched political power. In both cases the gains to nationalism were negligible, though how negligible was only to become apparent in the aftermath of the First World War.

VII

Emile Durkheim and other late nineteenth-century sociologists saw society, organised in the nation-state, as a means of directing the ego of the individual at a time when it was disoriented by the impact of industrial capitalism and the division of labour. The alternative was the condition they termed *anomie*, in which individual wills either conflicted destructively with each other, or drifted into undirected apathy. Scotland had, before 1914, lacked the apparatus of the nation-state, but the functional linkage of industrial growth, emigration and imperial involvement provided both practical contexts and plausible myths for Scots fulfilment during a period of revolutionary social transformation. During the First World War this came to an end. The economic dynamic which held together the relationships of 'greater Scotland' ceased; the limitations of economic integration with the rest of Britain were exposed. Robert Rait, the Principal of Glasgow University, wrote in the *Encyclopaedia Britannica*:[63]

> Like other portions of the Empire, Scotland has, since the end of 1918, suffered from the weariness produced by stupendous effort and from a consequent restlessness and impatience which has found vent in industrial disputes and in an eager adoption by some of the youth, of new social ideals, in which the influence of Russian Bolshevik experiments and propaganda has been conspicuous.

The classic ingredients of anomie were here, yet any prospect of integration through nationalism was denied by the weakness of the nationalist movement. Rait's own expectation, that disruption would be quieted by 'the restoration of commercial and industrial prosperity', turned out equally false. Between the wars, Scotland was a disoriented society.

This was partly the result of the war itself, partly the result of the political ideologies it validated. Economically, the war took a heavy toll of Scots manpower; the militarist myth had worked to the extent that the Scots enlisted enthusiastically – 26·8 per cent of the miners joined up in the first year – and a disproportionately high number were killed.[64] It also encouraged the further development of the heavy industries, just at the time when some faltering attempts were being made to broaden the country's industrial base. The result was that dependence on traditional markets for railway equipment and steamers increased, despite the increasing challenge these transport methods faced from new technologies, which were scarcely represented in Scotland. After the war this competition and excess capacity in the heavy industries took their toll. The Scottish economy not only experienced the effects of the slump, but entered a distinct and irreversible decline. Unemployment was the most obvious evidence: from 1·8 per cent of the insured work-force (on the whole skilled men) in 1913 (the figure for London in the same year was 8·7 per cent) it rose to a minimum of 10 per cent between the wars, and sometimes rose as high as 25 per cent.[65] This was not simply the result of Scots economic problems: the international impact of the depression shut the safety-valve of emigration, which had peaked in the decades 1911–31, when as many people left as had left in the preceding forty years. But a larger – and consequently cheaper – work-force did nothing to stimulate economic development. In 1908 Scots industry had provided 12·5 per cent of UK production; by 1930 this had fallen to 9·6 per cent.[66]

Present-day nationalists tend to see this decline as the consequence of Unionism. Contrasts between the prosperous Scotland of 1913 and the problems of subsequent years still feature in speeches at Scottish National Party Conferences. Yet the weakness of the inter-war Scots economy was largely the result of decisions taken in Scotland by Scotsmen while the economy was still prosperous and relatively autonomous. Nationalist writers – or at any rate some of them – were aware of this at the time. George Malcolm Thomson, an Oxford-educated journalist, marshalled a scathing indictment in his *Caledonia, or the Future of the Scots* (1926):[67]

> Scotland is already a land of working men and petty tradesmen, a land, that is, in which both work and trade are destined to wither. She is sinking slowly in an economic and racial quagmire. . . . She is an annex, half-industrial, half-sporting, of English civilisation, and tomorrow she will be a proletarian state, blind, resentful and submerged, populated by a nation of machine-minders doing the bidding of foreign capitalists. . . . There is no intellectual community capable of producing the friction of minds from which ideas are generated. It is a land of second-hand thoughts and second-rate minds, inapt to improvise or experiment, an addict to the queue habit in the world of ideas, and woefully unaware of the time-lag that makes a visit to it a voyage in time as well as in space for most West Europeans.

As an exercise in destructive criticism, Thomson's assault was effectively and timely. The option of non-national Scottishness was at an end; assimilation as drastic as that of a century earlier was now under way. In 1928 Scottish government was put under the London civil service. In 1929 the Free Church and Auld Kirk, whose brawling had permeated national affairs for almost a century, quietly amalgamated, and in the same year, without any prior investigation, Scottish local government was drastically reorganised. The parish councils, the first institutions of local democracy in rural Scotland, were abolished, to the dismay of radicals in the Labour Party as well as traditionalists in bodies like the Convention of Royal Burghs. The tendency was aptly summed up by one Labour MP, William Adamson, in 1924:[68]

> We believe that government policy is to subordinate Scottish administration to Whitehall to a far greater extent than has

> ever been the case, and to remove from Scotland practically the last vestige of independent government and nationhood and to have its centre in London.

Equally depressingly, it was a Labour government that he attacked.

The younger men who had survived the war, like Thomson and MacDiarmid, were gravediggers for the old order, but they could scarcely be said to represent a nationalist alternative: they and their contemporaries had to create one. We have already seen the mixed fortunes which attended their efforts. The problem was not just that nationalism was divided between left and right, but that on the left, where it was potentially strongest, it faced the competition of a new assimilationist ideology. The effect of wartime production demands on the heavy industries of the Clyde Valley, with their depleted labour force, strong craft unionism, and antiquated management structure, had been to produce a temporary but powerful alliance between craftsmen and socialist militants. 'Red Clydeside' was more legend than reality, but after the war its activists were to take a leading role in the formation of the Communist Party of Great Britain.[69] The Scottish revolutionaries were an articulate and able group, the first Scottish working men to rationalise an effective politics out of their own experience. Where the Chartists had adopted middle-class notions of self-improvement, and Keir Hardie had found that socialist organisation was only possible south of the border, they canvassed drastic remedies for the worsening economic and social problems of the Scottish industrial belt. But, under the programme of the Comintern, this involved the integration of the struggle for socialism in Scotland with the cause of world revolution. Temperamentally and organisationally, men like William Gallagher, J. R. Campbell, Arthur MacManus and Harry McShane, echoed the Covenanters who had tried to capture Britain for Calvinism in the seventeenth century: old presbyter became new Communist. Once again, religion had frustrated nationalism.

Between the wars the left had little success in Scotland anyway. If there was a consistent electoral trend, it was towards the right. In 1922 – the year the 'red Clydeside' MPs travelled to London to set the seal on an unusually tenacious myth – only 13 Unionists were elected in Scotland, against 27 Liberals and 29 Labour. By 1935 there were 43 Unionists, only 3 Liberals, 20 Labour and 5 Independent Labour MPs. Such success as Labour enjoyed was due largely to the migration of the well-disciplined Irish Nationalist vote, which the rise of Sinn Fein had left orphaned, from the Liberal Party. This owed more to the organisational gifts of Catholic Labour politicians like John Wheatley and Patrick Dollan than to any mass-conversion to socialism, as the government of Glasgow has demonstrated down to the present day. But it was not sufficient to enable Labour to fill the vacuum left by the collapse of the Liberals. 'Aristocratic and socially conservative', the Scottish Liberal leaders looked back to the days when they had underwritten the hegemony of their party in Westminster, with all the relevance of Jacobites toasting the 'King over the water'.[70] Neglecting the collectivist remedies offered by Lloyd George, most of them drifted quietly into alliance with the Unionists, imparting to the National coalition, which enjoyed a staggering 64–7 majority over Labour in 1931–35, a markedly antique appearance. In 1910 businessmen and lawyers had dominated Scots representation; in 1931, assailed everywhere by industrial problems, Scots MPs were largely lawyers, landowners and military men.

The deterioration of political Conservatism reflected the weakness of Scottish business leadership. If the inter-war British economy was imprisoned in the strait-jacket of financial orthodoxy, the position was aggravated in Scotland by the dominance of magnates from the traditional heavy industries, family dynasties which were keener to protect their own status and power than to experiment in new fields. The Census of Production of 1935 found that, in the growth industries of cars and electrical engineering, under 2 per cent of the work-force was employed in Scotland, but bodies which were formed to promote industry, like the Scottish Development Council in 1931 and the government-sponsored Scottish Economic Committee in 1935, achieved little because of dissension between the old industrialists and the new.[71] It was not until 1937 that government policy itself switched from schemes which encouraged the unemployed to move south to where there was work, to creating jobs in Scotland itself. But the Scottish Industrial Estates Corporation, set up in that year with a capital of £4 million to build an extensive estate at Hillington outside Glasgow, only created 15,000 jobs while, at the same time, armaments orders placed on the Clyde totalled £80 million.[72] As the Clydesdale Bank survey of the Scottish economy remarked, ominously enough, in February 1938, 'what building was to English recovery, rearmament has been to Scottish'. When war broke out, the economic problems of Scotland seemed as intractable as ever.

The problem was as much one of diagnosis as of prescription. Scotland shared the malaise of the British economy, but suffered from its own structural weaknesses, not the least of which was the lack of institutions, individuals and concepts capable of defining the scope of the reforms needed. The devolved departments dealt only with the traditional institutions, even if they were now situated in Scotland. They lacked any experience or authority in economic policy and physical planning. The universities, which were to provide almost a surfeit of prescriptions for the economy in the post-war period, were silent. The intellectuals were preoccupied with the doctrines of Marx or the mysteries of social credit, both of which were apocalyptic rather than remedial. In this situation there was an opening for a further extension of southern control, had the National Government bothered itself. But it did not stir, and it was in the circumstances of war that the new orthodoxy of a state-guided economy, formulated by J. M. Keynes, took effect.

By this time the men and ideas were available to give state planning a Scottish dimension. The men of Greater Scotland had come back to a nationality that they had ignored for nearly a century. In the course of his dynamic secretaryship (1941–5) Thomas Johnston drew on his experience on the Empire Marketing Board and took the Tennessee Valley Authority and the Ontario Power Company as precedents for his North of Scotland Hydro-Electric Board.[73] In 1939 James Bowie, the Director of the Dundee School of Economics, set up by an industrialist in 1931 to remedy the deficiency in economics teaching in the land of Adam Smith, applied Keynesian remedies directly to Scottish problems in his book *The Future of Scotland*. Bowie had spent most of his career teaching in America and his remedies smacked of the New Deal. He wanted a state-financed Scottish Development Commission to plan the economy, control the heavy industries, and assist the growth of light industries. His aims were only partially secured by Johnston's Scottish Council on Industry in 1942, but they were given widespread publicity by nationalist and left-wing organisations. Through Johnston's efforts, powers that might have gone south stayed in the north, and the authority of the Secretary of State was extended into new areas like physical planning and industrial development. The centralisation implied by post-war planning schemes would at least meet a countervailing force and a countervailing hope. In Bowie's words:[74]

> The best way to make Scotland a powerful partner in the Empire is to treat her as we have treated our dominions and to grant her successive instalments of power to set her own house in order. The present tendency to decentralise should be accelerated, and the next step is to give Scotland an effective instrument of diagnosis and prescription.

Chapter 3

The Intellectuals, 1707-1945

The deepest result of this complex involvement in British society was that the provincial's view of the world was discontinuous. Two forces, two magnets, affected his efforts to find adequate standards and styles: the values associated with the simplicity and purity (real or imagined) of nativism and those to be found in cosmopolitan sophistication. Those who could take entire satisfaction in either could maintain a consistent position. But for provincials, exposed to both, an exclusive concentration of either kind was too narrow. It meant a rootlessness, an alienation either from the higher sources of culture or from the familiar local environment that had formed the personality. Few whose conceptions surpassed local boundaries rested content with a simple, consistent image of themselves or of the world. Provincial culture in eighteenth-century Scotland was formed in a mingling of these visions.

John Clive, 'The Social Background' in *Scotland in the Age of Improvement*, 1970.

I

'The intellectuals had to create their own nationality,' A. J. P. Taylor observed of the subjects of the Hapsburgs. In the nineteenth century scholars compiling linguistic dictionaries caused Vienna more trouble than socialist revolutionaries.[1] Had he lived into the twentieth century Marx himself would probably have agreed. He had assumed that intellectuals alienated from capitalist society – 'a portion of the bourgeois ideologists, who have raised themselves to the level of comprehending theoretically the historical movement as a whole'[2] – would play a straightforward role in directing the mobilisation of the industrial proletariat. The nation-state was simply the 'historic' political framework in which they would act. But over much of Europe, after 1848, the anticipation of an industrial – or at least literate – society provided the intelligentsia with a different role. In this they confronted and even diverted the forces of economic change.

The intellectuals became the ideologues of the second wave of nationalism. Peasant societies, challenged by literacy, industrial development and centralised government, looked to them to provide a new national *geist*, a community which could withstand and contain the shock of social change. Their performance as educational reformers, philological researchers and cultural revivalists was backed by conservatives, attempting to confound materialistic and 'scientific socialist' forecasts of social evolution, and by radicals, trying to use the atavistic force of national loyalty to promote it. Thus the intellectuals helped create the institutions which promoted industrialisation and mass politics, but they also established at their heart the ethnic, religious and cultural components of a potent 'false consciousness'.

As Marx derived his theoretical model from England, where the social framework for industrialisation was established by the struggle for legislative supremacy between the King and Parliament in the pre-nationalist epoch, his over-simplification was understandable. England's apparent typicality masked a distinctive though understated national evolution. In the nineteenth century its political structure was to be challenged by the impact of the 'second wave' of intellectual-directed nationalism on its peripheral communities: Wales, where the political nation had long been in abeyance, and Ireland, where the linguistic revival helped shift the terms of nationalist rhetoric into the idealist and intransigent mould of Sinn Fein. In all this, Scotland was the dog which did not bark. Elsewhere nationalist intellectuals remedied the lack of national institutions by creating a nationalist imagination which served as a surrogate state. In Scotland they were silent, despite the presence of the traditional institutions of semi-independence. A rational case probably existed for legislative devolution, which the intelligentsia could direct through press and public opinion, but the most it contributed was a decorative and rather frivolous nostalgia. Only in the 1920s did intellectual nationalism become a reality, and only in the 1970s has it attained any real political significance.

But for most of the time after 1707 nationalism was never the only, or the most important, option for the Scottish intelligentsia. Its loyalty was a dual one, and only its weaker element concerned the home country and its institutions. The other loyalty was as powerful and protean as the achievement of 'Greater Scotland' itself. Its complex nature is aptly captured by C. M. Grieve's remark that the great Scottish novel is *Moby Dick*, a novel which has nothing to do with Scotland in any respect save its obsessive theme of a man's pursuit of his own destiny, an ego unconstrained by community or God; an intellectual ambition as huge and arrogant as the political wilfulness Grieve applauded in the reluctance of the Scots to behave like any other nation.

At the same time, however, Grieve's heroic view of non-national Scottishness had to coexist with the fact that the Scots prospered, materially and intellectually, in collaboration with the English. And English reluctance to explore the nature of the partnership communicated itself to the Scots. 'I hope you in Oxford don't think we hate you,' John Stuart Blackie asked Benjamin Jowett in 1866. 'We don't think about you' was the reply.[3] Yet Jowett's Balliol was a key Anglo-Scottish institution, one of the main channels of which ambitious Scots, the elite of a privileged provincial intelligentsia, assimilated themselves to metropolitan society on the best terms possible. Plainly, if they were going to play down the ambiguities in their own background, it was otiose to expect any greater enlightenment on the part of the English. What, for instance, were they to make of James Bryce, who told Gilbert Murray that he thought the traditional Scots university course the best possible, yet who disparaged the provincial English universities (on the whole following in the Scots tradition) as 'Lilliputian' and exalted the values of Oxford?[4] Was the distinctiveness of the Anglo-Scottish tradition no more than a range of institutions to be exploited as a means of advancement, and thereafter regarded with little more than nostalgic affection?

In 1809 Francis Jeffrey, who had headed the movement for political assimilation, sketched the anodyne picture of the country that the Anglo-Scots retained after they had made their way in the world:[5]

> It is connected in their imagination not only with that olden time which is uniformly conceived as more pure, lofty and simple than the present, but also with all the soft and bright colours of remembered childhood and domestic affection. All its pleasures conjure up images of schoolday innocence, and sports, and friendships which have no part in succeeding years.

Over a century later the novelist Neil M. Gunn, in his political allegory *The Green Isle of the Great Deep* (1944) offered 'the human familiarity, the life-warmth' of the Highland boy Art as the antidote to the subtle and insidious tyranny of a modern totalitarian state:[6]

> 'The later phase of life on earth has tended to destroy the wholeness of the child mind at a very early stage. The intensive pursuit of what is called education has also tended to disintegrate the young mind.'
>
> 'In what way does the boy Art differ?'
>
> 'In that he was still the complete boy. The country community he came out of was to him a complete and familiar community. Old Hector – and this is what some of us were slow to grasp – was his natural friend. The boy's simplicity was found again in the old man's – and the old man's was the simplicity refined out of experience. Added to that was the background of what they call Nature. Which means that the subconscious responses had a natural field of action . . .'

Was the residual Scottishness of the intellectuals merely a longing for Tir-nan-Og – the Land of Youth – irrelevant to mature industrial society? Or was it, in the words of Gunn's friend and publisher T. S. Eliot, 'to arrive where we started / and know the place for the first time', a complicated experience which offered a distinctive and positive identity for beleaguered modern man? Or could it be both?

Consciousness of the dual nature of the Scots intellect, torn between cosmopolitan opportunism and demotic roots which that opportunism had cheapened into nostalgia, is directly relevant to the current political upheavals, for it has been largely since the war that it has been rationally appraised, a process which has involved inverting the usual approaches to the intellectual history of nationalism. Notions of a continuum, of a developing interpretation, even of a consistent relationship with political change, have had to be left on a margin. The question why Scotland developed no orthodox national intelligentsia is now seen as far more important. It is a measure of the confidence of some contemporary nationalists that, at last, they have now faced up to this. It is a measure of the decay of the United Kingdom consensus that some of the most corrosive critics of traditional nationalism have now endorsed it.

Most nationalist intelligentsias see themselves as the servants of a national geist. They do not court metropolitan recognition; indeed, given their usual emphasis on linguistic distinctiveness, they cannot. Witness the private celebrations of the Welsh. The Scots have, by contrast, an ambiguous relationship to metropolitan culture: a desire to dominate it in the only way open to a provincial – by understanding and mastering its ideology – and an enduring suspicion that this path might, after all, be blocked by a socially-selective clique. Metropolitan culture might, or might not, be a sham; native culture might, or might not, be genuine. The enduring characteristic of the Scottish intellect since the reformation has been cultural insecurity at one pole or the other. The remedy has traditionally lain in the energy and acumen of individuals, and the openness of the national institutions to intellectual innovation – often in the teeth of opposition from those who see their role in classic nationalist terms. The significance of the present crisis is that it has occurred at both poles: political nationalism in Scotland has coincided with the intellectual and political atrophy of the British elite. And this time the modernisation of the universities has made the Scots intelligentsia acutely aware of the break-up, not only of the unitary state, but of monolithic theories of social change.

The most critical of these developments has been the reappraisal of Marxism. In the years after 1956 which saw the evolution of the New Left the old Marxian notion of governmental and cultural institutions being a 'superstructure' fairly straightforwardly erected on a basis of economic relationships came under intense criticism from historians and political writers like E. P. Thompson, Eric Hobsbawm and Raymond

Williams. They implied that the separate identity of Scotland, Ireland and Wales was to be respected if not (at this stage, at any rate) explained. A statement like Hobsbawm's in *Industry and Empire*:[7]

> . . . Scotland and Wales are socially, and by their history, traditions, and sometimes institutions, entirely distinct from England, and cannot therefore be simply subsumed under English history or (as is more common) neglected.

wouldn't have occurred to a Marxist thirty years earlier. It certainly didn't occur to Marx himself.

A consequence of this revisionism was that ideology was credited with a significance of its own: it was no longer seen simply as the projection of the self-interest of economic groups, but a factor whose importance could depend on other, non-economic influences. This both tended to affirm the contention of post-Namier historians that the process of political transaction was critically important, and to make them more aware of the role of ideology in providing the conventions which sanctioned it. It is in the matrix provided by this collaboration that the Scottish intellectual tradition loses its inscrutable quality and begins to show both the influence of a consistent ideology and of a distinctive politics.

II

Put briefly, the crisis of authority in early modern Scotland produced a situation in which ideology rather than social status determined the role of the intellectual in society, and in which a range of political relationships could be activated to ensure that it continued to do so. In this way the intellectuals, by David Caute's definition those who 'tend to apply theoretical arguments to the solution of practical problems or, conversely, search for the principles and symbols embodied in concrete instances',[8] were given a pre-emptive role in society that they lacked elsewhere in Britain. Their professions changed, priest to lawyer and scholar, novelist to administrator and technologist but they were able, for nearly four centuries, to recruit and to market their talents on their own terms. And these terms were co-terminous with the growth and development of the United Kingdom and its empire.

The Reformation was the critical discontinuity, intellectually as well as politically. A backward, semi-feudal northern country adopted a religious ideology – Calvinism – associated with advanced urban commercial communities. This was not altogether inexplicable: intellectual and commercial connections with the continent were strong; monarchial authority, which rapidly imposed Lutheranism on Scandinavia, was weak. The sponsors of the new religion occupied a powerful if uncomfortable position. They could arbitrate between competing political groups – the nobility, the Kirk, the towns, the English. But success was only achieved after 130 years of bitter religious-political power struggle, absorbing energies which could in other times have humanised the community. In the twentieth century Gramsci marvelled at the way in which the 'traditional intelligentsia' of the British professions had pre-empted the role of the 'organic intelligentsia' produced by industrial capitalism.[9] In Scotland this process had been telescoped: the 'traditional intelligentsia' that Calvinism created anticipated the 'organic' managerial intelligentsia of capitalism. All that was missing was capitalism itself.

Between 1560 and 1690 the balance remained delicate. Union contended with independence, absolutism with parliamentarianism, presbyterianism and episcopalianism. The aims of Knox and his fellows were only partly achieved, but materially and morally the Kirk had become, in R. H. Tawney's words, 'the real State in Scotland',[10] creating institutions and attitudes which the Union was to vitalise.

The Calvinist theology, with its stress on an autonomous and capricious God who

> Sends ane to heaven an' ten to hell,
> A' for thy glory.
> An no' for any gude or ill,
> They've done before thee.

both liberated and imprisoned. On the whole it led to a practical stoicism. Predestination recognised the same sort of lottery in life as in death. Over this pit, Calvinism constructed rules to keep civil society together. As James Hogg showed in *Confessions of a Justified Sinner*, it could mask tendencies far darker than those Burns caricatured in 'Holy Willie's Prayer', but it provided the hard and fast rules a frontier society needed. Areas of collective responsibility which the English state contracted out to the aristocracy or forgot about, in Scotland passed into the hands of the Kirk. Most notable were education and poor relief, subjects in which Calvinist values were expressed at their most emphatic. In England an empirical response to observed social conditions reflected existing hierarchies; in Scotland ideological prescriptions aimed at the reconstruction of society. The intellectual's role in this process was critical, yet the backwardness of the country inevitably frustrated his efforts, or redirected them.

The seventeenth century presented the Scots with the option of Calvinism in one country, or the export of revolution. They tried the latter course during the Civil War, but the result was direct rule by Cromwell, and after the Restoration a counter-attack by the episcopalians, only checked by the Glorious Revolution of 1688. Thereafter Scotland's religious distinctiveness was confirmed, and after 1707 the religious intelligentsia was tied to the Union, whose terms actually enjoined the persecution of episcopalians, and continued to do so until the nineteenth century. If Jacobites sought intellectual sanction for the old cause, they looked to Oxford, not to the Scottish universities. The way was at last clear along which the Kirk could lead society towards improvement.

The untimely religious revolution sent the Wandering Scot away on his Faustian pilgrimage, in search of a community which could contain his ambitions. But had the trauma caused by the change been altogether too severe to justify even the intellectual and material triumphs of post-Calvinist Scotland? Four centuries later, amid the debris of the achieving society, Neil Gunn and Edwin Muir looked back on the Reformation as a surrender of the idea of community long before it was challenged by industrialisation, a surrender which made it much more difficult to cope with the challenge when it came. In the words of George Mackay Brown, a pupil of Muir and a Catholic convert.[11]

> It was then that the old heraldry began to crack, that the idea of 'progress' took root in men's minds. What was broken, irremediably, in the 16th century was the fullness of life in a community, its simple interwoven identity. In earlier times the temporal and the eternal, the story and the fable, were not divorced, as they came to be after Knox: they used the same language and imagery, so that the whole of life was illuminated. . . . Innocence gave place to a dark brooding awareness. . . . From that time, too, the old music and poetry died out, because the single vision which is the source of all art had been choked. Poets followed priests into the darkness.

The struggle between what Coleridge called 'civilisation and cultivation' was joined in Europe and England in the nineteenth century, and one of its precipitates was the reinterpretation of the traditional community as the nation, an organisation which could sustain 'the fullness of life' in the industrial age. In Scotland, however, such foundations no longer existed.

III

Kirk and law were central to Scottish intellectual life after 1707. They were surrounded by, and linked to, other institutions – the aristocracy, the professions, the universities, the burghs, the commercial classes – which, in time, could provide the national intelligentsia, otherwise effectively excluded from politics, with other options to exploit. The Kirk, in particular, rapidly made the transition from near-heresy to an established centre of authority, under the control of men like William Robertson the historian, Adam Ferguson the social scientist and Thomas Reid the philosopher. More than any other group the Moderates – the archetypal red Scots – made possible the Scottish Enlightenment, which altered the reputation of the country from that of a barbarous and remote province to an intellectual centre which rivalled London, Paris and Vienna, not simply in the eyes of the Scots themselves, but in the opinion of savants like Voltaire and Jefferson. As the latter put it in 1789, where science was concerned, 'no place in the World can pretend to a competition with Edinburgh'.[12]

The Moderates were far removed from the passions of early presbyterianism. Robertson regarded John Knox as a boorish ruffian and said so. Neither this nor their resignation to the secularisation of society nor their tacit endorsement of the social *status quo* gave them any popular following, least of all among those who were reached by their evangelical opponents, the 'Wild' party, whose influence was swelling by 1800. Equally significantly, the writers of the Enlightenment drew the wrath of later generations for their apparent neglect of Scottish nationality. Carlyle was scathing about this. He wrote in his essay on Burns (1828):[13]

> Never perhaps was there a class of writers so clear and well-ordered, yet so totally destitute, to all appearance, of any patriotic affection, nay, of any human affection whatever.

The charge has stuck, not altogether justifiably. The vitality of the Enlightenment depended on an intellectual semi-independence analogous to the political status the country enjoyed. It was not the product of wholesale assimilation, but of conscious decisions by men working within Scottish institutions, who realised their strengths and weaknesses, and the power of the drive to assimilation. Edinburgh, whose carefully planned New Town of 1767 was its spiritual (or, more aptly, sceptical) home, was a substitute London, providing metropolitan amenities in a Scottish context. It was a fitting centre for such a transitional society. Its professional men and their clients could afford to think, but not to vegetate: landowners not wealthy enough to move to London, lawyers dependent on them for their briefs, merchants and manufacturers who still traded in a local market, ministers and teachers who had risen in the Scottish universities but could never meet the penal charges which entry into the English professions demanded.

The rise of Edinburgh would be remarkable enough even without the emergence around it of the institutions of classical nationalism. Yet, interestingly enough, many of the components of nationalism emerge in eighteenth-century Scotland: the romanticism unleashed by 'Ossian' MacPherson in the 1760s, the folklorist activities of Allan Ramsay, Burns, Grose and Scott, and the consciousness of community as something more than an aggregate of men in the work of Adam Ferguson and John Millar.[14] The difference was that the old Scots community displayed not the tranquillity and freedom from division that later nationalists postulated, but loyalties whose local and religious nature threatened to pull the state apart. Against this the specialised institutions and English orientation of semi-independence offered a stable basis for 'improvement'.

Yet an important element from the pre-industrial community underwrote the Enlightenment: the network of wide-ranging, collaborative, voluntary bodies which created a politics of intellectual co-operation and mutual reinforcement. The

Edinburgh Speculative Society of 1764 is as good an example as any. Its members later included Scott, Henry Brougham, Jeffrey and Cockburn – at daggers drawn in their politics but still prepared to spend their Wednesday evenings drinking and talking around the fire at the university. Both the condition for and the result of this was a remarkable versatility: ministers wrote plays; Law Lords and publishers discoursed on the descent of man; Charles MacLaren edited both the local paper and the *Encyclopaedia Britannica* (itself an Edinburgh project). When Adam Ferguson, minister and sometime infantryman, found that gaining the Edinburgh chair of philosophy meant that he had to teach physics and not, as he had thought, ethics, he set to and kept himself a fortnight ahead of his class. Polymathy was not a curiosity in eighteenth-century Scotland, it was a condition of survival.

'There appears in the genius of the Scottish people – fostered no doubt by the abstract metaphysical speculations of their universities – a power of reducing human actions to formulas or principles.' [15] Walter Bagehot's observation was just. One of the Enlightenment's main achievements – and the one which bound it tightly to industrial development – was the systematic collection and dissemination of knowledge. The *Encyclopaedia Britannica* was joined by the *Statistical Accounts*, a parish-by-parish social survey compiled by ministers to a pattern devised by the agricultural improver Sir John Sinclair of Ulbster. The Ordnance Survey had its beginnings in Scotland, and what C. R. Fay called 'the stream of social education' was forced along in the early nineteenth century by the 'monitorial' system of Dr Andrew Bell, which Dickens savaged as M'Choakumchild's Academy in *Hard Times*:[16]

> He knew all about the Water Sheds of all the world (whatever they are), and all the histories of all the peoples, and all the names of all the rivers and mountains, and all the productions, manners, and customs of all the countries, and all their

boundaries and bearings on the two-and-thirty points of the compass. Ah, rather overdone, M'Choakumchild. If he had only learnt a little less, how infinitely better he might have taught much more!

The excesses of the enlightened Scot drew the fire of Peacock and Cobbett as well as Dickens, but did not lead to Anglo-Scottish friction. However distinctive its origin, a society concerned to instruct and improve saw no boundaries to its efforts, and imposed no barrier to those wanting to join it. Eighteenth-century Scotland owed much to its English immigrants, to the surgeon-chemist John Roebuck, who helped found the great Carron Ironworks and patronised James Watt, to the iron and cotton magnates Dixon and Houldsworth, and to the protean Welshman Robert Owen who drew the crowned heads of Europe to his social laboratory at New Lanark. In turn, improvement opened the road to the south. Rather too much has been made of the way in which the Scots regretted their provincialism in polite English society; not enough has been said about the new, harsh *lingua franca* of calculation and organisation that they helped impose. The relationships which underpinned the golden age may have been temporary: the balance could not endure which ensured that sufficient talent remained, without developing into an intellectual proletariat. But the Enlightenment had allowed the Scots to create an unusually potent range of intellectual and educational investments.

The stream of social education was broad rather than deep. The obverse of polymathy and systematisation was a certain slapdash quality in Scottish intellectual life which increasingly began to irk not only those writers who sought a wider audience, but also those who wanted to preserve an organic community. Such discontents underlay the foundation of the Edinburgh Academy to offer a strict classical education on English lines in 1824, and the attempt to reform the Scottish universities two years later. This created the paradox that just at the time when nationality became significant in Europe, and explicit in Scotland, the impulses that propelled it were absolved into the movement for further assimilation. This was particularly important in the cases of Scott and Carlyle.

IV

In 1807, after a debate at the Faculty of Advocates in Edinburgh during which he had attacked proposed changes in the Court of Session as violations of the Treaty of Union, Sir Walter Scott turned to Francis Jeffrey. 'Little by little, whatever your wishes may be,' he said, with tears in his eyes, 'You will destroy and undermine until nothing of what makes Scotland Scotland shall remain.'[17] Parliamentary and legal reform, not the Union of 1707, would quiet the old song, Scott was a Tory partisan, and a fairly comprehensive reactionary, but he spoke with authority. As a novelist and folklorist, he was the acknowledged precursor of those reconstructors of historic identity who were to dominate European nationalism in the nineteenth century. As a politician and lawyer he stood at the nexus of the relationships which made up the society of eighteenth-century Scotland. As an historian, he was *ultimus haeres* of a great tradition. His perception of the evolution of the state since the Union of the Crowns was critical; no less so was his failure to extend this comprehension to include contemporary reality.

In the great sequence of novels, including *Old Mortality*, *The Heart of Midlothian*, *Waverley* and *Redgauntlet*, which spanned the century following the Restoration, Scott was historian and sociologist as much as romancer. Thomas Carlyle in the nineteenth century and Georg Lukacs in the twentieth congratulated him on filling the past 'by living men, not by protocols, state papers, controversies and abstractions of men'.[18] In this he dramatised the Scottish Enlightenment's preoccupation with the structure of society by setting his carefully delineated characters against complex, detailed and mutable environments. There are few tragic heroes in Scott: the freedom of choice on which tragedy depends is everywhere constrained by the conditioning of environment. But there is a continuing reappraisal of moral worth, as a changing society sanctions one form of behaviour and censures another. We see the progression of a nation from a society riven by conflicting statuses, social organisations and religious affiliations to one dominated by contract and the ideal of improvement. The armed dialecticians of the earlier age have been winnowed, by the later novels, into peaceable if litigious citizens on one side and picturesque bandits on the other.

Scott's preference for social description rather than plot made him treat the great events of eighteenth-century Scotland obliquely. The Union and the rebellions do not dominate; they are fitted into the milieu. *The Heart of Midlothian* is a novel about the consequences of the Union, although the Act itself is scarcely mentioned. By a characteristic mixture of meticulous historical reconstruction and sympathetic caricature Scott recreates the unsettled mood of Edinburgh in the pre-Athenian period, when its citizens regretted the absence of parliamentarians whom they could stone if they got out of line. Yet the period before the Union is also seen as one of religious bigotry, armed division and bad law. It was the Scottish parliament, after all, which had passed the Draconian statute – hanging for child-murder – under which Effie Deans was condemned. (It had also reimposed serfdom in the mines and salt-works.) The virtues which ultimately triumph are, indeed, those of the Scottish seventeenth century – Jeannie Deans's moral conviction and the Duke of Argyll's political grasp – but they make the transition from fanaticism and opportunism thanks to the security and wider horizons granted by the Union. Jeannie transmutes the hair-splitting pietism of her Covenanting father into sound morality; Argyll transmutes chieftainship into statesmanship and improving landlordism. In the sociological language with which the Victorians were familiar, both personify the change from a militant to an industrial mode of society, in which social relationships, and ultimately morality, will be founded on calculation.

Even the unsatisfying ending of *The Heart of Midlothian*, an odd combination of pastoral and melodrama, is significant as social commentary. Staunton and Donacha slaughter one another among pastures, once highland, now made rich by the husbandry of Douce Davie Deans: the men of violence of early eighteenth-century Scotland perish irrelevantly in the landscape of improvement.

The juxtaposition of violence, fanaticism and traditional authority with legality, rationalism and social change was to become a commonplace within the nineteenth-century novel, especially where it dealt with industrialisation and the extension of European influence. Scott stood at the beginning of an important literary tradition, at the other end of which are Conrad and Forster. But he had no heirs in his own country; nor did he deal at all with the new confrontation between a settled, landed society and the forces of capitalism, industrialisation and democracy. Scott, of course, viewed such challenges with unfeigned alarm and gloom, yet his self-avowed disciple, Balzac, who was equally conservative, revelled in dissecting the new politics. And even those of Scott's contemporaries, like John Galt, who described early nineteenth-century Scottish society with equal realism and insight, lacked successors. Why?

Failure of individual inspiration was not wholly responsible. Economic factors were also important. Capitalism was not just something to be observed. It penetrated the literary world; it made historic Scotland a marketable commodity. The ascendancy of Scott coincided with the breakthrough of Scottish publishers into the London book trade and the age of the 'Scotch reviewers'. Constable, Black, Chambers, Blackwood, later on Macmillan, Collins, Nelson and Blackie: publishing, not writing, built the Abbotsfords of the later nineteenth century. As editors and popularisers the reputations of George Gilfillan, Robert Chambers, George Lillie Craik and John Douglas Cook were ephemeral, but significant enough in their own day.[19] Not for nothing did Ezra Pound's Mr Nixon advise Mauberley to pay attention to the strictures of Dr Dundas. Together, such literary entrepreneurs dictated the sort of Scotland they wanted their readership to hear about, which was more or less the same sort of Scotland that increasing numbers of middle-class tourists, brought north by steamer and train, wanted to see. Far from extending his social analysis to comprehend the new industrial society, Scott provided it with its recreation.

After 1830, with the Whigs in office, the tide set decisively to the south. Scott died, fighting them to the last. Carlyle took the London coach. For their contemporaries and juniors, assimilation was eased by the number of prominent Englishmen – Lord John Russell, Sydney Smith, Lord Brougham – who had savoured the late Enlightenment when barred from the continent by the Napoleonic Wars, and by the contribution of Scots families like the Stephens and Macaulays to the evangelically-minded 'intellectual aristocracy' of public service. Social thought, as much as administration or technology, was to be dominated by men of Scottish birth or descent: Carlyle, Ruskin, Mill, Gladstone, T. B. Macaulay, Leslie Stephen. The dividend on past educational and social investment was impressive. But the result was an intellectual vacuum in the north.

V

'There is no sight half as impressive as a Scotsman on the make,' wrote J. M. Barrie at the end of the century. There was a harsh truth here, relevant to more than Barrie himself and the pawky careerists of the Kailyard school. The pursuit of success denominated red and black Scot alike. It did not make for profundity. There was even something second-hand about the high culture of the sages. They were organisers, activists, publicists, their eyes more on the main chance than on the reality of their society. Carlyle had noticed this as early as 1829, in 'Signs of the Times':[20]

> Not the external and physical alone is now managed by machinery, but the internal and spiritual also . . . Instruction, that mysterious communing of Wisdom with Ignorance, is no longer an indefinable tentative process, requiring a study of individual aptitudes, and a perpetual variation of means and methods, to attain the same ends; but a secure, universal, straightforward business, to be conducted in the gross, by proper mechanism, with such intellect as comes to hand.

The sage did not have to exert himself: the machine was ready. If he could supply it with suitable material, he would duly be projected. Carlyle at least saw, and said, where he was going. His contemporaries and successors did not. Whatever their success as public preachers – and in many cases it was salutary – they had effectively sacrificed the analytical intellect of the Enlightenment. By the middle of the nineteenth century it was easier for Karl Marx, a respectful student of eighteenth-century Scots social thought, to carry on its traditions than it was for the Scots themselves.

The regression was swift and alarming. Not only were the values of the Enlightenment not advanced, they were obscured by religious repression, pseudo-science and, by the end of the century, the comfortable acceptance of subordinate status in an Oxbridge-dominated world. The influence of the cult of phrenology, which had its centre among MacLaren's radical friends in Edinburgh, testified to one loss of direction. Samuel Smiles, founding economic progress on a simple set of moral injunctions, was scarcely an adequate successor to Adam Smith. By the 1880s, as the reformed English universities were gaining momentum in scholarship and research, the Scots were persecuting Robertson Smith, their greatest anthropologist, for heresy. His move to Cambridge in 1885 marked the capitulation: the humanities in the northern universities were to be left to the shallow and deferential schoolmen aptly commemorated by Professor William Knight in his *Some Nineteenth Century Scotsmen*. Nationality, not intellect, was their only distinguishing feature.

If the absence of a national focus is critical here, Carlyle's significance is that he was the man who should have supplied it, and did not. In his indictment of mechanism he was, in fact, paraphrasing words of Schiller's, written in 1796:[21]

> That polypus nature of the Greek states, where each individual enjoyed an independent existence, and in case of need, could act with the whole, now gives place to an ingenious engineering, in which a mechanical life forms itself as a whole, from the patchwork of innumerable but lifeless parts. The State and Church, laws and customs, are now rent asunder; enjoyment is now separated from labour, the means from the end, exertion from recompense.

German writers had seen nationalism as a means of reconstituting individuality in the age of industrialisation and rationalism. Carlyle agreed with them. His contempt for the detachment of the Scots Enlightenment was as scathing as his assault on the economists. Witness his essay on Burns. Yet he was too late. Although his social remedies were strongly nationalistic – and in their authoritarianism and race-consciousness they prefigured imperialism and possibly even fascism – the nationalism was transferred. Profoundly Scottish in speech, the 'greatest talker in London' was as individual in his prose style, which was much more alien to the English tradition than anything the Scots had produced in the eighteenth century. Yet he considered himself an Englishman, and was accepted as the arbiter of the English language's integrity in its struggle with the new industrial society.

The English language served and was served by Carlyle and the other Scots who migrated south in the early nineteenth century. It was a means of integration when the dual culture of the older Scotland was in decay; it had also to be protected from perversion by the new social order. The preoccupation of Carlyle or Mill or Ruskin with the definition of such terms as progress, liberty, representation or economics – as opposed to their customary usage – is something which is distinctively Scots. It is the response of intellectuals from a distinct but declining culture to a metropolitan culture under pressure from social change, a transfer of loyalty from a peripheral to what they saw as a central nationalism. It parallels the incorporation of the Jews within German culture during the nineteenth century,[22]

> alienated from a Judaism which they regarded as parochial, greatly attracted by the single-mindedness and relentless moral seriousness of a German cultural tradition which had profound affinities with that of the Jews themselves.

Ardent theoreticians of a language only then becoming prominent as a literary and scientific medium, Jewish intellectuals from Heine and Marx to Freud and Karl Kraus transferred to it the loyalty their fathers would have devoted to their own culture. The founders of the Pan-German Party in the Austrian Empire were Jews. Zionism only came with racial rejection and anti-Semitic propaganda. But the Scots never suffered from this. Assimilation, in the age of British imperialism, proved total. When the university intelligentsia campaigned for democratic reform in the 1860s in volumes like *Essays on Reform* (1867) they demanded 'a more national spirit in our politics'. Their arguments might be drawn from Mazzini, and almost half of them were either Scots or partly Scots, but the nation they invoked was Britain.

The search for social structures which could contain the

ambitions released by Calvinism and improvement became a central component of the 'emigration ideology' Carlyle played such a large part in creating. Foreign involvement in general and imperialism in particular satisfied this drive. One or two writers were bold enough to provide intellectual justifications, like John Davidson, the disciple of Nietszche, who saw the work of the empire builder as the destiny of the race:[23]

> I broke your slothful dream of folded wings,
> Of work achieved and empire circumscribed,
> Dispelled the treacherous flatteries of peace,
> And thrust upon you in your dull despite
> The one thing needful, half a continent
> Of habitable land! The English Hell
> For ever crowds upon the English Heaven.
> Secure your birthright; set the world at naught;
> Confront your fate; regard the naked deed;
> Enlarge your Hell; preserve it in repair;
> Only a splendid Hell keeps Heaven fair.

But it was more often accepted without qualification, morally justified by the concept of trusteeship, exemplified in the Indian administrators, the soldiers and the missionaries: in the respect shown Livingstone by the Africans he protected and the Arabs he fought.

It even penetrated movements which were ostensibly anti-imperial. The agitation about Turkish brutality and misgovernment in the late 1870s, which reached its peak in Gladstone's Midlothian campaign, was explicitly directed against Disraeli's 'imperialism', yet it also asserted the superiority of the values of protestantism, and Scottish Protestantism in particular, over the Turk, the Catholic and the Jew. It was a prelude to the energetic imperialism of Scottish Liberals, like Lord Rosebery, in the 1890s.[24] More complex yet is the case of R. W. Seton-Watson who, a decade later under the flag of 'Scotus Viator', set himself to lead the Slavs out of the bondage of the

Hapsburg Empire with, as matters turned out, considerable success. 'Scotus Viator' was a fairly impressive example of responsibility, although an excess of this probably helped bring about the collapse of the balance of power on which the new liberties depended. But he could not have existed in a non-imperial Britain.

At the very least imperialism provided a set of injunctions to which the individual could relate. Emile Durkheim connected the ultimate social breakdown of suicide with the degree to which society imposed its demands on the individual, 'a bolt that might snap if the nut of society held it too tightly or too loosely'.[25] For the Scot the constrictions of parochial society could be deadly, and the intermediate level of the nation-state was not available. The 'emigration ideology', exploitation and trusteeship, offered a structure which might hold. The resulting stress on responsibility produced a cast of mind which was less imaginative, more mechanistic, less hopeful. Conrad, possibly the most perceptive observer of the varying impact of the imperial experience on the European consciousness, drew it vividly in Captain MacWhirr, the Ulster-Scot captain of the stricken 'Nan-shan' in *Typhoon.* Kipling echoed him in the lines he gave engineer MacAndrew:[26]

> But – average fifteen hunder souls safe-borne fra' port to
>   port –
> I *am* o' service to my kind. Ye wadna blame the thought?
> Maybe they steam from Grace to Wrath – to sin by folly
>   led –
> It isna mine to judge their path – their lives are on my
>   head.

To opt out of this dialectic, to make one's own rules, above all to try to achieve something significant *in* Scotland, was to court disaster. Nineteenth-century Scotland is fitfully illuminated by genius flaring and then guttering into eccentricity or oblivion: Edward Irving trying to unify all the Christian churches,

Carlyle or Ruskin driving themselves into dementia with their rage against society, Hugh Miller trying to equate Genesis and geology and ending by shooting himself, Charles Rennie Mackintosh designing his buildings, whisky bottle in hand. Originality, if unconstrained by empire, nationality or community, seemed to lead to destruction.

Self-destruction against the background of a powerful nationalist movement, could send reverberations through a culture. Parnell's martyrdom in 1891 at the hands of the bishops and his party created a symbol which had baneful effects on the younger generation of Irish nationalist writers, from Yeats to Sean O'Faolain. But the fate of the 'uncanny Scot' was to vanish into the dark. The poet John Davidson, whose ambitions were the greatest, and who influenced talents as diverse as Hugh MacDiarmid and T. S. Eliot, walked into the sea in 1909, to be remembered by MacDiarmid as 'A bullet-hole through a great scene's beauty, God through the wrong end of a telescope'. The imperial experience highlights the crucial anomaly of nineteenth-century Scotland: the failure of the idea of development to coincide with nationalism. The national institutions which, in other countries, provided both the matrix for industrialisation – and the consequent division of society on class lines – and the means of socialising the intellectuals, failed to overcome their eighteenth-century limits: in fact, they generally regressed. The Kirk split, the law stagnated; by the 1870s any moderately gifted Oxford graduate stood a good chance of a chair at a Scottish university, if he couldn't get a fellowship. But Scotland remained distinctive, and the red Scots, the beneficiaries of an achieving society, wished to keep it so. At the very least it provided a relatively democratic means of recruitment for a metropolitan and imperial society otherwise dominated by aristocratic and professional privilege. A vacuum however, remained: of nationalist *expectation* in Scotland itself. It was soon filled by the treacly effluent of the Kailyard.

VI

The Kailyard had both a specific and a general identity. Historically it was a little constellation of novelists and short-story writers which emerged in the 1880s and 1890s around William Robertson Nicoll, Free Churchman, editor and confidant of Lloyd George, and Sir J. M. Barrie. They specialised in sentimental tales of rural Scotland and cunningly contrived to scoop a large market both in Britain and among the emigrants in North America. When he died of pneumonia in Mount Pleasant, Iowa in 1907, while on an American lecture tour, the Rev. John Watson, 'Ian Maclaren', had already sold several million copies of books like *Beside the Bonnie Briar Bush* and *The Days of Auld Langsyne* on both sides of the Atlantic. The Rev. S. R. Crockett did almost as well with *The Stickit Minister* and *The Lilac Sunbonnet*. There were others – rather less characteristic and consequently rather more durable – like Neil Munro and J. J. Bell, whose comic stories bore some relation to the urban experience of most nineteenth-century Scots, but on the whole the formula provided a commercially viable escape route into the nirvana of a rural past.[27]

The influence of the ideas which gave rise to the Kailyard – the word is Lowland Scots for kitchen garden – was more widespread than the definition would suggest. The Robertson Nicoll school was quite a late development. Burns, Scott, Galt and Hogg could lapse from time to time into sentimentality, but the countryside they wrote about was real enough. The Kailyard was the result of deliberate cultivation. Dismissing the Scottish Rights Association in the 1850s, Henry Cockburn wrote:[28]

> the memory of Old Scotland . . . can only live in the character of its people, in its native literature, and in its picturesque and delightful language. The gradual disappearance of the Scotch

accent and dialect is a national calamity which not even this magniloquent association can arrest.

This could be called its inaugural address. Five years later Edward Ramsey, Episcopalian Dean of Edinburgh, printed his *Reminiscences of Scottish Life and Character*, which had run through twenty-two editions by his death in 1872. While Cockburn had used recollection and anecdote to illuminate his own interpretation of the events he had experienced, Ramsay consigned the community to the museum of anecdote, producing what he thought was a harmless and heart-warming form of entertainment for an age which had forsworn the reading of pernicious authors like Richardson and Fielding. He was followed by many lesser talents, producing pawky and quaint characters by the hundred, catering for a secure middle-class market at home and abroad which wished to be reminded of a wholesome Scotland, untainted by urban and industrial problems.

The power of the stereotypes thus created was nowhere more obvious than in the work of the authors who attacked them. To read George Douglas Brown's *The House with the Green Shutters* or J. MacDougall Hay's *Gillespie* is simply to see the Kailyard inverted: a world of Scottish small towns whose inhabitants are preoccupied with doing each other down and killing each other off. Both books are satires on a genre; but the genre, and the preoccupation with it, diverted the novel, and Scots literature in general, from the inquiry into individual consciousness and social change for which it had appeared, in the early nineteenth century, uniquely well fitted. A novelist like Scott was – to quote F. R. Leavis on the proper stance of the poet – not far from being 'at the most conscious point of the race in his time'; the same could be said of John Galt, with his Balzacian studies of land and politics in the Scotland of Dundas. But this impulse then petered out: no Dickens or Bennett wrote in the shadow of the Scottish cities; no Hardy recorded the commercialisation of the land, and the experience of migration. In fact it was left to Hardy – the Wessex Hardy – to pin down the Kailyard Scot himself, sentimental and astute, in the character of Donald Farfrae in the *Mayor of Casterbridge*.

Why did the tradition of realist literature fail? It was certainly hard enough for any novelist to follow Scott, whose reputation cast a long shadow. It was also difficult to write honestly about the moral ambiguities of the 'emigration ideology' and imperialism, while benefiting from both. Yet the central constricting factor was surely this: Scott was at his weakest in exploring individual consciousness and in tackling the new social relationships of industrial society, and it was in these respects that his tradition had to be elaborated. Enough experiments had been made in this direction by Hogg and Galt to show that it was possible. But there experimentation stopped, checked by the growth of religious puritanism and the hypocrisy inherent within it. The moral indictment must be made. Scottish society was beset with terrifying social problems which any realistic treatment was bound to expose; and of these the customary targets of religious condemnation – alcoholism and promiscuity – were merely accompaniments of the deep-seated and intractable evils of poverty and overcrowding which the economic system was incapable of remedying. Realism in literature would not only expose these, thus posing a revolutionary challenge to society, it would also break the discipline of puritanism by mentioning the unmentionable. The Kirk enforced silence out of conviction, the middle classes out of fear. The bogus community of the Kailyard was promoted as an alternative to the horror of the real thing. 'Although expatriate Scots, like Thomas Common and William Archer, the first translators of Ibsen and Nietzsche, attempted to cope with intellectual change, the predicament of Scotland, as Robert Louis Stevenson found, remained a schizophrenic state which could only be suggested by allegory. Dr Jekyll and Mr Hyde remain the most potent symbols the nineteenth century in Scotland produced.

This social escapism also penetrated cultural activities in which the standard of work produced was far superior, and attained international recognition. If *fin de siècle* Scottish literature is forgettable, *fin de siècle* Scottish art and architecture is not. This was the period of the 'Glasgow Boys' – W. Y. MacGregor, E. A. Walton, John Lavery – who domesticated the techniques of Whistler and the French realists, of William MacTaggart, whose west-coast impressionism was quite *sui generis*, of the art nouveau designers and architects around Charles Rennie Mackintosh, of the arts and crafts revivalism of Robert Lorimer and the structural innovation of J. J. Burnet. The country houses and middle-class villas of Scotland, turreted, stone-built, step-gabled, but still convenient and manageable, bear witness to a generation of architects whose talents were widely but productively diffused. But, as far as both artists and architects were concerned, industrial Scotland did not exist. The painters' subject-matter was drawn from the land, from the small towns, from the seaboard. If they abandoned the folksiness of Sir David Wilkie and his less talented successors, and the sycophancy of the portraitist Sir Henry Raeburn, they also abandoned Wilkie's absorption with his society and Raeburn's delineation of the character of a ruling class. Apart from Muirhead Bone, an excellent architectural draughtsman rather than a painter, and John Quinton Pringle, a talented amateur, the artists totally ignored Glasgow, its industries and its slums. There was no Scottish Daumier or Van Gogh (although Scottish patrons and dealers bought both), not even an equivalent of Sickert and the Camden school. Even the breakthrough in photography made by Octavius Hill in the 1840s, which could have been the basis for stylistic innovation and the exploitation of new subject-matter – as in France – was never followed up. There was talent and skill in plenty, but it could not conceal a fundamental lack of inspiration.

The same could be said of the architects. The best of them, like Burnet, drew on the functional tradition – the plain, purpose-built factories and engine-shops of the industrial revolution – to produce an impressive urban style, comparable with the Chicago school in the USA. In the 1870s and 1880s there was even some prospect that architects might take the lead in social reform, when several bold experiments in workers' housing, employing standard modules, were carried out. Given the huge output of strictly functional architecture, in the shape of ships and railway equipment, innovation in architectural practice seemed almost inevitable. But it didn't happen: architecture in Scotland in 1914 was stylistically and socially as conservative as it had been forty years earlier. Burnet had set out to conquer new territory in London; Mackintosh, the greatest Scottish architect since the Adam brothers, was deserted by all but a few patrons and took to drink and water-colours; Robert Lorimer built meticulous reconstructions of seventeenth-century castles for millionaires; the Glasgow people went on living in their one- and two-roomed flats.

There was one dissenting voice: a throwback to the universal intellect of the Enlightenment. Patrick Geddes, biologist, sociologist, architect, town planner and socialist, established in 1892 at the Outlook Tower, at the top of Edinburgh's picturesque and squalid Royal Mile, a community hall which was to become a pioneer sociological research institute. Geddes, the pupil of Huxley and Haeckel, used concepts derived from biology to argue for an organic balance – an ecology – of the sexual, social and political life, which could become a goal for community planning. He took up the theme that Carlyle voiced sixty years before.[29]

> Everything I have done has been biocentric; for and in terms of life, both individual and collective; whereas all the machinery of state, public instruction, finance and industry ignores life when indeed it does not destroy it.

Geddes's fate was peculiar, but characteristic enough of red Scotland. He had no lack of patrons. He projected fifty town planning schemes in India and the Middle East, established a considerable reputation in America, chiefly through his disciples Victor Branford and Lewis Mumford, and in 1924 founded and settled at the Scots College at Montpellier in France where, in 1930, he received a knighthood from Ramsay MacDonald. His influence on social planning in the twentieth century has been incalculable if not wholly beneficial, as his ecological preoccupations precluded a realistic appraisal of the role of less inspirational factors like politics and economics. In a profession as morally ambiguous as presentday town planning, his name is more often than not quoted to conceal fairly ruthless commercial calculation. But in turn-of-the-century Scotland it was scarcely quoted at all. His pioneer town plan for Dunfermline, commissioned by the Carnegie Trust, was turned down by the council. None of his schemes bore fruit on his native soil: the opportunities provided by empire proved more engrossing than Scotland's intractable social problems.

VII

Geddes was one of the first to recognise the Scottish literary renaissance of the 1920s. Indeed, thirty years earlier he had tried to incubate something of the sort as a publisher at the Outlook Tower, along the lines of the contemporary Irish movement, but it produced no Yeats: nothing more durable than the 'harps in the twilight' fantasy of Fiona MacLeod. The 1920s renaissance certainly involved talents considerably superior to those of the nineties: Neil Gunn, Edwin Muir, Lewis Grassic Gibbon, James Bridie, Compton Mackenzie, Eric Linklater; and it had in the genius of Hugh MacDiarmid a figure comparable to Yeats and Joyce. It has been a continuing influence, important though also complex, on the post-war nationalist movement. But at the time, during a depression which compounded all the problems of industrial Scotland, it made only a marginal impact, scarcely more influential than the political movement.

Any discussion of the Scottish renaissance has got to begin with MacDiarmid because he is its central figure and, as an individual artist and literary entrepreneur, he deliberately stated the predicament of the national intelligentsia. MacDiarmid's aim was vast to pull red and black Scotland, thesis and antithesis, into confrontation, creating out of perpetual intellectual debate a continuing, vital culture. This was not achieved by any logical process; but logic and consistency figured nowhere in MacDiarmid's programme. Aristocrat and democrat, nationalist and cosmopolitan, communist and social creditor, urbane conversationalist and soap-box ranter, he set out, with all the energy of a Victorian sage like Carlyle, to comprehend everything:[30]

> I'll hae nae hauf-way hoose, but aye be whaur
> Extremes meet – it's the only way I ken
> To dodge the curst conceit o' bein' right
> That damns the vast majority o' men.

Thus his manifesto of 1926 'A Drunk Man looks at the Thistle': a pledge which he has consistently kept. Yet it has only been since the Second World War, and in particular since the late 1950s, that the scope of his ambition – and the size of his achievement – has been recognised. This is a tribute to the maturity in recent years of the Scottish intelligentsia, but it raises the question: why, after producing poetry, political and lyrical, of rare insight, wit and beauty, and a vast and challenging output of critical writing, was he neglected by a society which, in all conscience, was crying out for such transfusions of activism?

MacDiarmid was not ignored in the twenties and thirties – the intelligentsia did shift some way along the road he attempted to push it. But then it stuck. Alternately ogre and martyr,

MacDiarmid remained (sometimes literally) in the wilderness, his work circulating almost in 'samizdat' form. Where he was appreciated, it tended to be for the wrong reasons, sometimes for the wrong poems (an inveterate and often haphazard employer of quotations, some of his quotations became, in time, attributed to him). On the whole, he tended to be regarded as a gifted vernacular lyric poet, with a taste for grinding an excessive number of linguistic and political axes. The reasons for this were various, and not the least of these was his own complex personality. Not everyone was eager to revive the old tradition of 'flyting' or intense literary argument, to talk politics, literature and music for twelve hours at a stretch, and to drink opponents to a standstill. Yet this combination of private conviviality and public aggressiveness was matched, intellectually, by the tension between his Scottish loyalties and his universal ambitions.

MacDiarmid was not affected by the Scottish crisis alone. As a member of the *New Age* avant-garde he was aware, as were Yeats, Eliot and Pound, of the trauma an 'industrialised' war had inflicted on the values and coherence of European civilisation in general and Britain in particular: a society already grown mechanistic and spiritually empty had suffered a moral as well as a material blood-letting. These intellectuals from societies which had once been provincial to an English centre saw its collapse and sought alternatives, all the time aware of the extent to which their own identity had depended on it. Eliot's invocation of Anglo-Catholicism, Pound's identification with the European revolutionary right, Yeats's return to Ireland were all attempts to construct an alternative reality. MacDiarmid's combination of cosmopolitanism and nationalism stood in this tradition, as did its complement, his Anglophobia. Nationalism was a synthetic construct, an alternative to the mediocre provincialism that English culture had itself become. Even MacDiarmid's definitions of Scotland were imprecise. In *Albyn* he claimed it as 'the old Brythonic kingdom', taking in England down to the Humber and the Mersey.[31] His friends and allies, Denis Saurat, Pound, K. S. Sorabji, Sean O'Casey, were closer to being an international 'Salon des Refusés' than a provincial intelligentsia. His conviction of the mission of the small nation to redeem civilisation was drawn from the dubious but stimulating source of Spengler's *Decline of the West*. Neither this heterogeneity nor the variability of his own output bothered him much. In his own engaging way he described himself as a volcano 'producing heat and light and also a great deal of rubbish'. Activism was all. The trouble was that the correspondence between the European breakdown and the Scottish opportunity was far from exact.

For a start, the Scottish literary movement had itself no ideological homogeneity. It was an *ad hoc* coalition brought about largely for defensive reasons – a sideways glance at Ireland and a preoccupation with the break-up of Scottish society – in which linguistic revivalists coexisted with local journalists, ex-Kailyarders, established or hopeful Anglo-Scottish writers and romantics of left and right. It lacked the strength of the coalition between mass organisation, academic activity and aristocratic patronage which had created the Irish literary movement in the 1890s, and in the absence of this sort of backing, the linkage of ex-home rulers (backed up by the journalists, Kailyarders and Anglo-Scots) and root-and-branch separatists (backed up by the linguistic revivalists) could not be expected to last. For the moment, however, the use of the vernacular by the generation of poets which MacDiarmid headed gained general approval from both sides, as a means of conserving national distinctiveness. Much play was made with the survival of the *Landsmaal* dialect in Norway and the Frisian dialect in North Germany. 'Lallans' or the Lowland Scots dialect, elements of which were still common enough in working-class talk, seemed to provide a linguistic line to be held against 'creeping Anglicisation'. At the very least it was a compromise which bought off the real wild men who wanted to restore the Gaelic. The Lallans revival, however, provided the rock on which the literary movement foundered.

Vernacular poetry had continued after Burns, and the growth of the local press stimulated its quantitative expansion. Sixteen dreadful volumes of *Modern Scottish Poets*, exhumed from newspaper back-files for the most part, were published in the latter years of the nineteenth century:[32]

> Frae mony a but and ben,
> By muirland, holm and glen,
> They cam' an hour to spen' on the greenwod sward;
> But lang hae lad an' lass
> Been lying 'neth the grass,
> The green, green grass o' Traquair kirkyard.

Not Harry Lauder but an Oxford professor of poetry in demotic mood: Principal Shairp's 'The Bush aboon Traquair' amply demonstrates the thinness of the dialect tradition; Swinburne and Kipling, who were not Scots, could, and did, do better. But, MacDiarmid believed, with a properly exploited traditional vocabulary, Lallans was capable of handling a wide range of subject-matter with greater force and subtlety than standard English. More than any Scots predecessor his model in this was James Joyce, who in *Ulysses* (1922) had used a reworked language, and the peculiar discomfort of the Irish literary and political experience, as a springboard into the complex and subtle exploration of human consciousness.

Lallans was particularly rich in words and idioms denoting action, physical shape, destruction and disorganisation, and abuse of all sorts, while it could retain the dignified cadences of the Makars, the mediaeval court poets. MacDiarmid took full advantages of this variety in his greatest poems, ranging from knockabout to cosmic speculation to images of the fulfilment of body and mind. 'A Drunk Man looks at the Thistle' is a statement about the relationship of the individual to culture, community and the life of the intellect comparable in scope to the contemporary extended poems of Yeats, Eliot and Pound. This is not the place to attempt comparisons of quality, but 'this lurching, inebriate's progress from Milne's Bar to the Absolute Idea and back again',[33] as Tom Nairn has called it, carries tremendous power, not simply because of its ambitions, but because argument and deflating wit continually burst in to bring the poet back to the reality he has to vitalise:[34]

> Sae God retracts in endless stage
> Through angel, devil, age on age,
> Until at last his infinite natur'
> Walks on earth a human cratur'
> (Or less than human as to my een
> The people are in Aiberdeen);
> Sae man returns in endless growth
> Till God in him again his scouth.*

The thistle, mutating throughout the drunk man's vision, is not a symbol of nationalism: it is the eternal negation of man's present state, on which his mind must act, as thesis on antithesis, to secure his liberation. The nation, on the other hand, is a human construct, a necessary matrix of traditions and institutions, which can be – indeed has to be – used to cope with and homogenise this process:

> Thou, Dostoevski, understood,
> Wha had your ain land in your bluid,
> And into it as in a mould
> The passion o' your bein' rolled,
> Inherited in turn frae Heaven
> Or sources fer abune it even.
>
> Is Scotland big enough to be
> A symbol o' that force in me,
> In wha's divine inebriety
> A sicht abune contempt I'll see?

* Scouth = scope.

For a' that's Scottish is in me,
As a' things Russian were in thee,
And I in turn 'ud be an action
To pit in a concrete abstraction
My country's contrair qualities,
And mak' a unity o' these
Till my love owre its history dwells,
As owretone to a peal o' bells.

And in this heicher stratosphere
As bairn at giant at thee I peer. . .[35]

MacDiarmid's intentions for Lallans went far beyond the liberal-minded *gemeinschaft* ideals of most vernacular revivalists. In his political poems written around 1930 – the first two 'Hymns to Lenin' and 'The Seamless Garment' – he used it to communicate directly with working people to promote communism and political mobilisation:[36]

Hundreds to the inch the threids lie in
  Like the men in a communist cell.
There's a play o' licht frae the factory windas.
  Could you no' mak' mair yoursel?
Mony a loom mair alive than the weaver seems
For the sun's still nearer than Rilke's dreams.

The recent international recognition of the size of MacDiarmid's achievement has given him a significant place in the English-speaking cultural tradition. His experiments with language, both Lallans and his later 'scientific' idiom, place him alongside those writers whose cultural bearings were re-oriented by the First World War. The depth and authenticity of his political commitment makes him a much more important socialist poet than the public school radicals of the 1930s. In this he fits into the 'red Scottish' tradition. But if he is the twentieth-century counterpart of Scott, his relations with nationalism seem as ambivalent. In his own day, Yeats or

Joyce were similarly placed. But to a much greater extent even than Yeats, he suffered from the 'the day's war with every dolt' that organising a national movement implied. Yeats was at least given, by his patrons among the Anglo-Irish Ascendancy and in America, a theatre in which to transform the mob into a nation, and a stage from which to berate it when its notion of nationality diverged from his. MacDiarmid, among journalists and popularisers, found that an apparent unanimity about the plight of Scotland masked a general hostility to his own goals and standards.

VIII

For MacDiarmid, Lallans was a vehicle for national differentiation and political mobilisation. The idea of preserving the old community was always secondary, although it was always present. Langholm, his boyhood home in the Scottish Borders, continued to supply symbols for his later work – 'the ground-plan of my mind' – and his dislike of cities has led him to spend most of his life in the country.[37] A retrospective idea of community was even more powerful in the other writers of the renaissance, in Gunn, Linklater and Muir. Gunn rarely strayed out of the Highlands, and couched his political and philosophical allegories in terms of the natural and social life of the society he knew. To the Orcadians Linklater and Muir, the communities of the northern islands were always an alternative to the brittle and changing relationships of the south. But the opposition of community and progressive politics was seen at its most intense in the work of James Leslie Mitchell, 'Lewis Grassic Gibbon', whose achievement as a novelist came close to MacDiarmid's as a poet. In three novels written in an arresting vernacular prose-poetry, *Sunset Song* (1932), *Cloud Howe* (1938), and *Grey Granite* (1934), collectively called *A Scots Quair*, Gibbon described the decline and dispersal of an east-coast farming community under the pressure of war and industrialisation. The novels, strongly influenced by Marxism, move from the passivity of the crofters in the face of the destruction of their community by war and profiteering, to the conversion of the heroine's son, in the final novel, to 'a faith that will cut like a knife' and a role in the militant labour movement of the Scots cities. Yet the heroine herself, Chris Guthrie, who moves through this enforced social evolution, completes the circle by returning to the land, symbolising Gibbon's other, near-mystical faith in 'the great, green international' which links peasant communities throughout the world and in other ages, back to the men who reared the megalith circles which loom over the parks of Kinraddie.[38] Between traditional community and international revolution, Gibbon found no place for Scottish nationalism, which appears in the *Quair* only to be ridiculed. Although he joined MacDiarmid in shooting up bourgeois Scotland in *The Scottish Scene*, published just before his tragically early death in 1934, he had little sympathy with the compromises involved in his friend's nationalist projects.

The problem was that the literary revival was a political movement: not in the ideological sense, but in the sense that the cohesion of potentially fissile elements had to be maintained by continual balance and negotiation. And MacDiarmid was – almost by his own definition – no politician. But he had acted for so long as arbiter of what should, or should not, come within the pale of the literary movement, that he became identified with it more than with his own views: a battleship sailing uneasily in convoy with pleasure-steamers. His discomfort increased as the literary movement became more explicitly political towards the end of the 1920s, as the politics of most of its journalistic and Anglo-Scottish adherents were not his own revolutionary brand, or even those of the National Party he had helped found in 1928, but gravitated towards the moderate Scottish Party. When, in preparation for the amalgamation between two parties, the left wing of the Nationalists was purged in 1933, MacDiarmid was the first to go. The implications of the defeat were considerable: MacDiarmid seemed to make intellectual concessions to promote the political movement, but it had failed to show any signs of ideological maturity, and rejected him for the conservative establishment that he loathed. The political nationalists soon found that their attempt at consensus did not pay off, and were left with the enduring stigma of being hostile to the intellectuals.

This attack was pressed home in 1936 by Edwin Muir in *Scott and Scotland*, written, ironically, in response to a commission from MacDiarmid. Muir was scarcely a lesser figure and, as a nationalist, socialist and social crediter, shared several of MacDiarmid's political enthusiasms. An Orkneyman who had migrated in poverty to Glasgow, he had been, in fact, more deeply affected by the experience of industrial society. He had struggled out of it via the ILP and socialist journalism, settled in Europe, and gained an international reputation – at that time more as the translator of Kafka and Rilke than as a poet. Although he had sympathised with the Lallans movement in the 1920s, he saw Scotland in the following decade as the casualty of its own offspring, industrialisation and repressive puritanism. His remedies were socialism and a regenerated community, in comparison with which nationalist politics and the vernacular revival threatened to cut Scotland off, permanently, from the European cultural mainstream.[39] Muir was no provincial. Life in Czechoslovakia in the 1920s and 1930s had led to sympathy with the new European nations; but he had also become aware of the totalitarian threat. His cosmopolitanism was as great as MacDiarmid's, but the gap between community and nationalism was real enough. Moreover, he reflected the regrouping of the European intelligentsia in the face of fascism, which had succeeded the centrifugal tendencies of the 1920s. Scottish nationalism of MacDiarmid's militant variety seemed to him to divide, where unity was needed.

Muir's stance was, however, marginal to the Scottish intellectual predicament. To blame Scotland's problems on the Reformation was to neglect the achievements of Calvinism and the Enlightenment, and the persistence of a unique form of Scottish, if not national, consciousness in both. So, not surprisingly, he misinterpreted as parochial MacDiarmid's programme, which was anything but:[40]

> To prove my saul is Scots I maun begin
> Wi' what's still deemed Scots and the folk expect,
> And spire up syne by visible degrees
> To heichts whereo' the fules ha'e never recked.

On the other hand various of the lesser talents in the MacDiarmid convoy were easy meat. Political poetry is the great soft option for cultural critics with more opinions than evidence. MacDiarmid the politician, already thrown over by the nationalists, rounded on Muir and attacked him without mercy and without any vestige of political *nous*. At a time when personality counted in establishing the credentials of the vernacular revival, MacDiarmid appeared an unhelpful amalgam of Calvinist ranter and Stalinist commissar, persecuting the diffident and gentle Muir. At the same time he forsook Lallans for the elaborate quasi-scientific vocabulary of his later work, with a grand Carlyleian curse:[41]

> The idiom of which constructive thought avails itself
> Is unintelligible save to a small minority
> And all the rest wallow in exploded fallacies
> And cherish for immortal souls their gross stupidity.

He had intended the revival to be promoted by continual dialectic; but it wasn't strong enough for this.

The 1930s were as much a decade of eclipse for MacDiarmid, assailed by personal and money problems, as for literary nationalism. Despite his radicalism, he fared no better with the Communists than he had with the National Party. Despite a membership and leadership which included a large number of Scots, the Communist Party had always looked to the south. In the 'popular front' atmosphere of the 1930s it was, moreover, eager to court the anti-fascist establishment, notably the Labour Party, and not nationalism (scarcely the decade's most presentable ideology). The Scots who had fought for the International Brigade in Spain evoked great sympathy; the Scottish Tories even produced an anti-fascist aristocrat in the shape of the Duchess of Atholl; pacifist, internationalist and left-wing causes were strongly backed at the universities, hitherto the stronghold of nationalism. In 1936 the Rev. Dick Shepperd, founder of the Peace Pledge Union, was elected Rector of Glasgow in a campaign which attracted national attention, soundly beating Winston Churchill. In fact, in terms of the liberal-left dissent which dominated the decade, the red Scots found (as it happened for the last time) that they were well served by the United Kingdom. Lord Reith was telling the masses what they ought to hear, John Grierson what they ought to look at, Boyd Orr what they ought to eat, and J. B. S. Haldane what they ought to think.

By the Second World War literary nationalism seemed to have made only limited progress among the Scottish intelligentsia, whose definitions of 'Scottishness' within the Union still appeared to have continuing validity. The ideology which underlay the national institutions – Kirk, law and education – was still intact, as were the channels for promotion by merit within the United Kingdom and the empire. The economic component of the Union had cracked, but its political and intellectual components had held, and so had ensured that remedies for economic ills would largely be couched in Unionist terms, whether from right or from left. While the wartime devolution of authority meant that nationalism of a ceremonial sort was more in evidence – the *Scots Independent* applauded the fact that St Andrew's day in November 1944 was celebrated by the government and the BBC on an unprecedented scale – the most this seemed to offer was the resurrection of the Kailyard.[42] Political nationalism of this sort appeared so innocuous that it was almost an aid to integration into United Kingdom society. 'Actually, I'm a bit of a Scottish nationalist' conveyed a vague centrism, more acceptable than socialism or even, in an age of waning faith, profound religious conviction.

But seeds had been sown. Younger poets, like Sidney Goodsir Smith, Douglas Young and Robert Garioch, writing in Lallans, or like Norman McCaig, George Bruce and Maurice Lindsay, writing in English, were the inheritors both of MacDiarmid's rigour and of his conviction that real creativity was possible in Scotland. From the Highlands, the Skye schoolmaster Sorley Maclean contributed lyrics in Gaelic of a quality unknown since the eighteenth century. The great treasury of song and ballad created by fisherfolk, farm labourers, crofters and textile workers was gradually being explored. A dictionary of the vernacular had been started in 1931. In the schools younger teachers, like Bruce or McCaig or Hector MacIver at the Royal High School in Edinburgh were convincing the next generation that the Scottish revival was important within the European tradition. Whatever their metropolitan ambitions, the red Scots now felt that the renaissance could no longer be dismissed as a parochial outburst, that MacDiarmid, Gibbon and Muir, whatever their differences, were speaking with their accents, and had isolated in a Scottish context problems about the relationship of culture and society which the more hierarchical tradition of English social criticism had neglected. At this stage the feeling might only express itself in a mixture of guilt and irritation when others used the old stereotypes of black Scotland. But it existed.

PART II

Chapter 4

From Tendency to Transaction

1945 is the line of division, the hinge. Before then, the course of Scottish politics can be explained in terms of the main tendencies which had governed it. Thereafter, a different story has to be told in a different and more detailed way as politics become more unstable, more dependent on actions and reactions. The change is partly one of consciousness. The themes of the previous chapters have been retrospective ones, which only become distinct after 1945. The war had proved that nationalism, if marginal, was persistent. The depression had shown that Union and assimilation remained different things. The abstention of the intellectuals from "classic" nationalism through a sort of 'transferred nationalism' showed signs of coming to an end, and the intellectuals were now giving the Scots a consciousness of their experience which they had hitherto lacked.

After 1945 the British political establishment had to define its position *vis-à-vis* nationalism, which was something it had never done for up to a century. Whether the nationalist political challenge would have continued is debatable, even given its acceleration during the war, but the important thing is that the war changed the rules. In British society the state now took a leading role. The continuity of a Scottish society detached from party politics was no longer possible.

This had the consequence that, in Scottish affairs, activists consciously made use of such devolution as existed to secure reforms in the interest of specific social groups. Nationalists were only one group among many, but they could become an interest to be appeased. Such actions enhanced the distinctiveness of Scottish government, but they did so against a background of central government growth. During the nineteenth century Westminster was frequently insensitive to Scotland out of ignorance and indifference, but now, at some stage or other of decision making, sins of commission were also involved. Despite their promises, ministers' decisions inevitably had to hurt Scottish interests, while growing political fluidity gave the resulting resentment a cutting edge and channelled it into distinct types of response, around which activists could coalesce. The rise of the Scottish National Party was not itself inevitable. The other parties could have pre-empted it. They failed to do so partly because political tendencies were unfavourable, but also because of failures of leadership. And this may have been sufficient to deflect Scottish politics on to a course which they were unable to cope with.

Post-war politics in Scotland have hinged on two factors. The first is internal. The exercise of power has passed from the owners of the economy in alliance with the traditional institutions to political and administrative groups consciously concerned to provide collective answers to economic problems, with or without the assistance of external interests. The second factor stems from the ambitious economic aims of post-war British governments. The failure to combine sophisticated planning with either adequate finance or adequate consultation has helped promote a revolution of rising, but continually frustrated, expectations. Nationalism is only one of the possible responses but, in alliance with other factors on the Scottish scene, it has been able to move to the centre of the stage.

The distinctive quality of modern Scottish politics, especially since the late 1950s, has been their indeterminate and unpredictable nature. Far from an economic substructure responsive to certain simple fiscal controls underlying political behaviour, the Scottish economy had been the product of substantial, if not always sensitive or successful, political intervention. The behaviour both of the Scottish electorate and of power groups in Scotland has both depended on and influenced these transactions. This complexity is remote from the relatively simple equations between economics, class and political behaviour used by 'behaviourist' political scientists, whose 'psephology' has provided the market research for the essentially manipulative politics of the social democrat consensus. The failure of this consensus to come to terms with Scottish politics, as much as its failure to solve the country's economic problems, has provided the Nationalists with their opportunity.

Chapter 5

Leaders to no Sure Land: Unionist Scotland, 1945-1976

Consider these, for we have condemned them;
Leaders to no sure land. . . .

C. Day Lewis.

I

In 1936 a visit to Motherwell decided Edwin Muir to write his *Scottish Journey*. The sprawling, silent steel-manufacturing town seemed to him to exemplify, in its total subordination of community to material development, the fatal impact of industrialisation on Scotland.[1] With the slump it had ceased both to work and to exist as a community. It, and the hundreds of industrial settlements like it in the Scottish central belt, were simply accumulations of buildings and people, whose only reason for existence was their contribution to the organisation of capitalism.

Capitalism, wielded by Scots against Scots, not the depredations of the English, was the spectre that had to be exorcised before any valid community could be re-established.

Nine years later Motherwell was, however, to provide the Scottish Nationalists with their first election victory, and forty years later it remains significant as a paradigm of the Scottish predicament. The predicament, and Motherwell, has, however, changed. Few of the houses of 1936 remain; new housing schemes and multi-storey blocks, a new civic centre, a new station, have created a town Muir would scarcely recognise, a town that is strange to me, and I was born and brought up in it between 1944 and 1949.

The critical factor has not been capitalism, but government. In 1936 the vast majority of the working population was employed by several large privately-owned steel and heavy engineering companies, and rented its houses from private landlords. Now the state-owned British Steel Corporation is the main employer, and the Motherwell and Wishaw District Council is the landlord of 83 per cent of the households. More fundamentally, a series of policy decisions aimed at preserving employment and population have retained in being a settlement originally established for the convenience of capitalist industry. And what is true for Motherwell is even more true for the other settlements of the Scottish central belt, from the former colliery villages of Ayrshire to the former textile villages around Dundee. A combination of policies to attract work to areas of unemployment and to disperse the congested population of the Glasgow conurbation has created a new Scotland, neither urban nor rural, which straggles westwards from the fringes of the Firth of Forth to the lower Clyde. It is this unknown Scotland, not in the guide-books, away from the motorway, seen fleetingly from the express, that holds the key to the modern politics of the country.

After the war government action became critical at national and at local level. It meant that the traditional dialectic between autonomy and assimilation was superseded. Both tendencies grew, and competed, with the result that it was no longer easy to identify gains and losses. The decline or takeover of a traditional Scottish industry could be counterbalanced by specifically Scottish initiatives to attract substitute industries, or by the devolution of administration to Edinburgh. Conscious or unconscious, these responses reflected a changed balance in Scottish politics. Before the war they had been determined by economic performance, institutional conservatism and intellectual abstention. During it this gave way, albeit temporarily, to a dependence in personalities and political initiatives. Although this development subsequently slowed down, it created a framework in which people expected that a Scottish response would be made to economic difficulties. At the same time, the Labour councillors who fell heir to the local government of most of industrial Scotland were preoccupied with urban reconstruction, the attraction of industry and the highly political business of allocating council housing, to the exclusion of any long-term assessment of the future of their communities.

II

At both levels Scottish government was functional rather than deliberate. Despite wartime innovations no institutions existed which could discuss and plan for future social changes. Labour created a Scottish Economic Conference which was intended to continue the work of Johnston's Council on Industry. It met a few times in the late 1940s but lapsed when Labour left office in 1951. It was only a half-hearted gesture. Expansion in Scottish government was outpaced by the centralisation of decision making in London which followed the establishment of economic controls in 1941. This was not simply a wartime innovation. It was a victory for the reformist politicians and administrators of the centre-left who had advocated economic planning before the war, and it was perpetuated into peacetime as an essential aspect of economic policy. As well as a new ideology, a new élite had taken over, an academic oligarchy drawn from the two old English universities. Whatever gains Scottish autonomy had made during the war had to be set against this, and against the fact that a relative decline in population had weakened her bargaining-power as a region.

In a formal sense, the recognition of Scottish distinctiveness by central government became more pronounced after the war. The French Canadian politician René Levesque told a conference in Edinburgh in 1975 that when he had been stationed in Scotland during the Second World War government had emphasised its 'Britishness'. Now, although there had been no constitutional change, it was emphasising its 'Scottishness'. He contrasted this with the Canadian situation, where in a federation the power and self-confidence of the Federal government seemed continually to be stressed against the nominal sovereignty of the states. This shrewd perception reflected the way in which the devolved administration had expanded. In 1937 the Secretary of State supervised, along with one parliamentary under-secretary, 2,400 civil servants. Johnstone secured another under-secretary in 1941, and ten years later the Conservatives added another, along with a Minister of State of cabinet rank. By 1970, with addition by Labour of a second Minister of State, there were six political heads, as well as the two law officers, supervising 8,300 civil servants.[2] At the same time the competence of the Scottish Office was steadily extended. It took over electricity in 1954 and roads in 1956, and acquired the Scottish Development Department in 1962, the Highlands and Islands Development Board in 1965, and the Scottish Economic Planning Department in 1969. During the 1960s the pace of growth increased. While a chronology of Scottish administration and legislation during the 1950s would be fairly sparingly filled, in the 1960s it would be crammed with boards, commissions, inquiries, plans and bills.

Far from being a logical progression, however, the devolution of administrative authority was the result of two mutually opposed philosophies: socialist planning and Conservative hostility to it. The growth of the Scottish Office in the early 1950s stemmed directly from Churchill's promises of decentralisation. In his appeal to Scottish nationalism Churchill almost sounded like his father 'playing the Orange card' in Belfast sixty-four years earlier:[3]

> The principle of centralisation of government in Whitehall and Westminster is emphasised in a manner not hitherto experienced or contemplated in the Act of Union. The supervision, interference and control in the ordinary details of Scottish life and business by the Parliament at Westminster has not hitherto been foreseen, and I frankly admit that it raises new issues between the two nations . . . I do not therefore wonder that the question of Scottish home rule and all this movement of Scottish nationalism has gained in step with the growth of socialist authority and ambitions in England. I should never adopt the view that Scotland should be forced into the serfdom of socialism as the result of a vote in the House of Commons.

Churchill's rhetoric, like his promises of 'a senior member of the cabinet to be constantly in Scotland' – a Viceroy? – and the return of the Scottish university MPs, was the nationalism of noisy inaction, but the ministerial team was strengthened. By contrast, the next major accession of authority, in the mid-1960s, was carried out by a Labour government committed to centralised planning and (at least until 1968) eloquent against legislative devolution of any kind.

Despite this ambiguous history, St Andrew's House, and its newly-built and hideous satellite office blocks, had become by the late 1960s the terminus for an increasing amount of Scottish business. Its civil servants were 'much more accessible to the general public than those in Whitehall' and thought of their careers 'almost entirely in Scottish terms'. This was the opinion of Professor Hanham, a critic of its continued subservience to the south. His judgement that 'the creation of a Scottish parliament appears on the face of things to be the only way of revivifying the present administrative machine' was not in 1969, likely to provoke much dissent in St Andrew's House itself.[4]

The relative independent-mindedness of the Scottish administration was not something that any government, whether Labour or Conservative, had premeditated. It was the outcome of frustration when the functional role that it had been promised was, through economic circumstances, denied it. Had the Labour government's ambitious planning strategy worked, the Scottish Office would have continued to fulfil its role within the traditional administrative structure. Yet the economic problems it had to face seemed constantly to swell beyond its own capacities. The problem was that it was attempting to fill a role which had, before the Second World War, not been performed by government at all, but by the most powerful of the traditional Scottish institutions, the business community.

III

The only major business reputations made in post-war Scotland were those of the retailers Sir Hugh Fraser (Lord Fraser) and Sir Isaac Wolfson. Before the war, on the other hand, the leaders of the Scottish heavy industries played a major role as representatives of British as well as Scottish capitalism, and as senior government advisers and (in times of emergency) executives. Sir James Lithgow, the owner of the largest shipyard on the Clyde, also dominated the Federation of British Industry and the National Shipbuilders' Security Corporation, which 'rationalised' the industry in the 1930s. Sir William Weir (Viscount Weir), another Clydeside engineering magnate, took charge of aircraft production during the First World War, set up the electricity grid and the beet sugar industry in the 1920s, and replanned the transatlantic steamer services in the next decade.

Sir Andrew Duncan ran the Central Electricity Board and later the British Iron and Steel Federation. Lords Maclay and Inverforth dominated merchant shipping, and Lord Macgowan ICI, while Sir Robert Horne headed the Great Western and William Whitelaw the London and North Eastern Railways. These men represented the old school of business: the heavy industries. Their markets lay abroad, their solution to economic difficulties was wage reductions, their attitude to the new consumer goods industries one of unveiled hostility: 'sheltered industries' was the contemptuous epithet they used. They were realistic about the role of the state, and made admirable administrators of state or semi-state industries; they were also capable of quirky acts of goodwill to unorthodox bodies (Lithgow financed the Iona Community, run by the outspoken left-winger George MacLeod).[5] But their Cobdenite economics alienated them from the left, and their Unionism was fervent. In 1933 Scottish industrialists organised an energetic attack on the infant nationalist movement, which provided them with a secure place in its demonology. In the government of Britain, the victory of the centre-left in the early years of the war meant their departure from the right hand of the politicians, while in Scotland they appeared doubly damned as the architects of the country's dependence on a narrow and insecure industrial base. Deprived of power, their survivors and their sons sulked. They had little to do with bodies like the Scottish Council (Development and Industry) which depended heavily on largely Labour-controlled local authorities in the early post-war years. Yet neither it, nor the civil servants, could fill the void they left, and provide the link which bound Scottish industry to central government.

Yet the legacy of the heavy industries remained critically important. When the economics department of Glasgow University carried out a pioneer inquiry into the Scottish economy in the early 1950s it found that 'this dependence on heavy industry has grown rather than diminished'. The gloomy forecasts made during the war about their future were not borne out by events. Unlike the First World War, the Second World War left the shipyards of Germany and Japan in ruins, while Scottish yards suffered very lightly and were in a strong competitive position. The inquiry editor, Professor (Sir) Alexander Cairncross, noted:[6]

> it is neither surprising nor inappropriate that the products by which Scotland is best known abroad and of which she is proudest are the great liners that have been launched on the narrow Clyde.

The words 'liners' and 'narrow' were to have an ominous significance within very few years, especially when taken in conjunction with Cairncross's other, less flattering, observation about

> the comparative indifference of Scottish industry to new equipment, new knowledge, and new opportunities for development.

Four years later, the *Third Statistical Account* volume on *Glasgow* could still regard 50,000 tons as the upper limit of size for a freighter (the average size of a Clyde-built ship being 6,000 tons), and conclude that, all things considered, 'there is no fear of competition from the air' for the passenger liner.[7]

To take the *Queen Mary II* 'doon the watter' in the mid-1950s was to pass through a world which had changed little for half a century. The twenty-odd yards still employed 27,000 men, as many as they had employed in 1900. The old dynasties were still in control – Stephens, Yarrows, Lithgows – just as the old shipowners stuck to their traditional routes and their traditional liveries: black and red funnels for the Clan lines, black and buff for the 'Hungry Hogarths'. The Irish steamers still loaded at Anderston Quay, the MacBrayne coasters at Kingston Dock, Robertson's little puffers still butted down the Firth to Crinan and the beaches of the Outer Isles. The supertanker, the container ship, the vehicle ferry, the Boeing 707, seemed far away.

They were not. State-financed or subsidised yards in Europe or Japan or factories in America were already building them, with modern equipment, efficient management and a flexible labour force. On the Clyde purchases of new equipment made up barely half of annual depreciation, management was only equalled in conservatism by the unions. When nemesis came, it came fast. Between 1950 and 1954 Scotland's share of world shipbuilding output was 12 per cent; by 1968 it was 1·3 per cent. Only seven yards were still in production and of these only two were economically viable. When the *Queen Elizabeth II* steamed down the Firth on a maiden voyage which completed the disasters which had punctuated its construction, it left a river which was only marginally more lively than the Styx.

The collapse of the railway engineering industry was even more spectacular. In the early fifties it employed about 10,000 men in Glasgow, Motherwell and Kilmarnock. With 5,000 workers and three plants the North British Locomotive Company was the second-largest of its kind in the world, with a near-monopoly position in several Commonwealth countries. Practically every week a huge truck crawled down the streets from Springburn, bearing a gleaming locomotive to the great crane on Lancefield Quay which would swing it like a toy into the hold of some Singapore- or Durban-bound ship. Practically all these locomotives were steam: the technology of diesels and electrics was somewhat alien to Springburn, closer to that of the motor industry. And the market for steam locomotives was shrinking fast. Springburn tried to compete, taking advantage of the huge British Railways modernisation programme of 1955, but its products were disastrous. By 1960 the company, ironically under the chairmanship of Lord Reith, was moribund. By 1963 only one waggon works at Wishaw and a small locomotive works at Kilmarnock, together employing less than 1,000 men, remained.

The rapidity of heavy industrial decline was unexpected, but, through the intervention of government, new and at the time exciting industries were coaxed north to fill the vacuum. The Wiggins Teape group was persuaded to build a pulp and paper mill near Fort William, on a railway threatened with closure. In 1962 the British Motor Corporation announced a truck plant at Bathgate in West Lothian, and the Rootes Group a car plant near Paisley, promising a total of 11,000 jobs. To serve these the government loaned the steelmaking firm of Colvilles £50 million to build a strip mill at Motherwell, after a decision-making exercise characterised, in the words of an authoritative commentary, by 'secretiveness and lack of candour . . . (and) deliberate withholding of information'.[8] In such inauspicious circumstances did Scotland move into the new age of growth industries and regional economic policy.

The northward march of the motor industry was the result of government pressure. The other major growth sector of the Scottish economy owed much to pressure from Scottish bodies, notably the Scottish Council. This was the expansion of foreign-owned factories, mainly American. Such concerns were not new to Scotland. During the nineteenth century, while massive capital exports flooded from Scotland to America, there was a fairly strong counter-flow, bringing over the Singer sewing-machine factory at Clydebank, the North British Rubber Company in Edinburgh, and Babcock and Wilcox, 'the largest boilermaking works in the world', at Dumbarton and Renfrew. Dundee, which only a few decades earlier had been the fountain-head of investment in the American West, began the new wave by attracting National Cash Register in 1946. An energetic public relations campaign followed, aided by the legendary expatriate David Ogilvie of Ogilvie, Mather, with the result that in 1973 148 plants employing 14·9 per cent of the Scottish manufacturing work-force, were American-owned.[9] Of all American firms established in the United Kingdom since the war, over a third found sites in Scotland. Between 1958 and 1968 they accounted for 30 per cent of the employment created in Scotland.

But while this expansion sustained prosperity in several areas otherwise threatened with mass unemployment, it created numerous structural disadvantages. Industries like business machines or electronics, in which the American firms had a dominant role, were well adapted to female labour. They required high manual dexterity rather than craft specialism, and settled rapidly in areas like Dundee where the run-down of the traditional textile industries provided them with an inexpensive and adaptable work-force. This meant that the female labour force increased, while the male labour force continued to decline. Whatever this did to overall employment statistics, the absence of jobs for heads of families probably played a major part in promoting growing emigration during the 1950s and 1960s. Further, by depending on American managerial techniques and personnel, the American firms restricted upward mobility, research and development, and graduate recruitment. Although they employed 87,730 in 1973, they took on only 250 graduates between 1965 and 1969.[10] The industrial continuity which their high technology promised, masked an essentially colonial relationship in which decisions were 'taken' at head offices in New York or Chicago instead of being 'made' in Scotland.

IV

Manufacturing industry provided some sort of continuity with the Scottish past. It was still largely privately owned, and market-responsive. The role of government, though important. was marginal. Elsewhere, however, actions by the state proved critical, creating frameworks for economic and social change. Agricultural subsidies enabled the modernisation of farming on a scale unparalleled since the eighteenth century, but as a result the agricultural labour force fell between 1951 and 1971 by over 70 per cent, with a profound effect on the countryside of the Lowlands, the Borders, and the north-east of Scotland, as the activity of local centres declined, bus and train services became uneconomic, cinemas, halls and schools closed. Hitherto scruffy farm cottages, tidied up for weekend visits by the professional classes, belied a clearance as drastic as that of the nineteenth century. Rural Scotland was, increasingly, a country of the old.

In the Highlands and Islands, by contrast, past intervention by government had precisely the opposite effect on agricultural efficiency. The 1884 Crofters' Act had granted the crofters security of tenure, but its main intention, to produce holdings of viable size, was realized only in the Orkneys and Shetlands.[11] Elsewhere, the demoralisation bred of a century of eviction and emigration, and the continued indifference of landlords, sustained the slow dissolution of a society which seemed not to care all that much about achieving anything at all:

O that the peats would cut themselves,
  the fish chump on the shore,
that we might lie intil our beds,
  for ever and evermore!

North and west of Oban and Dingwall, an altogether different time-scale and logic seemed to take over. The roads became indescribably bad, trains, buses and steamers paid only nominal attention to timetables, crofting communities seemed to break records for Sabbatarianism, reliance on national assistance, and whisky drinking. The legend had a fair degree of reality behind it, not least the fact that the Highland way of life seemed somehow magically protected from the attentions of economists or anyone concerned in getting a return on investment. The prudent tourist travelled by motor coach or the S.S. *Killarney*, which cruised up the western coast in summer. Hardened gamblers could take a chance on public transport. Motoring from Southern Scotland to the north-west took days rather than hours, once the accumulated perils of elderly cars, single track roads, inadequate ferries and queasy children were taken into account. The Highland frontier still held, but only just.

Throughout the Highlands the traveller would encounter the dams and pylons of the North of Scotland Hydro-Electric Board, the major achievement of Johnston's secretaryship, which he now headed. £50 million had been spent on them by the time he retired in 1959, yet despite the powers the Board had to 'collaborate in the carrying out of any measures for the economic development and social improvement of the North of Scotland'[12] there had been none of the Tennessee Valley sort of industrial development that its proponents had hoped for and its opponents had feared. The only heavily capitalised industrial plants in the highlands were the distilleries and three aluminium works which had built their own hydro-electric schemes, and the withdrawal of the navy from its northern bases was actually diminishing the industrial element in the highland economy. By the 1960s the hope that cheap hydro-electric power would aid the Scottish economy seemed increasingly forlorn. At the limit of its development, in 1963, hydro-electricity provided under 30 per cent of Scotland's generating capacity; by 1973 this had dropped to 18 per cent. Could the money spent on Johnston's great vision not have been better employed re-equipping the Clyde shipyards and engineering works?

In a way the Hydro Board symbolised the relationship of government and the economy in the 1950s. Its purposes were vaguely nationalist and vaguely socialist. It served a myth, that of the Highland way of life. Its elegant power stations commemorated some sort of autonomy, an autonomy respected by a Conservative government. The Conservatives, in fact, intervened only gingerly in Scottish affairs, and respected the other great shibboleth of the Scottish left, the provision of subsidised housing. Although in 1961 42 per cent of Scottish households rented from local authorities, and in 1971 51 per cent – more than double the proportion in England – rents were on average less than half those in the south. This situation had existed since the First World War, and no attempt had been made to change it, despite the fact that losses on the housing accounts of Scottish burghs and counties were made good by the ratepayers, who could pay up to 25 per cent more than their southern counterparts.[13] The low rent policy of Scottish Labour councils was the nearest they came to imposing the 'dictatorship of the proletariat', and led to a direct political cleavage along owner-occupier/tenant lines. Edinburgh alone of the four cities had an owner-occupier majority, and Edinburgh alone was controlled by the right wing. Low rents were frequently gained by sacrificing amenities on housing estates: Billy Connolly's description of Glasgow's Easterhouse as 'a desert wi' windaes' is all too true. They also impeded mobility of labour, while the resulting high rates penalised commerce and industry. Yet the Conservatives retreated from confrontation, despite the fact that low rents had been shown to contribute little to solving the problem of the slums.

If the economic politics of Scotland were the politics of illusion, then illusions ended in the slump of 1957–8. The Glasgow economists had sounded a muted alarm in 1954:[14]

> The picture that emerges is of an industrial economy that shows signs of lagging behind the rest of the country.

By 1959 even the usually euphoric Scottish Council was announcing that 'on balance, the short term prospects for industry and employment in Scotland are not good'.[15] Besides the troubles of the heavy industries, which were now showing signs of terminal disease, the slump checked American investment. In October the Scottish electorate announced to Prime Minister MacMillan that it had had it better, and the Conservatives lost five seats. Thereafter Scotland began to figure more prominently, if not always consistently, in the thinking of both government and opposition.

V

1960 saw a general reorientation of Conservative policy in the direction of planning, and regional planning in particular. MacMillan had been the friend and publisher of Keynes, and the MP for Stockton during the depression. Despite his Edwardian aura, he was keenly aware of the problems of the older industrial areas, and this awareness was increased when Cairncross came south as chief economic adviser in 1961. (Macmillan seems to have had a predilection for Scots economic advisers, as Allan Young played a major part in forming his 'Middle Way' policies in the 1930s.) Conservative regional policy was seen at its most spectacular, or outrageous, in north-east England, whither Lord Hailsham, cloth-capped, was sent to liaise with the equally ambiguous socialist magnate T. Dan Smith, but in Scotland, besides extending local employment assistance, a planning group was set up to work on West Central Scotland and assistance was given to the Scottish Council in their preparation of an authoritative report on the Scottish economy.

The Inquiry into the Scottish Economy which reported in November 1961 was chaired by (Sir) John Toothill, the English-born managing director of Ferrantis. Toothill had been closely involved with the Scottish Council since 1946, he also represented one of the few new industries with heavy research and development investment in Scotland. The Toothill Report was neither a detailed plan nor a statistical investigation, but a straightforward statement of the requirements of new industry and the value judgements underlying these. Its conclusion was that a major shift in policy, away from palliating unemployment in the older industries to stimulating a totally new industrial structure, was vital.[16]

> A given industry may be expected to adapt itself to change provided the change is not too drastic in terms of the industry's technology and trading practices. Successful shift is less likely

> where there is a fundamental change in the nature of production and in the marketing relationships. The newer growth industries have been of kinds which would have meant just such a shift or adaptation in Scottish industry and this – not any sudden or general collapse of entrepreneurial calibre – is the basic reason why it has not in the main diversified itself.

The Toothill report had little to say about the heavy industries, and less about devolution. Yet although it laid particular stress on transport links with the south, this stress on assimilation was countered by its insistence that these would make it possible for Scots to control industry in Scotland, as it would no longer be considered a remote province. To this end it supported the decentralisation of research, development and physical planning, and large-scale investment in education at all levels. A new industrial structure had to be created, a new and adaptable labour force, and a new managerial and technocrat class, and the responsibility for this was placed firmly on government. Government responded. The Science Ministry was set up, the Scottish Development Department created, the Robbins Committee into higher education and the Brunton Committee into Scottish secondary education promised wide-reaching reforms; the Buchanan Report not only sanctioned massive urban redevelopment but called for the creation of powerful regional authorities; the Beeching reorganisation of the railways provided fast passenger and freight connections with the south. An approach was also made to the Highland problem, in a style far different from that of Johnston. A partnership between the Glasgow retailer Sir Hugh Fraser, various commercial concerns, and the Scottish Office was set up to build an 'integrated tourist complex' at the railway junction of Aviemore in the Grampians, whose ski-runs would provide an all-the-year-round attraction. Fraser's architect – for a project of surpassing vulgarity – was the well-connected Yorkshireman John Poulson; his government liaison man was the senior civil servant 'Gorgeous George' Pottinger. Much was subsequently to be heard of both gentlemen.

'The white heat of the technological revolution' was appropriated by Harold Wilson as a Labour slogan in November 1963, but it was in fact common to both parties. The opposition, however, reserved the right to make what capital it could out of those social groups the new consensus rejected, and to minister to the faithful who found their cherished myths tossed aside. Labour, headed in Scotland by William Ross, a former Ayrshire schoolmaster with a Knoxian line in invective, exploited these options for all it was worth. Pit and shipyard closures were hurled at the government, the discontent of every organised group in Scotland was channelled by Labour MPs and activists to arrive on the doorstep of Michael Noble, the innocuous and reasonably progressive Conservative Secretary of State. The Liberal revival, which had centred on Edinburgh University, where David Steel and Russell Johnston had secured the election of Jo Grimond as Rector in 1960, also contributed, especially in the highlands, which were threatened by the Beeching Report's proposal to close down most of their railways and by a landlord-backed campaign against the Hydro Board. Despite the radicalism of his government's policies, the appearances of Mr Macmillan in the north, impersonating various John Buchan characters, suggested that the Tories still viewed Scotland as a huge sporting estate, and were doing their best to keep it that way, Images were important, and when the Earl of Home, one of the country's largest landowners, was 'evolved' into Macmillan's place, reality seemed to have caught up with them.

Sir Alec, as he rapidly became, got into Parliament in a by-election which seem to have come straight from a Buchan novel – *Castle Gay*, to be precise – fought in the mountains and bars of Kinross and West Perthshire. The Liberals had high hopes of a split in the Tory Party, Labour backed their candidate, a fairly typical product of the right-wing establishment of the Glasgow University Labour Club, with their full Scottish team, the veteran Arthur Donaldson stood for the Nationalists, purveying, as the *New Statesman* snidely put it, 'a totally new kind of boredom'. Besides these there were three independents, including the cartoonist William Rushton, a sort of reincarnated Macmillan, who was supposed to be backed by the publisher John Calder. Convoyed by retired colonels (the constituency held the record for Old Etonians per square mile), Sir Alec was exhibited in the villages. The Nationalists paraded with pipes, drums and flags, while Labour declaimed against the Beeching cuts (which shortly removed about half of the constituency's railways) and promised a Highland Development Board. To no avail. Sir Alec was returned with an absolute majority. One myth had been at least partly confirmed. A large number of Scots actually liked being ruled by a laird.

Nevertheless, the subsequent failure of the Conservatives a year later, when their representation in Scotland fell from 31 to 24, owed much to the archaic nature of the party. Despite the level of support it received, it had never been an authentic part of Scots capitalism. It had never managed, as it had in England, to digest the fragments of the Liberal Party and establish itself as the legitimate mouthpiece of the business community. The continued existence of some sort of Liberal loyalty probably helped it electorally as it split the 'radical' vote which would otherwise have gone to Labour, but it meant that it remained socially archaic, dominated by English-educated landowners, farmers and professional men, and severed from urban right-wingers, who had their own independent Progressive or Moderate parties. Paradoxically, the majority of Conservative Secretaries of State after 1932 were drawn from commercial or industrial backgrounds. Sir Godfrey Collins, 1932–35, headed the publishing concern; Walter Elliot, 1935–38, came from an auctioneering family and was a distinguished scientist in his own right; John Colville, Lord

Clydesmuir, 1938–40, was from a Motherwell steel firm; John S. Maclay, Viscount Muirsheil, 1957–62, was the son of Lord Maclay, shipping magnate and shipping controller in both world wars; while Michael Noble, 1962–64, came from the dynasty which had run Armstrong-Whitworths. Yet their perception of Scottish politics seemed to be that of the custodians of the picturesque political museum whose exhibits – Clydeside reds and grousemoor lairds alike – were to be cherished rather than challenged.

VI

Labour's return in October 1964 set the seal on the regional planning consensus. It had been through Johnston's initiatives and under Labour's Town and Country Planning Act of 1947 that development plans had been drawn up for the main critics and regions of Scotland, mainly by the disciples of Patrick Geddes. These had lain in pigeonholes for over a decade. Now they could be used as the foundation for something much more ambitious: not just a series of district plans, but an interlocking system of national and regional planning, directed from London by the new Department of Economic Affairs. Throughout Britain Regional Economic Planning Boards (of civil servants) were set up, advised by Regional Economic Planning Councils (comprising business interests, trade unions and local authorities). In Scotland the board and council were further supplemented by the Regional Development Division of the Scottish Office. The first two years of William Ross's secretaryship were as energetic as he had promised they would be. In 1965 he carried legislation to set up a Highlands and Islands Development Board – an executive as well as a planning body – against appropriate Tory grumblings of 'undiluted Marxism', established a permanent Law Reform Commission under Lord Kilbrandon, and issued a circular to Scottish local authorities requiring the reorganisation of education on comprehensive lines. In the following year the Scottish Plan appeared, along with a White Paper on Social Work, while a Royal Commission under Lord Wheatley began to examine the reform of local government. The groundwork for a new Scotland seemed well advanced.

When the Highland Development Board was set up the *New Statesman*, at its most Webbian, drooled.[17] It seemed to represent an almost perfect example of Voltairian enlightened despotism. There was little that was democratic about the socialist new order; indeed with Ross dispensing some four hundred posts through patronage the eighteenth-century parallel was only too apposite. Labour's attitude to nationalism was more ambiguous. It had, as *The Scotsman* commented when Ross left office in 1976, 'been preparing well the soil in which the seeds of nationalism could take root', yet its endorsements of nationalism were more explicit in Wales, where it raised the Welsh Secretary to the cabinet and established the Welsh Office, than in Scotland. Many of Ross's reforms either paralleled similar legislation in England, or were intended to increase assimilation. The circular on comprehensive education was always seen in this light, probably unfairly, as Ross, for all his 'dominie' manner, had strong radical views on educational change. But the feeling was always there that, because of the criteria of regional planning, notably the stress on city-regions and car-commuting, nation would shrink to region. Indeed, in the mid-sixties, some plans were being bandied about which created a new cross-border region centred on Carlisle.[18] Sir Walter Scott's expectation that Scotland might end up being run like Northumberland – if not by Northumberland – seemed closer to realisation than it had been before.

Assimilation through a dynamic policy of regional development might not have been all that unpopular. George Brown's raid on Clydeside in the autumn of 1965 – which saved the Fairfield shipyard from closure, placed it under the tripartite control of private industry, government and the unions, securing radical management and co-operative unions – was widely praised, although it effectively placed under state control a hitherto Scottish-owned firm. The *Plan for Scotland*, when it came out in January 1966, was not just qualitatively more advanced than the *National Plan* of October 1965, but aimed to remove Scotland's traditionally higher rates of emigration and unemployment and lower rates of wages – elements of national distinctiveness no one was proud of – through direction of industry and preferential grants. The initiative appeared to rest securely with Labour, which at the March election pushed its total of seats to 46. In ten years, Tory MPs had declined from 36 to 20.

Labour's exultation did not last. The seamen's strike, which aroused the well publicised complaint of the island communities that their plight was being neglected by Westminster, was followed by the economic crisis which brought the fight for supremacy between the Department of Economic Affairs and the Treasury to a head. The DEA lost, deflationary policies were brought in, the grand design of a planned, expanding economy was deferred. Retribution came swiftly in England in the form of staggering by-election reverses, on a scale unprecedented in peacetime politics. The Tories were the main beneficiaries but on 12 July 1966 Welsh nationalism scored its first success, when Gwynfor Evans took Carmarthen with a personal poll of 39 per cent. It had been a Lloyd George rather than a Labour seat, but the *Blaid* had only polled 16 per cent at the general election. The precedent was an ominous one for Labour's Scottish fiefs.[19]

It was not a situation which the Labour Party in Scotland was well fitted to meet. Despite its victories in three successive elections, its internal state was parlous. The legend of the red Clyde was only legend; the Glasgow Labour Party was right-wing, badly organised and poorly supported, and the same went for most constituencies and burghs where Labour had traditionally secured majorities. Radicalism and enthusiasm were mainly found in marginal or hopelessly Tory constituencies, among students or young professional people, or the numerous ex-Communists who had 'come over' in 1956. It was rarely reflected by the elected representatives. The standard of Labour MPs in Scotland was lower than in the rest of Britain, and as local government work was unpaid, many party activists found it difficult to get time or permission to serve on councils. Labour councillors tended to be small businessmen, trade union officials and housewives, whose level of political consciousness, if it existed at all, was low. The key to success in the Labour Party, as one weary left-winger maintained, was 'the law of the rise of the charismatic numskull':

> Go to meetings, become minutes secretary, organise jumble sales, canvass, but don't say anything. Never express a political opinion. Then nobody will know what you stand for, and they'll sort out everyone whose line they do know. That way you become an MP, as they can't think of anything against you.

But in 1967, as the Pollok and Hamilton by-elections were to show, even the most charismatic of numskulls was in for a very rough time.

Planning hung around Labour's neck like an albatross, big, dead and smelly. Targets had been set which could never now be reached, regional development teams were at work on plans which had little hope of fulfilment, inquiries were set up into Scottish social problems which could not be solved without enormous public investment. All of these blew up in Labour's face. The Cullingworth Committee's Report on *Scotland's Older Housing*, published in 1967, found, for example, that 'one in three persons lives in a house considered either substandard or unfit for human habitation'. It placed the blame squarely on central government:[20]

> For, though local authorities by no means come through our examination unscathed, the problem, especially in

> Glasgow, is of such huge dimensions as to place it beyond the resources of any single authority, even though it be the biggest authority in the country.

Ross was made responsible for the failings of his Conservative predecessors, as well as for Labour's management of Glasgow (which Cullingworth, in the circumstances, probably let off rather lightly). With the mounting tide of left-wing criticism of Westminster policies in general, he had also to cope with activists who seceded to single-issue groups, and flung the conclusions of inquiries like Cullingworth's back at him. The Highlands and Islands Development Board's new powers went to its head and it began thinking in terms of a city of 300,000 based on Inverness. It ran into accusations of neglecting the Gaelic-speaking west and enriching its own members. In turn it accused the Secretary of State of niggardliness and interference. An imaginative development plan for the Central Borders, an area of high emigration, coincided with the determination of the Ministry of Transport to close the only railway which served the area. At all turns the Secretary of State had to take the blame for the shortcomings of Scottish local government and Scottish industry, while he was unable, through the financial constraints imposed by the Treasury, to take much initiative on his own. A lot was done. Government expenditure per head was about 20 per cent higher in Scotland than in the rest of the UK. But the promises of the planners always held before the Scottish voter an ideal of what things ought to be like, and Ross was probably not the man to explain tactfully the realities of the situation. The dominie's pointer rapped the figures on the blackboard, and, if his critics weren't careful, he hinted that it would rap their fingers as well.

Ross was the greatest Secretary of State, in the sense that he developed the post to the limit of its powers. He used his weight in the Cabinet and kept his civil servants under control, while, along with his Permanent Secretary, Sir Douglas Haddow, accelerating the transformation of the Scottish Office from an administrative to a planning agency. He knew where power lay in the Scottish Labour movement, and he never lost contact with it. He was a Scottish administrator of the classic type, rather than a politician. He served the system that he knew better than it has ever been served, but he had little knowledge of, and less desire to co-operate with, those who wanted that system changed. Ironically, he had much more in common with the rank and file of the Scottish Nationalists than he had with the younger members of his own party, who were distressed at his aversion to liberal reforms and his delight in the worst excesses of the Kailyard. The qualities which made him a good Secretary of State were the same ones which made it so difficult for him to meet the challenge of the new Scottish politics, or, for that matter, to solve the country's persistent and worsening economic dilemma.

VIII

The problem was that the Scottish economy did not just lag behind the English in terms of aggregate performance. It still remained a different kind of economy, with a much greater dependence on the production of capital goods on the one hand and on the service industries on the other. This made it difficult to fit into the system of controlling the economy by regulating the demand for consumer goods, as the conditions which stimulated investment in the capital goods industries were not always the same as those which stimulated consumer demand. The National Plan was seen as a means of producing a general identity between the two economies, after which the Scottish economy would respond to the same stimuli as the English. This did not happen. Not only that, but by the end of the 1960s grave doubts were being expressed about whether the exercise ought to have been undertaken in the first place.

Undercapitalised and antique though they were, the heavy industries – shipbuilding, coal, steel, railway and mechanical engineering – had good reason to remain in Scotland. A skilled labour force existed, the universities supplied highly trained technical staff like naval architects and metallurgists, a range of associated concerns manufacturing things like navigational equipment, machine tools and mining machinery provided its own type of diversified economy. This was something that the new transplants like the motor industry failed to do. Linwood and Bathgate were branch factories, and none too successful branch factories at that. The industries which supplied them did not follow them north. As Peter Jay, the *Times* economic correspondent, told the Scottish Council in 1974:

> If these had equal non-labour cost advantages with the traditional industries, they would have been traditional industries as well.

They could only have taken off into self-sustaining growth if wages had been reduced, something which the increasing power of trade unionism made impossible. What happened was therefore that:[21]

> The initial once-and-for-all penalty of losing its traditional industries with comparative international advantages [was] transformed into a perpetual dynamic of decay.

In 1970 a sub-committee of the Scottish Council produced a report which was diametrically opposed to the Toothill orthodoxy. The concept of *Oceanspan* involved a return to the rationale which had underlain Scotland's growth in the eighteenth century: the nation as entrepôt, with the Common Market supplying the political framework that the Union had then provided. The Clyde, the largest natural harbour on the European Atlantic seaboard, could accommodate and turn round the largest bulk carriers anyone would be likely to build, vessels which could be a menace in the restricted confines of the English Channel. Cargoes could be transferred in the Firth to smaller ships and barges which could bypass the European ports by using the rapidly developing river and canal systems of the EEC countries. The mid-Scotland ship canal which generations of nationalists had urged came back into prominence. Moreover, the Clyde as a transhipment point would be bound to attract industries which would benefit from the enormous economies of scale involved, like steelmaking, shipbuilding and oil refining. It meant, in other words, the resurrection of the heavy industries.

The man behind *Oceanspan* was in fact the last great magnate of the heavy industries, Sir William Lithgow, who had inherited the family shipyards at Port Glasgow, amalgamated them with those of Scott's at Greenock, and made the resulting combine the largest and most successful shipbuilding firm in Scotland. He was no less resolute a defender of capitalism than his father had been, and to this extent stood out on his own when other Scottish business leaders had made their peace with Labour and planning. Yet *Oceanspan* put this whole consensus in question. As the first drilling rigs were towed into position off Aberdeen, and the assault of the Nationalists on local and national politics ended in relative ignominy, opinion about the industrial future of the country was more fragmented and volatile than it had been since the war.

Chapter 6

Nothing Abides: Civil Society, 1945-1976

As far as the United Kingdom is concerned, the Scots have at least some consciousness of their 'Kailyard' as a problem; the English are still largely unaware of having arrived there.

Tom Nairn, 'Old Nationalism and New Nationalism' in *The Red Paper on Scotland*, 1975-7

I

In 1962, when David Keir, the editor of the *Edinburgh* volume of the *Third Statistical Account*, wanted to convey the timbre of life in the capital, he got together a dinner-party at Sir Compton Mackenzie's house in the New Town, and recorded the conversation of the guests. They were Anne Redpath, the artist, Sir David Milne, former Permanent Secretary at St Andrew's House, Lord Cameron, Dean of the Faculty of Advocates, Alastair Dunnett, the editor of *The Scotsman*, and Sir Compton himself: fairly typical representatives of the middle-of-the-road, quasi-nationalist establishment which had presided over the country since the war. Their discussion was doubtless cosy and self-satisfied enough to provoke a snarl or two from the cottage in the Lanarkshire countryside where, like Yeats in his tower at Ballylee, MacDiarmid stood guard over the Scottish intellect but it reflected a society in which the institutions which wielded power could readily be identified, and for the most part identified as Scottish. Administration and the direction of public opinion were recognisably centred in Edinburgh. Lord Cameron thought that the description in Scott of the benefit of having a parliament in Edinburgh was again relevant: 'We could aye peeble them wi' stanes when they werena gude bairns.' Sir David Milne agreed:[1]

> That's because Scotland is the right administrative size. In general, this goes for government as well as for running newspapers, and for a lot of other things . . . it hasn't the remoteness of England, say, as an administrative unit. The contacts and the relations between the centre and the periphery in England are nothing like as close as here.

As they talked, the certainties of post-war Scotland were already crumbling, and with them the prestige of the institutions they represented. The light that slanted into Sir Compton's windows faded on the slums and empty slipways of the Clyde, and on the disused shale mines of West Lothian.

The institutions of Scottish civil society – Kirk, law, local government and education – not party politics – had traditionally provided the means of bringing national consciousness before the public. While imperfect economic strategies and regional plans meant that pressure for devolution among civil servants and the electorate grew almost by default, such traditional institutions were directly at risk in an age of waning belief, increased collective intervention, and doctrinaire educational prescriptions. But the progress and prospect of decay had an ambivalent effect: in nineteenth-century Europe it had accelerated the emergence of formal nationalism, strengthening resistance and calling new institutions into play. Overdue by a century, a process something like this took place in post-war Scotland.

There was nothing particularly democratic about the traditional institutions. Indeed Anne Redpath's Royal Scottish Academy, which selected its members, was in some ways a paradigm for the rest. A system of corporations, with relatively easy admission for the trained and the talented, which then exercised an important degree of social control: this summed up their *raison d'être*. No pluralist society lacks such institutions: Scotland, however, was unique in having, for so long, depended on them for its government.

Challenged by the growing power of central government and the waning of their own internal dynamic, and given an effective regional policy, they might have been quite painlessly assimilated. I remember a young Labour activist, now an MP, arguing in 1966 that St Andrew's House was itself a barrier to reform and ought to be phased out in favour of direct rule from London. The failure of planning meant the survival of the traditional institutions, but it also coincided with a period in which distinctively Scottish alternatives to them were created.

In his *Modern Scotland*, a book which on its publication in 1968 focused attention on the continuing distinctiveness of Scottish civil society, the Glasgow political scientist James Kellas devoted only 20 of his 230 pages to economics. In the nineteenth century these proportions would have had to be reversed, although Kirk, law and education then played a much more powerful social role. National development was no longer directed by the entrepreneurs. The decline of the economy – oriented towards Britain and the empire – paradoxically increased the influence of bodies which had survived from the pre-industrial period. The decline both of industry and of the 'industrial politics' of the Clydeside magnates left a vacuum, which they entered. Scottish local authorities, for example, put up nearly half of the money for the Scottish Council: Development and Industry in 1946, while nearly all the great shipyards and the North British Locomotive Company contributed no more than the basic £3 subscription.[2] The universities, which had almost totally abstained from economic and social inquiries between the wars, took on large commitments in these fields in the 1950s and 1960s. The churches were always ready with prescriptions for the country's social and political ills. The social values they represented were enfeebled, but, as spokesmen for a society whose problems remained obstinate and distinctive, they remained relevant. Out of this dialectic, by the end of the 1960s, a new synthesis, closer to classic European nationalism, was beginning to emerge.

II

Of the traditional institutions the legal system was the most prehensile. Based on different principles from that of England, the authority of its own elite of solicitors and advocates was unquestioned. If they could not practise in the English courts, neither could English lawyers practise in Scotland. They were a powerful, but exclusive and patrician group. They were also, by the mid-1960s, becoming conscious of the penalties of their anomalous position.

Scots Law had been threatened by the development of administrative law during and after the late nineteenth century, but there was always an irreducible minimum of legislation which had to be translated into its categories, and while this remained any prospect of thorough assimilation of the two countries could be ruled out. The nationalism of the legal system was vitiated, however, by the party affiliations of many Scots advocates. To say that their politics were adopted in the hope of attracting political patronage would be an unkind exaggeration, but any change of government meant that the posts of Lord Advocate, Solicitor General and the Advocates Depute (crown counsel) would fall vacant. A candidate for a hopeless constituency or membership of some political organisation was always a useful gambit to play. The judges – Senators of the College of Justice – were political appointments, and many had been Lord Advocates or Solicitors General. Most were Tories, but the independent Charles Dalrymple Shaw, Lord Kilbrandon, and the former Labour Lord Advocate John, Lord Wheatley, were both to play a significant role in the reforms of the mid-sixties. The law faculties of the universities, which had produced Dewar Gibb in the 1930s, were also a potential redoubt of legal nationalism.

Besides the business of patronage, law had its own surrogate politics. The elaborate and extended cases, often concerning quite trivial issues, which punctuate Scottish legal history can in a sense be seen as almost ceremonial assertions of the independence of the Scottish courts. Often undertaken as a result of disputes between or within the traditional institutions, they were an embodiment of the 'ideology of noisy inaction'. However, by the mid-1960s, a more positive role was being demanded of Scots Law and Scots lawyers, both in providing technical assistance to the numerous inquiries and plans, and in the modernisation of Scots law itself through the Scots Law Commission, set up by Labour in 1965.[3] The prospect of entering the European Economity Community, moreover, meant that the Scots system would no longer be an isolated and rather parochial freak, but a much more logical component of European jurisprudence than English common law. After a hundred years of decline, hopes were high for innovations in organisation and in legal philosophy. *New Society* commented in July 1965:[4]

> The Universities are seeing the start of a legal renaissance in Scotland. The Edinburgh law curriculum, for example, has

> become an articulated full time course displaying an awareness of the social and international implications of the law.

There was some progress along this road. Legislation on young offenders, which integrated the former juvenile courts with social work departments, was a notable breakthrough for the new conception of law, but it appeared to many that the reform of law could only be carried through with the aid of a devolved legislature. Not the least of these was Kilbrandon, who had secured the Young Offenders' Act and was Chairman of the Commission. In March 1972 he became Chairman of another Commission: on the British Constitution.

It was to be the Law, the most conservative of institutions which, in October 1968, quietly provided the Scottish National Party with its main platform for the 1970s. By the Continental Shelf (Jurisdictional) Order, the activity of extracting oil and gas north of 55° 50′ was placed under the Scots courts. In the opinion of nationalists, and some, though not all, lawyers, the Scots now had title to this potential wealth. To support this, the SNP was able to produce the Professor of Public Law from Edinburgh University, whose 'legal renaissance' had led to a considerable preoccupation with European public and commercial law. Shortly afterwards, another nationalist, Neil MacCormick, the son of 'King John', was appointed to Edinburgh's Regius Chair.

Nationalism among lawyers was important but not unanimous; the fear of parochialism was too great. On the other hand, for the ambitious, the old unionist tradition now had little appeal. In the days of Cockburn and Jeffrey, legal reformers had led the campaign for assimilation, while trying to retain their dominance in the north. This had not greatly changed, but the question was now: assimilation to what? It was not surprising that in 1975 a Scots lawyer should see the future axis of Scottish politics as Edinburgh – Brussels, not Edinburgh – London. Nor that his name should be Lord Kilbrandon.

III

In Scotland local government changes were more directly linked to public opinion about nationalism than legal affairs. The Local Government (Scotland) Act of 1929 stimulated the growth of the National Party, as it dismantled a structure of local autonomy whose defenders believed it to be guaranteed by the Act of Union. Such drastic and unpopular changes had the effect, profound if temporary, of destroying traditions while failing to provide an immediate identification with the new unit. They may well have contributed to the loss of community Edwin Muir mourned; and they certainly heralded forty years during which very few people bothered themselves with local government. Polls in municipal elections were low, councillors were elderly and unimaginative, political issues rarely transcended those of rates and council-house rents. Labour held on to the larger towns and most authorities in the industrial areas. The Moderates or Progressives (until the late 1960s Conservatives were virtually unknown in local government) held Edinburgh, several of the medium-sized country towns and some suburban burghs around Glasgow. There were still large numbers of independents in the Highlands, the east coast and the Borders, the last representatives of a community identity being swamped elsewhere by industrial change and population migration. Burgh status was still successfully claimed by a place as small as New Galloway (population 331 in 1971) while it was denied to Bellshill (population 10,000 in 1971). The Border burghs of Galashiels, Hawick, Selkirk, Jedburgh and Kelso kept alive a tradition of local independence which precluded much collaboration between them, as well as any cross-border co-operation. The settlements around Glasgow fought hard against the city's encroachments; those at a greater distance co-operated with it in settling large numbers of 'overspill' families. Such anomalies were compounded by the appearance of five entirely new towns. East Kilbride was designated in 1947, Glenrothes in 1948, Cumbernauld in 1955, Livingston in 1966 and Irvine in 1969. Planned to provide centres for light industry and eventually to house nearly 10 per cent of the country's population, these constituted an exercise in the 'direction' of Scottish society as drastic as that of the eighteenth-century planned villages, and as autocratic. The problems and opportunities they created were, in the late 1960s and 1970s, to have a considerable effect on Nationalist successes.

A major overhaul of Scottish local government was plainly overdue by the late 1950s. The Scottish Office advanced a scheme in 1963, drawn up by the ill-starred George Pottinger, but, largely through Pottinger's own diplomatic failings this was rejected.[5] In 1965 Ross appointed a Royal Commission under Lord Wheatley to produce a scheme for a wholesale reform. Unlike the corresponding Redcliffe–Maud Commission in England, Wheatley's intentions for the 'top tier' of authorities were from the start ambitious. Regional government on a grand scale was thought of as a rationalistic alternative to nationalism, although some authorities, notably Professor John Mackintosh, considered that an 'all Scotland' top tier would be both administratively efficient and politically attractive. Mackintosh's scheme had the merit that it avoided the main difficulty that beset Wheatley: how to replan the congested central belt while representing the mass of the population which actually lived there.[6] Wheatley's solution, announced in September 1969, was the division of the country into seven large regions: Strathclyde, Lothians and Borders, Highland, Grampian, Tayside, Central, and Dumfries and Galloway, under which were to be forty-nine district councils. The regions were to have authority for transport, town and country planning and education, while the districts would handle housing and social work. The new Tory government published a White Paper in 1971, granting, in response to public controversy, two further regions, Fife and the Borders, and special types of district council for Orkney, Shetland, and Outer Isles. Legislation followed quickly, and although the Crowther Commission on the Constitution was already in session when Wheatley reported, no attempt was made to co-ordinate the reform of Scottish government with the new regions, neither were the various nominated semi-regional bodies controlling the health service, water supplies and police included in the new scheme. Since both governments evidently regarded the Crowther/Kilbrandon Commission as a means of deferring devolution to a date when it could quietly be buried, this lack of co-ordination made sense, but the resurrection of nationalism after autumn 1973 meant that the introduction of the new system coincided with the questioning of the whole principle which underlay it.

Intriguingly, there is no mention whatsoever of the Commission on any of the 836 pages of Harold Wilson's *The Labour Government, 1964–70: A Personal Record*, published in 1971. Both Labour and Tory governments had doubtless hoped that, once established, regional government would meet Nationalist charges of 'remote government' while enabling higher standards of administration and economies of scale. The Kilbrandon Report, and the need to implement it, removed the first advantage, while inflation after 1973 and the need to compensate employees of the old system removed the second. As well as favouring the Nationalists by removing old loyalties, regionalisation gave them a wide range of grievances to exploit.

Besides having to adapt to the new system, local government created its own problems. Labour councils with their housing debts were condemned for profligacy by right-wingers otherwise noted for their reluctance to spend money on anything. From time to time scandals erupted which reflected low standards on both sides. Sometimes these were relatively minor – backhanders for granting licences, giving planning permission, or allocating council houses – but, with the growth of council expenditure, a more disturbing trend began to emerge. Major corporation contractors both began to take an active role in local politics – usually on the right – and, where their interests were concerned, attempted to influence the votes of Labour councillors by offering them employment compatible with the sizeable demands of council work. The amateur tradition of local government thus led to its direct domination by powerful interest groups.

This was particularly worrying in the 1960s, as councils undertook a wide range of new and expensive responsibilities, like urban reconstruction. The Buchanan Report, which appeared in November 1963, called for the almost total re-planning of cities to accommodate a constantly rising level of car ownership. The flaws in Sir Colin Buchanan's logic – his neglect of public transport, walking or cycling, his underestimation of regional variations in income and car ownership, and his conviction that there was some sort of causal connection between roadbuilding and economic performance – seem now to make his rise from a relatively humble town planning official to the doyen of his profession in a couple of years one of the more mystifying phenomena of the 1960s. But his report was given the hard sell by its steering committee under Lord Crowther, by the Minister of Transport, Ernest Marples, and by the British Road Federation. Nowhere was its prescription swallowed as enthusiastically as in Glasgow, which actually had one of the lowest proportions of car ownership in Britain (in 1966 1 car to 11 people, compared with 1 to 4 in Surrey).[7] The resulting destruction certainly removed some slum properties whose clearance was overdue, but it also laid waste a townscape which had been one of the liveliest and most ingenious achievements of industrialisation. In the late 1960s Scots socialists could be forgiven if they were baffled by a Labour council which provided the middle-class motorist with urban motorways and a remarkable suburban electric railway system, while it filed away the working classes who elected it in thirty-storey blocks of flats. Some observers, like the poet Edwin Morgan, at that time in a rather futurist frame of mind, saw this as the Glasgow spirit renascent: the city transfiguring itself like its American counterparts. But the cash was no longer there: the industries displaced by the roads closed down or went away; money was diverted from areas, like housing and social work, where it was already in desperately short supply; the population projected for the city in 1980 fell from 900,000 in 1961 to 750,000 or less in 1973.[8] Like the model aeroplanes that South Sea islanders built to induce their gods to bring them Western consumer goods, the great six-lane roads were a sort of cargo-cult. But prosperity did not come.

The entrenched conservatism of Edinburgh, by contrast, saved the city from destruction. The city engineer thought up a grandiose ring road project in 1965, and in 1967 the leaders of the Labour group joined with the right wing to force it through. There was a revolt in both parties and among well-heeled amenity societies, the public inquiry into the city development plan rejected the scheme, and Sir Colin Buchanan, no less, was called in to advise on a new one. When, two years and £500,000 later, he reported, opinion in the city had swung – much to his disgust – against big road schemes of any kind. One result of the brief foray of the Scottish Nationalists into local politics between 1967 and 1969 was to eliminate many of the dimmer Labour councillors, and the new generation, largely from the universities, was more left-wing and more articulate. Not only were the road commitments dropped, but there was a general reappraisal of policies on housing, health and town planning. The changing face of Labour was most apparent in the east, but matters began to improve even on Glasgow Corporation, with the assistance of several court cases which disposed of the less reliable comrades. The problem was that such improvements came when the old councils were facing reorganisation, and experimentation and innovation were curbed by their extinction.

In the early 1970s, just as the second, oil-powered, Nationalist assault was beginning, Scottish local government was in its most confused state for over forty years, with no real consensus apparent about its status and future role. Socialists in particular, who looked to the new units to provide a practical alternative of 'good government' to the claims of the Nationalists, had to admit that the record of the authorities in the past did not augur well. If a lesson was to be drawn from the disasters of the 1960s, it was that the Scottish administration should intervene more positively in local government affairs. In turn, this would only be possible with some sort of representative government. A Conservative Secretary of State like Gordon Campbell, who represented only the majority party in Westminster, could never hope to take such initiatives.

IV

In nineteenth-century Europe the decline of religious observance had a particularly important influence on the transference of denominational loyalties to national communities. In Scotland, given the central position of the Kirk in society, the preoccupation with religious affairs during and after the Disruption, and the arrival of a large Irish immigrant community, religious affiliations continued resilient into the second half of the twentieth century. In 1950 church membership, at 60 per cent of the adult population, was nearly three times as great as in England. At that time 25 per cent of the total population were still members of the Church of Scotland, and 13 per cent of the Catholic Church, and the power of the Churches was proportionately effective in social and educational life. Authoritarian and conservative, the Catholic hierarchy played a leading role in the Labour-dominated politics of West Central Scotland, while the Church of Scotland's General Assembly continued to exercise a quasi-parliamentary function, commenting on a wide spectrum of British and Commonwealth politics. By the mid-1960s, however, a permanent decline in observance and influence had set in. The number of communicants in the Kirk dropped by 1 per cent annually, rising to 2 per cent between 1970 and 1974. Decline in Catholic numbers only began in 1970, but recruitment of religious personnel and teachers shrank.[9] Various factors lay behind this. City clearance and overspill schemes shifted a large proportion of the population away from established congregations, and the middle-class activists who had organised them. Television and the belated impact of materialist and rationalist ideas also took their toll.

The Kirk was aware of the challenge, but its response was not the combination of nationalism and social intervention associated with George MacLeod and the Iona Community. Instead it fell back on American evangelism. Emphasising personal conversion at mass rallies, this began with the 'Tell Scotland' crusade of the Rev. Tom Allan in 1947 and rose to a climax with the Scottish Crusade of Dr Billy Graham in the winter of 1954–5. Based on the Kelvin Hall in Glasgow, widely broadcast by radio and television and relayed by land-lines to churches and halls throughout the country, it had a greater impact than Moody and Sankey in 1873–5. But even on evangelical terms, personal conversion in the Nuremberg-like atmosphere of Kelvin Hall had to be sustained by fresh parochial resources in the new housing schemes. It was not. As a result the Church found that it had regressed intellectually while making no significant gains in communicants.

During this period the progressive element in the Church remained influential. But, like the Moderates, it was an unrepresentative group. Its strength lay in its links with other churches, in its industrial and urban involvement, and in the mission field. Under the leadership of men like George MacLeod, Geoffrey Shaw and Kenneth MacKenzie, its links with the Labour Party and with anti-colonial and disarmament movements were strong, but its roots in the largely middle-class rank and file of the Church were limited. The influence of the left probably rose to a climax in 1960–4 with CND and the agitation over the future of the Central African Federation. But thereafter, as well as suffering from the ebbing of left-wing confidence, the progressives within the Church were also disadvantaged by the retreat of a numerically declining Church on its middle-class laager.

Within the Catholic Church, paradoxically, intellectual developments were more radical and sustained because of the rise of a Catholic middle class.[10] If the hierarchy was – in contrast to the Church of Scotland – both populist and reactionary, the progressives began at last to lose their identification with the old Catholic families and upper-class Anglo-Scots whose nationalism was of a rather intellectualised and condescending kind. By the 1950s the younger members of a new Catholic middle class were beginning to chafe both at the authoritarianism of their hierarchy and at the residuum of Scots presbyterian prejudice. The association of Catholicism with left-wing social criticism, which Edwin Muir had made in the 1930s, from outside the Church, was restated in the 1960s by influential Catholics like the Dominican Father Anthony Ross, Chaplain to Edinburgh University. Ross, a convert in the 1930s both to Catholicism and to nationalism of the MacDiarmid variety, offered hospitality and encouragement to students of all faiths and none, playing a major role in setting up the literary periodical *Scottish International* in 1967. Deeply involved in social work, especially in the forgotten Edinburgh of the Grassmarket doss-houses, Ross carried conviction among a generation adrift from political and religious orthodoxy, with his plea that:[11]

> Before deciding what it is to be Scottish we need to examine our ideas as to what it is to be human, and to be Christian, and make at the start an act of contrition for ourselves and the community in which we live.

Religion had never been in Scotland the opium of the masses. Since the Union the politics of the Churches had been closer to the mass of the people than those of parliament or town council. But they were elitist and male-dominated, and in the 1960s they were steadily losing their grip, partly because of secular social change, and partly because of genuine doubts about the future of organised religion. For younger people, to whom a generation earlier religion was a kind of surrogate politics, politics now became a surrogate religion, a fitting vocation for Christians with a strong desire to identify with the community, and a distrust of their own conservative establishments. This motivation did not lead directly to nationalism, but it created expectations of politics which the system itself could scarcely fulfil.

V

But the most spectacular crisis of confidence came in the educational system, traditionally the link between the Scots institutions and the opportunities provided by Britain and the empire. In the late 1950s educational change on a large scale appeared imminent, as the trained cadres of the new economic order would have to be produced. It was also plain that such change would be imposed according to English, not Scottish, ideas. Half a century of neglect and complacency had left an educational system which both needed reform and was incapable of generating that reform internally, through its neglect of research and experiment. The implications of this were focused by a remarkable book published in 1961 by the Edinburgh philosopher George Davie, *The Democratic Intellect: Scotland and her Universities in the Nineteenth Century*. Davie argued that in the years after 1832 the democratically recruited and unspecialised nature of Scottish liberal education had suffered from a 'trahison des clercs'. It had been modified to fit the English demand for specialisation and elitism and the result had been its reduction to an anomalous provincialism:[12]

> The democratic intellectualism which had distinguished Scottish civilisation was being allowed to disappear and the peculiar polymathic values it supported were, increasingly, at a discount among the cultural leaders . . . there has been a marked reaction in twentieth century Scotland against the historic heritage, but one will misunderstand the situation unless one sees it not as a collapse but as a slow surrender. The ideal of a balanced breadth of mind still remained entrenched in wide educational sectors; what was being swept away was rather the intellectual sharpness required to secure its survival . . .

In some ways Davie's book was an apologia for the old tradition rather than a realistic description of it. He underestimated the practical domination of the universities by the clergy, the lawyers and the medical men. He ignored the superficial nature of the instruction in the huge lecture classes, and the intellectual conservatism of the country in the age of 'vital religion'. He also underestimated the impact on the 'democratic' nature of the universities of the reorganisation of secondary education, a move which benefited the middle class, whose children could be sustained through two extra school years. But, these apart, Davie's book was a powerful tract, which seemed to indicate that slow surrender would soon turn into outright capitulation.

Four years later the battle was joined, when Labour began its reform programme, encouraged by Willie Ross, who concealed radical ideas about education under a headmasterly exterior. The system was challenged from three sides: from new forms of teaching, from new types of school organisation, and from new ideas about the role of education in society.

Despite occasional subversives like A. S. Neill, Scottish education has always been teacher-, not child-centred. 'The teacher should consider carefully whether . . . time is being used to the best advantage',[13] as the Scottish Education Department handbook on Primary Education put it in 1950. This orthodoxy was challenged by new methods of primary instruction developed mainly in the south. In the revised handbook for 1965, these were accepted in Scotland. Regardless of their scholastic merits, they implied considerable changes in the status of teachers themselves, always a politically articulate group.

In the same year a policy of comprehensive reorganisation throughout the country was announced. Again, the precedents involved were English, although district secondary schools in the Scottish counties had traditionally catered for all the children in their locality. Associated with this, the reduction of pupil/teacher ratios required more teachers than the ordinary degree courses of the universities and the established teacher training colleges could supply. The latter started to offer a Bachelor of Education degree, and were supplemented by four new colleges, with the result that the tradition of a teaching profession in which all the men were university graduates was weakened.[14] This unease was rapidly given political shape. In 1965 a General Teaching Council was set up to govern the profession in Scotland. Initially, this was seen as a means of imposing lay control; then when teachers' representatives formed a majority, it seemed to reflect the numerical majority of non-graduates in the profession, and so be a means of securing dilution. To this end an Aberdeen schoolteacher, J. S. Malloch, backed by the graduates' union, the Scottish Schoolmasters' Association, conducted a series of court cases to challenge the power of the Council to bar unregistered teachers from employment. This lengthy and tortuous litigation testified to the continuing influence of the 'surrogate politics' of the old institutions, and to the real concern of the teachers about their changing status, but it seemed to be a defensive response to narrowing horizons. The teachers were no longer the recruiting-sergeants for an army of opportunity.

The universities, however, provided the crisis with its epicentre. Their relative strength in numerical terms had been steadily declining since the turn of the century, when Scotland provided nearly half the university places in Britain. With the growth of the English provincial universities this proportion had fallen by 1960 to 16 per cent. The Robbins Committee Report in 1961 promised a numerical expansion, but one which would slightly lessen this proportion. Fifteen per cent was still an advantageous proportion for the Scots, but on closer examination their position was much weaker. Sixty per cent of the degrees awarded were ordinary degrees, whose recipients would, in England, have gone to teacher training colleges. Scotland also lacked the polytechnics which were rapidly developing in the south. On top of all this, a larger proportion of staff and students (frequently the abler ones) were coming north from England.

Robbins brought matters to a head. The expansion of the universities, which took the form of a new university at Stirling and university status for the Dundee outpost of St Andrews and the technical colleges at Glasgow and Edinburgh, had to be staffed and, especially in the arts and social sciences, the native tradition showed itself woefully deficient in supplying the necessary teaching and research skills.

Scotland had always lagged in research; able graduates, if they wanted to persevere, usually went on to Oxford, Cambridge or London. So the deficiency was made up by English or English-trained professors and lecturers. By 1974 there were as many Oxford graduates as there were graduates of the Scottish universities teaching history subjects north of the border, and the proportion of the latter was never higher than 33 per cent in any department. Although this became a major focus of nationalist grievances later in the decade its results were as much stimulating as infuriating. The Scottish universities were enlivened by digesting new techniques and new research interests, and postgraduate studies at last started to develop.

Even this, however, had its perils. In the early 1970s, as the first generation of Scottish postgraduates began to emerge with their PhDs, the expansion of the universities came to an end. Those lecturers in post were mostly English, recruited at the peak of the post-Robbins boom, when there had been an academic sellers' market. A very able generation of young Scots, now denied academic careers, confronted an establishment which was itself young. The rivalry of the two groups underlay the conflict which developed increasingly stridently in the mid 1970s about who should control the universities, the proposed Scottish assembly or the British University Grants Committee.

Thus in 1971 Donald Macrae, Professor of Sociology at the London School of Economics, recollected a Scottish education dominated by injunctions to the young to seize a future which was always outside Scotland. That time was now past:[15]

> The prestige, the cash value and the cultural importance of what universities do and the qualifications they give, all fall as they are more widely distributed.

In the late 1960s and early 1970s unease about the educational system, its organisation and purposes, grew widespread among teachers, hitherto strong supporters of the Labour Party. In the changed circumstances of post-imperial Britain, nationalism, and the recovery of traditions and values which the schools had on the whole neglected, seemed to offer a plausible alternative. By 1974 a substantial minority of the profession – somewhere between a third and a half – had demonstrated this conviction with their votes.

VI

In the 1960s Scottish civil society suffered a series of alterations and reverses which left its self-confidence weaker than it had ever been before. Law, its most conservative, and most explicitly nationalist, component, was the least affected; religion and education found that they had to accustom themselves to a new role in a changed and rather unfriendly world. Hitherto the problems of such institutions had generally been dealt with internally, as part of the essential federalism of post-Union politics. Now their weakness became a matter of general concern. But whose concern? Local government had problems enough of its own, and could scarcely extend its competence to cope with them. The Scottish Trades Union Congress, which might have provided a left-wing counterpoise to the declining sector of Scottish-owned industry, was itself suffering from the steady southward drift of union authority. As a result, not only did civil society try to compensate for loss of authority by backing devolution, but the discussion of Scottish social problems passed increasingly to the nationally-oriented institutions which had developed since the nineteenth century: to the press and the literary intelligentsia.

The Scottish press in the early 1950s had changed little since Lord Beaverbrook and Rothermere had bought their way in twenty years earlier. In the interval the Mirror group had purchased the Glasgow *Daily Record* so that the mass-circulation dailies were all in English hands, but considerable autonomy was granted to the Scottish papers and none of their English stablemates, like the *Mirror* or the *Herald*, was widely on sale in the north. The two quality dailies, *The Scotsman* and the *Glasgow Herald*, remained in Scottish hands; the *Press and Journal* in Aberdeen was independent. The Dundee *Courier and Advertiser*, famous for its ferocious Toryism and one-sentence paragraphs, remained the possession of the inscrutable Thomson family, the reclusive brethren who also owned the *Beano* and the *Dandy* as well as that Kailyard gold-mine, the *Sunday Post*. Most of the Scottish dailies had companion, and usually much more profitable, evening papers, and survived on a fairly unvarying diet of crime, court reporting, and sports coverage. Localism was the main reason for their distinctiveness. Their readers were not interested in what was happening in other Football Leagues, let alone in other countries.[16] This was something which all the centralising impulses in the British press found it difficult to beat. (In June 1976 the Aberdeen *Press and Journal* referred to the Italian election results in half a column inch: it was the only mention of foreign affairs the paper carried that day.)

In the 1950s the challenge to the old establishment came, once again, from a Scots Canadian. In 1954 Roy Thomson, the proprietor of several Canadian provincial papers and radio stations, wanted to break into the British press. He saw that the junior of the two Scottish quality papers, *The Scotsman*, was for sale and, remarking that the outfit wouldn't have lasted six months in Canada, took it over.[17] *The Scotsman* was plainly only a stepping-stone to further possessions; within three years Thomson had taken over the *Press and Journal* and, in England, the Kemsley group of papers, including *The Sunday Times*. More critically, he had bid for, and captured, the franchise for the first commercial television channel in Scotland.

Thomson was an affable philistine. He added to his definition of editorial content as 'the stuff that fills the spaces between the ads' a description of Scottish Television as 'a licence to print money'. He was, in fact, initially alone in backing it. The Reithian tradition died hard. But the investment paid off handsomely. So too did the Edinburgh papers, though not before the rival and more prosperous *Evening News* had been amalgamated with Thomson's *Evening Dispatch*. Thomson was a Tory but he had no great wish to impose any line on his papers. Dunnett, his appointee as editor of *The Scotsman*, had a leftish and nationalist background and, although until 1966 the paper usually made a rather belated swing to the right just before elections, it maintained for the most part a critical stance and provided a platform for left-wing and liberal views. The pre-war situation in which journalists had to use pseudonyms and anonymous pamphlets to make their voices heard while avoiding the wrath of their proprietor was over.

Scottish Television was scarcely an ornament to the cultural scene. Its dramatic output was negligible and its light entertainment abysmal. It had for a time the services of John Grierson, but it made no attempt to develop documentary, although *Seawards the Great Ships*, made in 1958, showed that Grierson had lost none of his gifts. Only in sport and in news coverage did it provide competitition for the BBC, which had been plunged in provincial inertia for the best part of two decades. Parties and pressure groups were not slow to grasp the value of the increased coverage, and the emergence of newscasters, announcers and reporters with a Scottish reputation provided the products of the university debating societies with new routes into politics. Commercial television, and the BBC's reaction to it, reinforced in a much more explicitly political manner the national identity which the decline of the traditional institutions was currently eroding. That identity might only take the form of the small-screen parochialism of the Scottish news bulletins or the neo-Kailyardery of *Dr Finlay's Casebook* and *Sutherland's Law*, but it existed and it was capable of development. It took an English director, Peter Watkins, to show what could be done to dramatise, and de-mythologise, Scottish history, which he did, brutally, in *Culloden* (1964). But standards were improving by the end of the 1960s. The talent of James MacTaggart brought a rare sense of place to the work of writers as different as Edward Boyd in *Good Morning Yesterday* – the first of a series of thrillers about a seedy Glasgow investigator, Daniel Pike, who ultimately ended up as a sort of west-of-Scotland Sam Spade – and George Mackay Brown in *An Orkney Trilogy*. His vision of Scotland was bleak and uncomfortable, and its qualities survived his death in the work of Tom MacDougall – *Just Your Luck* and *Every other Saturday* – and the austere films of Bill Douglas – *My Childhood* and *My Ain Folk* – both of whom won major European prizes. Their Scotland fitted no cosy nationalist stereotype, but its predicament was real enough.

VII

In 1936, *in Scott and Scotland*, Edwin Muir had written that, despite the efforts of MacDiarmid, the prospect of creating an integrated Scottish literature was remote:[18]

> In an organic literature poetry is always influencing prose and prose poetry; and their interaction energises them both. Scottish poetry exists in a vacuum; it neither acts on the rest of literature nor reacts to it; and consequently it has shrunk to the level of anonymous folk-song.

This criticism had stung MacDiarmid to violent rejoiner yet, thirty years later, it still appeared valid. The only major novel-writing talent to appear comparable to the poets had been Lewis Grassic Gibbon. Periodical production and short story writing limped along from year to year. Muir's own commitment to Scottish culture, his wardenship of the Scottish Adult Education College at Newbattle, gifted to the nation by the imperial administrator and diplomat Philip Kerr, Lord Lothian, ended in disappointment and estrangement. Individual sorts of cultural communication developed, but without critical standards, intellectual interchange or – all too frequently – social relevance. In an article on Scottish Literature published in 1971 the critic Alexander Scott sounded like a company director announcing record-breaking productivity:[19]

> Even Scotland, where the poets have always outnumbered the novelists – and most of them have been poets too – has never experienced such a pullulation of poetry as in the last decade, and while the cascade of slim volumes pours from the presses, there seems no reason to believe that anything short of a major slump, and a consequent catastrophic cut in Arts Council subsidies, can stem the flood in the foreseeable future.

Poetry, since MacDiarmid the imaginative centre of Scottish culture, seemed, in the 1960s, closer to politics than to literature, not because its practitioners were nationalist, but because they produced the pattern of internal validation familiar in nationalist movements. It was not a large world: apart from MacDiarmid and Norman MacCaig, Edwin Morgan and George MacBeth, few Scots poets were widely known out of the country, but it was a community with a high degree of participation. As many seemed to write poetry as to read it. Parties were formed; small magazines assaulted one another; a little Arts Council money went a long way. Much of the output was mediocre or derivative: too many periodicals foundered under the weight of imitations of Ginsberg, Lowell or Brecht. 'Vigour and variety', as Edwin Morgan pointed out 'don't guarantee a direction or consolidate an achievement.'[20] But at least the Scottish scene was vibrant, compared with the well tuned provincial gloom which predominated in London. Kingsley Amis ruled out 'philosophers or paintings or novelists or art galleries or mythology or foreign cities or other poems' as fit subjects for poetry. Booze, copulation and death were enough to be getting on with. Sexual freedom led to a paradoxical imprisonment of the imagination. In Scotland sophistication may have been lacking, but so was the coterie spirit. The nature of the place meant that to acquire freedom of any sort the forces of darkness had to be challenged, and as time went on the limitations of conventional poetry itself as a means of surveying a rapidly changing society became apparent. It was against this background that the influence of MacDiarmid reasserted itself, not just the accomplished vernacular lyricist but the Carlyleian sage of the uncompromising dialectic prose and the 'catalogue poetry' who sought to evolve a language complex enough to deal with the industrialised materialistic world.

Paradoxically, the relatively weak pre-war nationalist movement seemed to attract more attention from literary men than its powerful post-war successor. Some political scientists have argued from this that modern nationalism has owed little to intellectual or cultural values. Yet this divergence is more apparent than real. MacDiarmid excepted, the contribution of literary nationalists in the 1930s was either playful, like Eric Linklater and Compton Mackenzie, or journalistic, like William Power and Lewis Spence. Political nationalism may have got publicity from such writers, but it was scarcely subjected to fundamental discussion. The responses of the greater writers, Muir, Gunn, MacDiarmid and Gibbon, were much more complex, and political nationalism was, justifiably, allocated only a marginal place. Their problem, mentioned earlier, was the difficulty of establishing an image of Scotland which was credible and resonant. The reality was too riven; the alternative loyalties of local community or cosmopolitan opportunism still held good: Grassic Gibbon's line – and he was the cosmopolitan opportunist *par excellence* – 'out of the world and into Blawearie' epitomised them. He also forecast the consequences of its collapse, in the address of the Minister at the end of *Sunset Song*:[21]

> Nothing, it has been said, is true but change, nothing abides, and here in Kinraddie where we watch the building of these little prides and little fortunes on the ruin of the little farms, we must give heed that these also do not abide, that a new spirit shall come to the land with the greater herd and the great machines.

In *Grey Granite*, the last novel of the *Scots Quair* trilogy, Gibbon penetrated through to the political life of industrial Scotland in the depression, but the imaginary city in which the action is set remained a projection of general industrial tendencies rather than an actual Scottish place. As Gibbon's biographer, Ian Munro, has written:[22]

> Duncairn has no identity, none of that indefinable yet inescapable atmosphere known to the natives of any Scottish

town. Gibbon's city is anonymous and voiceless despite the tumult of traffic and noise of its inhabitants.

But Gibbon had at least tried: a more or less wilful failure to tackle urban life – or to deal with it in terms other than those of outright rejection – characterises his contemporaries Muir and Gunn, and even, for all his communism and materialism, MacDiarmid. It left a gap which could all too easily be filled by comfortable character studies and anecdotes, the sort of urban Kailyard carefully tended by the feature writers of the Scottish local press. Writers like Jack House and Cliff Hanley in Glasgow, Wilfred Taylor and Albert Mackie in Edinburgh and Cuthbert Graham in Aberdeen maintained some sort of corporate memory with wit and sometimes imagination, but they failed to show any real understanding of the social and economic dynamics which had changed and were changing their cities. They seemed able to offer only a nostalgic response to the ruthless and mindless destruction of urban life which was carried out in the 1950s and 1960s by businessmen, councillors and – most notoriously – the universities. It was only in the 1960s that Gibbon's inquiry was resumed, not only into the life of the cities but into the 'unknown Scotland' of the half-urban, half-rural central belt, in the work of novelists like Alan Sharp, Archie Hind, Gordon Williams and William MacIlvanney. Their achievement has been uneven, and in the case of the two most successful, Sharp and Williams, has led them away from Scotland to the lusher pastures of London and Hollywood. Enough may have been done only to show the limitations of the novel as a way of capturing and conveying social reality. But the predicament delineated is important enough, if depressing.

Gordon Williams's *From Scenes like These* will suffice as illustration. This study of a doomed Scottish adolescent, Duncan Logan, trying to struggle out of an industrial village in Ayrshire – ironically, in practically the same area as the Dalmailing that the Reverend Micah Balwhidder presided over two centuries earlier in Galt's *Annals of the Parish* – accurately delineated the signpostless life of the 'unknown Scotland'. Life is grim, but meaningless rather than earnest. The tradition of 'getting on' no longer leads to great things, only circuitously to the vacuous existence of Logan's vague nationalist schoolteacher. Sex, when available, is coarse and unsatisfying through lack of sensitivity and compassion. Love is a formula which leads to marriage and a council house. Drink and the mindless enthusiasm of the football terraces offer, at the end of the book, the dependable conditioning which makes life in Kilcaddie tolerable. At one level there is little enough in this that distinguishes Logan's predicament from that of the youths in the novels of Alan Sillitoe and Stan Barstow a decade earlier, but at a deeper level there are resonances which are peculiarly Scots, like the booze-propelled *machismo* (Scotland has five times the alcoholism rate of England), the weakness of working-class political activism, the decay of promotion through education, and, penetrating everything, a lapsing in and out of dialect to suit different situations, an optional Scottishness which could never be taken as wholly honest or wholly false. Williams's book was not about nationalism, but in the situations he described, the almost classic environment of anomie, nationalist politics were to put down their roots.

The problem remained of how to make the Scottish novel artistically symmetrical as well as documentarily accurate. In this sense most of the new practitioners were deficient; they lacked the grasp of historical process and pattern that both Scott and Grassic Gibbon had, through their vast reading, come to possess. William MacIlvanney's translation of Hamlet to Kilmarnock in *Remedy is None* was forced, though his *Docherty* produced a credible and powerful hero-figure from Scottish mining life. Was it worth it anyway? The novel-reading public was desperately limited, nowhere more so than for novels about working-class Scotland. The ingenious formula was still the fastest way out, as A. J. Cronin had found it in the past. and George MacDonald Fraser and James Herriot were finding in the 1960s. Indeed, with practitioners like Mary Stewart, Jean Plaidy, Alastair MacLean, Dorothy Dunnett and Nigel Tranter working flat out – and throwing in the contribution of Ian Fleming for good measure – the Scots seemed to have cornered the market for escapist fiction.

The realistic treatment of Scottish social life coincided with a corresponding realism in portraying personal relationships. On the surface, this concerned the explicit description of sexuality in the arts, but deeper questions about the relations between the individual and society were involved, the same questions which the puritan repression of Victorian Scotland had done its best to silence. There was something worrying about the opinion of the *Scotsman* columnist Wilfred Taylor, that:[23]

> The late Annie S. Swan . . . wrote about the relationship between the sexes more imaginatively and adventurously in our opinion than D. H. Lawrence.

The fear of offending the gentility of the Edinburgh suburbs which lay beneath this facetiousness was much more offensive than straightforward puritanism. Annie S. Swan was never more than a third-rate Kailyard writer. But in early 1960s Scotland it did not do to suggest that unorthodoxy could be equated with honesty and talent.

It seems, in retrospect, amazing that MacDiarmid and Grassic Gibbon got away, over thirty years earlier, with a treatment of sexual relationships which was as explicit, and in social terms much more realistic, than that of Lawrence. Possibly the Lallans vocabulary acted as a linguistic fig-leaf. The value of what both were saying about sex and consciousness, and sexual roles in society, extended beyond conventional ideas about freedom and fulfilment, and beyond the Burnsian dualism of sentimentality and bawdry. If it was their Scottishness which made them permissible reading while the old puritanical canons still applied, their conviction that personal liberty involved sexual equality and social involvement became relevant after the novelty of permissiveness had worn off. At the same time another element of the Scottish intellectual tradition surfaced in R. D. Laing's investigation of the social origins of schizophrenia, *The Divided Self* (1960). The notion that madness was a protest against a constricting society went down well in the country of James Hogg and R. L. Stevenson. When Laing came north for a visit in 1967 he was lionised at the universities. Despite – or possibly because of – the puritan presence, the Scots were well placed to exploit the new freedoms, without becoming obsessed by the bizarre and the outrageous.

Leslie Stephen likened the impact of secular ideas on English intellectual society in the 1860s to the cumulative effect on an ice-cap of the slow sapping of warm currents. Suddenly and apparently without warning, the old environment split and crumbled and altered beyond recognition. Something like this happened over a century later in Scotland. The collapse of religious constraints and prescriptions meant that the stability of institutions like marriage depended more on consent than on convention, with a resulting fragility which was only partly borne out by an increase of 400 per cent in divorces between 1960 and 1974. The responsibilities of individuals to work out their relationships for themselves was brought home as never before, with results which were as painful as they were liberating. It did not require the frequent production of Ibsen and Strindberg plays at the local repertories to convince those of us who were students in the 1960s that the preoccupations of these great subversives had at last taken root among us. We knew our Brands and our Lovborgs; all over the place Noras were slamming doors; in every drowsy fishing town on the eastern coast there were Bernicks and Manders to be fought and Stockmanns to be supported. Freedom was indivisible. The people who wanted to shut down the Traverse Theatre, ban 'filth' at the Edinburgh Festival, and prevent the publisher John Calder from addressing the General Assembly were, we argued, also likely to think well of South Africa and the atom bomb. Our convictions were increased by the attentions of the Moral Rearmers, assiduously peddling their three Absolutes at the most unlikely meetings, and by the occasional reassuring fatuities of MPs (not always Tory), councillors and bailies.

Now there was nothing specifically nationalist about all this, although it was one of the factors which contributed to the belated recognition of MacDiarmid's achievement. It was much more important in a negative sense, calling into question all the traditional institutions, and the values which had secured them in position: marriage, religion, law, the educational system, patriotism (however defined). In their place came ambitions which were either individualist – like sexual freedom or freedom of expression – or collectivist, like the reorganisation of industry and regional government. The connection between the two was direct. Wilde's *The Soul of Man under Socialism* seemed, more than any of the speeches of the Labour leadership, to embody what was expected from 'the white heat of the technological revolution':

> Unless there are slaves to do the ugly, horrible, uninteresting work, culture and contemplation become almost impossible. Human slavery is wrong, insecure and demoralising. On mechanical slavery, on the slavery of the machine, the future of the world depends . . . the community by means of organisation of machinery will supply the useful things, the beautiful things will be made by the individual.[34]

I remember quoting this to a left-wing trade union leader at a party in 1965 or 1966 and being told that reading Wilde's essay had converted him to socialism. Not only the university-educated youth regarded the Wilsonian future in this sanguine light. But the new order did not establish itself, while there was little enough of the old left to return to. However alien the antics of the nationalists in the late 1960s seemed, the goals of the earlier part of the decade seemed even more remote.

It was, however, during this interregnum – 'between two worlds, one dead, one struggling to be born' – that political writing became an accepted institution of cultural communication, for the first time since the heyday of the *Edinburgh Review*. Before the late 1960s, books and articles dealing with contemporary Scottish society and politics had mainly been propagandist: Professor H. J. Paton's *The Claim of Scotland*, which appeared in 1967, was one of the last of the genre. Now the focus shifted to the task of understanding why Scotland was different, and what long-term factors, if any, underlay the current political upheavals. Book-making about Scotland became almost an obsession among the red Scots, at home and abroad; it seemed no less attractive to the recent immigrants. There were several symposia: Glasgow academics produced *The Scottish Debate*, which was edited by John MacCormick's son Neil, now a Balliol law don; Edinburgh University retorted with *Scotland: Government and Nationalism*, edited by its American economics professor J. N. Wolfe; two literary expatriates set to work as well, Duncan Glen, Hugh MacDiarmid's biographer, in *Whither Scotland* and Karl Miller, then editor of *The Listener*, in *Memoirs of a Modern Scotland*. Contributions to these were variable, and when the boom caused by the Nationalist upsurge had passed, all too often they found their way fairly rapidly on to the remainder shelves. But they contained enough of value – Nicholas Phillipson's discussion of semi-independence within the Union, Tom Nairn's exploration of the post-Reformation dualism in the Scots intellect, Harry Hanham's studies of the development of Scottish administration – to stimulate a continuing and serious inquiry into the nature of Scottish society. Even the Ross administration appeared to recognise this when it appointed Dr Gavin McCrone, the historian of the post-war Scottish economy and regional policy expert, to head the new Scottish Economic Planning Unit at St Andrew's House in 1969. With books like Hanham's *Scottish Nationalism*, James Kellas's *Modern Scotland*, Christopher Smout's *A History of the Scottish People*, the treatment of the Scottish experience began to move away from myth, recollected grievance, and the romanticism which had penetrated earlier popular accounts. There was a long way to travel yet, especially in transmitting this new objectivity to the public. The Canadian journalist John Prebble found a ready audience when he recounted the vivid traditions of Highland deprivation. Messrs Berresford Ellis and Seumas Mac a'Ghobhainn invented, in *The Scottish Insurrection of 1820*, some new legends of their own. The Messianic figure of John MacLean was reincarnated in two biographies published in 1972, rather than understood.

But now there was at least an apparatus of criticism which would ensure that some objective standards were applied. With half a dozen more or less durable periodicals, the later 1960s were a far cry from the poverty of the earlier decade, when serious Scottish periodicals were confined to the limping *Saltire Review* and the infrequent poetry periodical *Lines Review*. Political parties, and political clubs at the universities produced their periodicals, and funding by various foundations was now available for several independent publications. At one level the whole thing might be explained by the 'duplicating revoluion' and Arts Council subsidies, and certainly the quality of output varied enormously, but it was also an indication that more fundamental changes were taking place. There were more people to write, and there was more to write about.

As elsewhere in Europe in the 1960s, the universities took the lead. For all their political importance, the Scottish universities had traditionally exerted only limited influence on the lives of their students, many of whom commuted from home towns up to thirty miles away. In the post-Robbins era, more students lived in flats and in residences. A student bohemia of a type hitherto unknown in Scotland – though familiar enough on the continent – began to emerge. In many ways it was pretentious, immature and self-indulgent, but its attempts through little magazines and the student press to articulate and rationalise its life-style were valid in that they were the only communication possible. The attempts of the international student lefty to settle down in Scotland were hilariously illustrated by the exploits of an invention of the future student Rector of Edinburgh University, Jonathan Wills. Gaston le Jobbe, in beard and beret, persistently encountered big thick workies who referred to him in expansive mood as 'Djimmeh' and otherwise as 'wan o' they fung studints'. 'Fung studint' became in 1968 the Scots equivalent of 'Juifs Allemands', and was properly worrying to the students themselves. In the next few years, as some minor disturbances came to a head, with more official panic than student cohesion, the total absence of any linkage between students and working classes became all too apparent. Much subsequent student literary activity was directed at discovering why this was the case, and what could be done about it. On the whole this produced its dividends. The Edinburgh University Student Publications Board graduated from publishing guides to pubs and students and charity newspapers, to producing a quarterly, *the New Edinburgh Review*, in 1968, the *Red Paper on Education* in 1969, the first publication in English of essays by Gramsci in 1972, and in 1975 the *Red Paper on Scotland*, a hefty and very valuable symposium on Scottish government and society, edited by the second student Rector, Gordon Brown. Students who had served their apprenticeship on such ventures moved out, not only into television, Fleet Street and the Scottish papers, but into small publishing concerns and a rash of community newspapers, of which the *West Highland Free Press*, founded in 1972, provided a durable and effective radical voice in the Highlands on the eve of the oil boom.

In all this upheaval the government, in the shape of the

Arts Council played a major catalytic role. Until the Labour government took office in 1964, Arts Council funds had been very limited and about half had annually been spent on opera. The Scottish allocation had actually dropped from 8·4 per cent in 1948/9 to 6·3 per cent in 1963/4. Thereafter things improved, under the godmotherly influence of Jennie Lee. The Council's grant-in-aid rose by a factor of three and a half between 1964 and 1970, and the Scottish allocation climbed to 11·4 per cent. Hitherto most of the Scottish allocation had gone to the Edinburgh Festival and the orchestras, now it was much more widely distributed. The major coup was still a musical one, the rapid expansion of Scottish Opera, which had been founded in 1963, but funds were now being channelled towards literature – not simply poetry, but critical and even political magazines. For the first time these had some financial stability, and were even able (occasionally) to pay contributors, while bursaries to writers went some way to stemming the drift south.

Assistance from the Arts Council also helped *Scottish International*, which despite being run by three poets, Robert Garioch, Edwin Morgan and Robert Tait, changed from being a rather glossy, self-consciously artistic magazine into an impressive platform for dissenting and critical views, culminating, shortly before its regrettable demise, with a conference, 'What Kind of Scotland', in April 1973, at which for many of the participants the full implications of the oil boom suddenly became clear, and from which John McGrath's 7:84 Theatre Company set out to capture the Highlands for socialism with *The Cheviot, the Stag, and the Black, Black, Oil*. *Scottish International* succumbed to a fit of the trendies a year later. Mistakes were still being made, but the literary-political momentum was now strong enough to survive them. The *New Edinburgh Review* continued and was joined by the left-wing *Galgacus* and the political monthly (now fortnightly) *Question*. The Edinburgh Student Publication Board followed the *Red Paper* with the *Yearbook of Scottish Government*. When, in 1976, the *Scottish*

Educational Journal republished MacDiarmid's *Contemporary Scottish Studies*, the veteran could reflect that:[25]

> one of the aims of my *Contemporary Scottish Studies* has now been realised – the recognition that anything that purports to be a contribution to Scottish literature must be judged by the standards applied to literature in all other civilised countries.

VIII

In his 'Parliamo Glasgow' sketch, the comedian Stanley Baxter translated 'Erra perra toon cooncillors' as 'here come two intellectuals'. Before the 1950s the Scottish definition of the word was scarcely more comprehensive. In Scotland an intellectual meant a professional man, who lived a life dominated by a limited range of institutions and relationships, most of which were closely bound up with civil society: family, Kirk, golf club, former pupils' club. Except when decorously mediated through Scottish Orchestra concerts, the Royal Scottish Academy and touring drama companies, culture, in any creative sense, was alien, part of a Mr Hyde world of Rose Street bohemians. Some could cross the divide, but usually only by assuming another identity. For those bold enough, it was almost the same in politics: one set of views for employer and colleagues, another for propagandising. This was the context in which the pseudonym flourished, the land of Alias MacAlias. With the post-war decline of the traditional institutions, the creation of alternatives and the loosening of traditional strictures on behaviour, something much closer to a classic European intelligentsia began to emerge, with a direct correspondence between social situation, style of life, and political conviction.

At one level, Scottish intellectuals realised that they were constrained by geography, resembling for the first time their counterparts in nineteenth-century Europe. At another, an ideology was available which enabled them to rationalise their position. In a country which had for over a hundred and fifty years eschewed the tradition of political dialectic, it is impossible to overestimate the intellectual role of 'revisionist' Marxism after the mid-1950s in challenging the traditional anti-nationalist stance of the red Scots.

This significance was fourfold: the schism in the Communist Party in 1956 led to greater ideological awareness among the Scottish left; its attempts to establish a base among the Scottish working class encouraged a national identification; and the Marxism of the New Left paid unprecedented attention to the political and cultural superstructure and its relations to the economic base. Finally, this more complex historical analysis led to two quite different patterns of intellectual integration with society and politics, north and south of the border. While the scholarship of left-wing historians like E. P. Thompson and Christopher Hill went some way to creating – for the first time – an English nationalism, the New Left opened to the Scots the prospect of new links with Europe.

The Communist Party had always been strong in Scotland and its break-up over the invasion of Hungary in November 1956 released a number of highly articulate and effective writers, thinkers and organisers, who coalesced with non-party activists to create the New Left. (With typical perversity, MacDiarmid chose this occasion to rejoin the Communist Party, although he had protested at the Hungarian invasion.) By 1962 there were New Left Clubs in all the university towns and one development unique in Britain, the Fife Socialist League, a successful independent left-wing political party run by Lawrence Daly, the ex-Communist organiser of the Mineworkers' Union in Fife. But, this apart, the New Left illustrated the lack of direct political involvement among left-wing intellectuals in Scotland, and the absence of the sort of close identification between working-class power and creative political thought that they admired in Italy and Yugoslavia.

There was little that was specifically nationalist about the New Left. Indeed, in some ways it seemed an organisation tailor-made for the English academics who had been coming north in such numbers, analytical and withdrawn from anything except the rather moralistic political commitments of groups like the Campaign for Nuclear Disarmament. The Edinburgh University philosopher and playwright Stanley Eveling, interviewed in 1963, was fairly typical in his attitude to the plays of Arnold Wesker:[26]

> If one belongs to the New Left, as I do, you know exactly what Wesker's people are going to say next. It's a kind of left-wing sentimentalism which produces the notion that if human beings are allowed to be spontaneous, they become good, that if human beings are given the opportunity of becoming sensitive and intelligent, they become sensitive and intelligent.

This sort of attitude expressed an apprehension about the nature of working-class activism, as well as a positive desire to find out what precisely were the links that bound base to superstructure. Other activists, notably among the ex-Communists, were both more positive about political action and more preoccupied with the Scottish context. Under its Scottish General Secretary, John Gollan, the Communist Party had paid particular attention to Scottish economic problems and since 1951 had been committed to a Scottish parliament. This solution was revived by Lawrence Daly in a *New Left Review* article in 1962:[27]

> A Scottish Parliament would certainly contain a majority of Labour and radical members. There is every chance that it could not only revitalise Scotland's economic and cultural life but that it might well set the pace for the progressive social transformation of the rest of Britain.

Even where this was not endorsed, socialists connected with the New Left, like Norman Buchan and Hamish Henderson with their folk-song and folklore studies, and David Craig with his important *Scottish Literature and the Scottish People* (1961) set out to explore the connections between national culture and political mobilisation. They believed that popular culture had to be investigated and employed to re-create links which the formal structures of politics had allowed to decay, even although their conclusions seemed all too frequently to indicate that, with the collapse of the old institutions, the chances of achieving this integration in a Scottish context were minimal.

Politically, this activity flowed not into nationalism but into the concentration on regional policy which marked Labour's response during the late 1950s and early 1960s. By 1966 several of the New Left activists, like Norman Buchan and Neil Carmichael were in Parliament and further committed to the Labour Party programme. To them, the nationalist upsurge seemed an outbreak of lower middle-class false consciousness, irrelevant in its ideology and propaganda to the economic issues which had led to regional imbalance. As Buchan wrote in 1970:[28]

> If Scotland suffers from the uneven development of capitalism in common with other areas then it is right that the entire UK resources should be used to restore the imbalance . . . if we remove all Scottish political control and influence over what all accept is a single economic entity . . . then we are left inevitably to be controlled by that total economy . . . Paradoxically, total separation means less real independence.

There was logic behind this position, given the Nationalists' rather wilful attempts to prove that English taxation was robbing Scotland blind, but the point remained that regional policy had not been effective and that 'false consciousness' had been – not only in Scotland but, more ominously, in Northern Ireland. The problems that Scotland faced might be the same as the North-East and Lancashire, but the responses were distinctive in each area, and were not such as to bear out the existence of a 'real' working-class consciousness. Moreover, the rather Knoxian tendency among Scottish Labour politicians to anathematise colleagues whose views differed from their own did not add much conviction about their own democratic credentials. To younger people on the left, who had had some opportunity to see beyond British politics, the attitude of the Labour left seemed dogmatic and intellectually conservative, even if the Nationalists themselves appealed little. There did seem to be a divide between those members of the New Left who had been integrated into Labour's 'patronage state' and were concerned to defend it, and those who wanted, from a position of disillusionment, to examine the roots of the revolt against it.

A similar divergence existed by 1968 in English left-wing politics, with the publication of the New Left's *May Day Manifesto*, and the withdrawal of support from the Labour Party by many who, like Raymond Williams, the editor of the *Manifesto*, had given it tentative endorsement in 1964. The *Manifesto* 'wholeheartedly welcomed'[29] the success of the nationalists – rather optimistically conflating nationalism with radicalism – something the left in Scotland was scarcely likely to do. But the revisionism which Edinburgh students would be familiar with in the work of Victor Kiernan, whose 'Notes on Marxism in 1968' in *The Socialist Register* proved a notable landmark, made them treat nationalism as something much more significant than 'false consciousness', especially when, in the following year, Tom Nairn of the *New Left Review* started the first of several bouts with the beast. 'The Three Dreams of Scottish Nationalism' was dismissive, but it did recognise that nationalism in Scotland had a chronology different from that of the rest of Europe, and that Scottish civil society – in being both nationalist and assimilationist – was unique.[30] Nairn's conversion to nationalism was in the future, but his work, and the rediscovery of Gramsci, was to ensure that the question preoccupied the intellectual left in the early 1970s.

There was no equivalent activity on the right. It was difficult to see how there could be, as Enoch Powell, at that time the prophet of the market economy, saw emigration as the only solution to the problems of the Scottish economy. But 'scientific' middle opinion surfaced in January 1972 in the *Ecologist*'s 'Blueprint for Survival', roughly a third of whose signatories were Scots. The 'Blueprint' scouted nationalism as 'a dangerous and sterile compromise' but in its invocation of small-scale industry and agricultural self-sufficiency it accorded with the views of some of the more visionary nationalists as well as those of the environmentally-aware young, Marxist or not.[31]

New thought had to come from the left. In a country so dependent on government, the prescriptions of the market economists had little relevance. The problems at issue were those of authority and control. As Neal Ascherson, who returned in 1975 from being European correspondent of *The Observer*, put it:[32]

> Scotland is not really within the category of 'capitalist economies' as they are usually classified. Neither is it socialist. It hangs somewhere between Eastern and Western Europe, a stateist economy without a state.

The links between the intellectuals and publicity and administration were strong. In an authoritarian state this was always important. But in another direction, where their formal loyalties lay, there was a serious weakness. However often they praised the Scottish working class as, in John McGrath's words, 'one of the strongest in Europe, with a considerable experience of struggle and great maturity as a result',[33] they had little real contact with it, and little knowledge of its political behaviour. Reviewing the *Red Paper*, Kiernan commented pessimistically that its editor, Gordon Brown,

> laments, as he well may, that after all these years Scotland has 'no socialist book club, no socialist labour college . . . only a

> handful of socialist magazines and pamphlets'. If any large part of the working class wanted such things, Scotland would have them.[34]

The university intellectuals who contributed to the *Red Paper* had moved to a position of political involvement. But their prospective allies were far from evolving the conscious proletarian intelligentsia of Gramsci's vision. Battered into waywardness by economic decline and the ineptitude of their own representatives, the working class – the people of the tower blocks and the bleak estates, the Scotland that no one ever visited – were responding to the old loyalties and the old songs. Fletcher's prophecy – that ballads and not laws made a nation – seemed to be coming true.

Chapter 7

A Dance to the Music of Nationalism, 1945-1977

At any rate, I think we should pay more attention to the small but violent separatist movements which exist within our own island. They may look very unimportant now, but, after all, the Communist Manifesto was once a very obscure document, and the Nazi Party only had six members when Hitler joined it.

George Orwell, *Tribune*, 14 February 1947

In the spring of 1962 Max Aitken, Lord Beaverbrook, returned briefly to Scotland. Thirty years before, he had been a sort of goblin godfather to Scottish nationalism; now, an old and sick man, he travelled to the village of Torphichen in West Lothian, an island of old Scotland in the wastes of the industrial belt, from which the Aitkens had emigrated to Canada over a century earlier. Bizarre coincidences are the bonuses of history. The dying prophet of a dying empire – the most restless of the red

Scots – chose to visit the place where, within a few weeks, the revival of nationalist politics was to begin. The Scottish National Party had one of its few branches in the village, but it was from this branch that the initiatives which were to transform it, and Scottish politics, were to come.

The party which William Wolfe, a local chartered accountant, had joined in 1959, had changed little since its victory at Motherwell fourteen years before. Its membership remained around the 2,000 mark, its leadership had changed only by resignation and expulsions – a resilient little sect, rather than a political movement. In 1946 it had adopted a new constitution, the work of a group of members around Dr Robert McIntyre, which was less a programme than a set of values. Influenced by social credit, populism, Catholic distributism, it repudiated size, centralism and the concentration of economic power in private or state hands. Beyond this, it was eclectic. As Hanham wrote, it found a place for just about everything 'except a frank acceptance of the modern state and of modern bureaucratized industrial, political, trade union, and commercial empires'.[1] McIntyre would later defend his rejection of contemporary ideologies by stressing the extent to which they imposed preconceived solutions to specific problems, simply for the sake of logical consistency,[2] but at the time his dominance in the party implied organisational constraints which were little less severe. The 'Sinn Fein' attitude of putting independence first – once a majority of SNP members was returned to Westminster, they would withdraw and found the equivalent of their own Dail – coexisted with a much more exclusive party spirit. The 'open party' principle which, despite their mutual hostility, Douglas Young and John MacCormick had both favoured was abolished in 1948. Young, and Christopher Grieve, joined MacCormick in apostasy.

Roland Muirhead, 94 years old in 1962, remained a member, but with little conviction. 'I am satisfied that the present policy of the party has proved a complete failure,' he wrote to another former member, Sinclair Dunnett, in 1957.[3] Apart from winning a few seats on the councils of small burghs, its impact had been negligible. But his own movement, the Scottish National Congress, founded in 1950, was no more successful. It was leftish and sent observers to Independent Labour Party conferences, but it simply mirrored the decline of the old libertarian left. Between 1945 and 1960, much to the chagrin of the SNP and the unattached radicals, the man who held the centre of the stage was 'King John' MacCormick himself.

When MacCormick set up his 'Scottish Convention' after leaving the SNP, little love was lost between the two groups. In a venomous squib 'On a North British Devolutionist' the *Scots Independent* commented in 1944:[4]

> They libbit William Wallace.
> He gar'd* them bleed.
> They dinna libb† MacFoozle.
> They dinna need.

Until the end of the war the advantage lay with the SNP, but thereafter MacCormick took the initiative. In March 1947 Scottish Convention held a National Assembly in Glasgow, rather like the one which had been planned for September 1939, to which representatives of political parties, local authorities, the churches, trade unions and so on, were invited. A resolution demanding home rule was passed almost unanimously, and a representative committee set to work to draft a scheme to be presented to a second Assembly in the following year. Once endorsed, this was made the burden of a Scottish Covenant, the signing of which started at the third assembly, in October 1949. Nearly two million signed it.

While MacCormick's gifts as an orator and organiser served him well, he showed little subtlety as a strategist. Scottish

* gar'd = made.
† libb = castrate.

Convention was campaigning for a consensus on home rule. Essentially, this meant holding Labour MPs to their election pledges of 1945, when, with Motherwell in mind, they had promised it high priority. But it was all too easy to swim with the anti-centralist, anti-socialist tide, and this he did. In late 1947, believing he had united the Unionist and Liberal Parties on a devolutionist platform, he stood against Labour at Paisley. The Liberals repudiated the 'pact' and MacCormick found himself being supported by some rather implausible converts like Walter Elliot and Peter Thorneycroft.[5] It was not a particularly auspicious opening to an all-party campaign.

MacCormick did not win the Paisley election, but he secured the enmity of the government, in the person of Arthur Woodburn, the Secretary of State, who had been very sympathetic to devolution during the war. No matter how many signatures the Covenant gained, or how many authoritative endorsements – from individuals like Tom Johnston and groups as varied as the Church of Scotland and the Communist Party – this factor was critical. Finding the usual crop of bogus signatures, the Labour government was able to laugh the Covenant off. The Conservatives could afford to make sympathetic noises but not commit themselves. Revivalism was not a very effective way of exercising sustained pressure, and MacCormick failed to exploit the opportunities presented by the two elections of 1950 and 1951. Instead, he recaptured his undergraduate past by becoming involved in the Buchan-like adventure of stealing the ancient Scottish Coronation Stone from Westminster Abbey on Christmas Day 1950 and smuggling it north to Arbroath, where it was recovered on 11 April 1951. The escapade was popular but inappropriate: it enhanced emotional nationalism rather than the moderate consensus MacCormick was trying to promote. It produced a catharsis after which the Convention's efforts seemed anticlimatic.

The Conservatives, despite their election rhetoric, went no further towards the Convention's aims than administrative devolution. The Balfour Commisssion on Scottish Affairs (1952) was instructed to avoid the home rule issue. The Convention involved itself in the *longueurs* of an elaborate lawsuit in which MacCormick challenged the title of the new Queen to be called Elizabeth II in Scotland. Some youngsters took matters a stage further and blew up pillar-boxes with the new royal insignia: these japes unfortunately coincided with an I.R.A. offensive, and did little to enhance the respectability of the home rulers. The Convention faded out. MacCormick had lost his health, and his lawyer's business, through his devotion to it. His old opponent, Muirhead, helped keep him going and he lived to contest Roxburghshire in the 1959 election, as a Liberal. He died in 1961.[6]

Scottish Convention demonstrated the benefits and the penalties of seeking consensus support from the traditional Scots institutions. When they thought themselves under threat – in this case from the Labour government – their assistance to a Scottish 'popular front' organisation could be impressive. The only problem was that MacCormick's popular front never really included the people, whose main loyalty was to the Labour Party. Only they could have given his schemes political continuity, as the Irish had a century earlier supported O'Connell. Once the equilibrium of the institutions had been restored, after 1953 and the emotional counter-attraction of the Coronation, they deserted. Scottish Convention, however, had sustained and transmitted some of the national consciousness developed during the war, and a reservoir of potential support awaited activists who could take advantage of the next combination of institutional unease and political uncertainty.

The leadership of the Scottish National Party might appear ineffective, but it survived and within its little organisation operated like a modest family business. It was not sectarian in the left-wing sense, with an elaborate liturgy and frequent backslidings. It had something of the simplicity of eighteenth-century Scottish religious dissent: a single political tenet which was the 'one thing needful'. As Robert McIntyre later pointed out, this simplicity was relevant when the policies of the major parties would produce a continuing drift towards centralisation: anything more complicated would trap itself in its own logic. This philosophy served the party well in its rise in the 1960s; by the time its drawbacks were apparent it was a far different organisation from the one which Wolfe, who had been a Convention and Saltire activist, had joined.

Scotland showed independence in the election of 1959 but the Labour Party was the beneficiary. The five Nationalist candidates had the curiosity value of the Independent Labour Party, or other remnants of the red Clyde who still cropped up. Only one deposit, Dr McIntyre's, was saved. Within two years, however, there were signs of change. The party started to do well at by-elections, and the quality of its organisation radically improved. The two were directly connected, as by-elections brought into the party leadership two men, Wolfe and Ian Macdonald, who were subsequently to play a central role in modernising it and creating an unparalleled publicity machine. Both in a way represented the 'unknown Scotland' and both were given their chance by the Labour Party's faltering grasp on the way that Scottish society was changing. Macdonald, born in India, was a farmer and had been a pilot in the RAF. He had become a Nationalist at Glasgow University, McCormick's former stronghold, now a nursery of ambitious young Labour politicians. In November 1961 he stood against Labour at Glasgow Bridgeton.

The late MP had been Jimmie Carmichael, once an ILP man, and his predecessor until his death in 1946 had been the most charismatic figure of the Scottish left, James Maxton. But the tiny Labour constituency party selected a pedestrian Glasgow councillor, James Bennett, thus presenting the SNP with a claim to the ILP tradition, the home rule commitment contemporary socialists had failed to uphold.

Macdonald was no left-winger, but he benefited from this

disillusionment and received 18 per cent of the poll, nearly beating the Conservative into second place. Encouraged by the result he gave up his farm and offered his services at £5 a week to the SNP as full-time national organiser, without guarantee of salary or tenure. It was the sort of gamble a nineteenth-century Scotsman might have made in business or colonial enterprise. Within a year it paid off: he had the West Lothian election on his hands.

In West Lothian in February 1962 the Labour Party went to the other extreme in selecting its candidate. Tam Dalyell of the Binns, descendant of General Dalyell, the scourge of the Covenanters, educated at Eton and Cambridge, could have stepped from the pages of George Meredith or Henry James, a charming, abrupt, enthusiastic aristocratic radical, but, on the face of it, rather an odd choice for the most depressed constituency in Scotland. The Tories had provided the traditional opposition to Labour, but they were struck a critical blow by their own government which, in the 1962 budget, removed tax concessions from hydrocarbon oils and killed the West Lothian shale oil industry stone dead. In the months after the Liberal triumph at Orpington, a third party now had a chance.

It was at this point that William Wolfe, recuperating from a bout of flu, was approached by a scratch SNP Constituency Committee to stand. Reading Grassic Gibbon's *A Scots Quair* had put him in receptive mood:[7]

> . . . I was moved to indignation and frustration not because of the loss of old and hard ways of life, but because I realised anew that the essence of Scotland was being so diluted and near destroyed without the people, the real folk of Scotland, being able to do anything about it. It was a kindly English imperialism that was destroying them, and their own vulnerability was was making it so easy.

One chicken of the literary revival had come home to roost, if hardly in the way Gibbon had intended. He had taken his

Kincardineshire folk into the new world of industrialisation and class politics. Wolfe was going to stop short and fight for the older ideal of community: his roll-call of the early activists of the West Lothian party – Kerr, Hamilton, MacDonald, McGillveray, Rankin, Kellock, Ross, Sim – and their jobs – papermill worker, watchmaker, seaman, painter, draughtsman, steelmill worker – is just like Gibbon's salute to the crofters of the Mearns at the end of *Sunset Song*: an invocation of a local, fraternal society under threat. In the circumstances, and combined with Wolfe's personality, it proved a remarkably potent symbol.

Wolfe's role – as Vice-Chairman and since 1969 Chairman of the Party – has been so unique in British politics that it has almost totally been ignored by political commentators, something which tells us more about British politics than about Wolfe. His biography is not his party's history but his importance reflects qualities in its organisation which distance it from other British political groups. Wolfe has never been a successful candidate, he is no tactician, no scholar, no theorist, not even an organiser. He does not dominate his party but he has since the early 1960s symbolised it through qualities rarely found among politicians – or even among other members of his own party – which may be summed up by what Orwell called 'decency'. Even the most articulate of his left-wing critics, like the playwright John McGrath, have to qualify political censure with personal regard. His role reflects the sense in which the SNP has regarded itself as a community as well as a movement, with Wolfe its conscience rather than its leader, conciliating and inspiring rather than manipulating. The closest parallel is probably with Keir Hardie and the ILP. Although no orator Wolfe, like Hardie, embodies the aspirations of his membership, and also manages, by instinct rather than skill, to equate with a commitment to democracy which would embarrass most political leaderships, in the agreeable chaos of the SNP annual conferences. Kirk Elder, scoutmaster, patriot, democrat, Wolfe embodies the old Scotland at its most responsible. If evidence is needed of the transference of its essentially religious values to secular life, Wolfe and the SNP are always to hand.

The West Lothian contest created, in embryo, the alliance which underwrote later SNP success. The activists included both the veterans who had fought the seat in the 1950 general election, when just over a thousand votes were polled, and recent recruits. Some of these were left-wingers who had left the Labour Party because of renunciation of 1962 unilateral nuclear disarmament, a cause with which Wolfe personally sympathised. Macdonald's publicity team battened on the shale oil issue – not the last occasion when oil and the fortunes of the SNP were to be intimately linked. Wolfe campaigned energetically throughout the constituency, which seemed to illustrate the economic and social problems of mid-twentieth-century Scotland: a mixture of elderly market towns, anonymous colliery villages, run-down factories and docks, and monumental industrial dereliction, typified by the vast red tips of burnt shale which disfigured it. Even with a run-of-the-mill Labour candidate he could have stood little chance of victory, and Dalyell proved (and still proves) a remarkably tough opponent, increasing Labour's majority from nine to eleven thousand. But Wolfe now lay second to him, with the Tory and Liberal lagging far behind. Both of these parties had good cause to feel concerned. The Tories had been the majority Scottish party only five years earlier, and the Liberals under Jo Grimond were bidding to become the 'third force'.

III

The SNP fought four by-elections before the 1964 general election – in Glasgow Woodside, Kinross, Dundee West and Dumfries – but without much impact. The party was, however, changing rapidly at the centre, with the influx of Wolfe and his

West Lothian activists. At the 1963 annual conference they made up about a quarter of the delegates and helped elect Wolfe Vice-Chairman, the first new recruit to the national executive for some time. These changes both shifted the party to the left on issues like disarmament and land nationalisation and, largely through Wolfe's shrewd patronage of younger activists, especially at the universities, managed to create a stronger central organisation. One perennial problem of the pre-war SNP – how to combine activism with cohesion – seemed to have been solved. The party had a flexible project-based organisation superior to that of the other Scottish parties. Given the depressed state of the Scottish economy, radical ideology was also generally acceptable, and the SNP could draw on individuals and groups which were otherwise agitating single-issue causes, like nuclear disarmament, opposition to railway closures, or the co-operative control of industry. These were to be of great value in directing the campaigns it subsequently mounted.

After 1963–4 the SNP had two executive vice-presidents. Wolfe directed publicity and development, Douglas Drysdale, a foundry-master from Falkirk, directed organisation and finance. In 1965 they were joined by Rosemary Hall, as honorary publicity secretary. Both she and Wolfe had been involved with the Saltire Society, and transferred its preoccupation with design standards to the SNP's publicity, which rapidly became the best and most effective of any British party. Central to this was the invention of a party symbol, a combined thistle and saltire, like an alpha sign stood on end. White and red on a blue ground, this looked effective on documents and badges, but (in a country addicted to graffiti) it could also, with a twist of the hand, be scrawled on walls, bus-shelters and lamp-posts. There had been nothing like it, opponents said, since the swastika: but this was sour grapes.[8]

Aptitude for organisation and a nose for promising issues were not enough. The SNP faced a rival under Jo Grimond. The Liberal revival had been particularly effective in Scotland, with a lot of support in the universities. The Liberals, further, promised an extensive measure of home rule: in any head-on clash, they would probably have wiped the floor with the Nationalists, despite what happened in West Lothian. However, in February 1964 Wolfe and his allies persuaded the National Council to offer the Liberals a pact. This was furiously opposed by older members but Wolfe argued that it would force the Liberals to come clean about their Scottish policy: were they primarily a home rule party or was their Scottish policy simply one among many commitments? Although a precedent existed in the pact of 1938, this request placed the Liberal leadership in a quandary, from which it only emerged, badly battered, four years later. It replied that home rule was an integral part of the Liberal policy and could not be advanced as a joint demand; yet enthusiasm for a pact remained among certain prominent Liberals, and during the 1964 general election both parties were on the whole careful not to contest the same seats.

In hindsight, this partial truce cost the Liberals dear: for the price of a few deposits they could, in the election of 1964, have shattered the confidence of the SNP. Only where they were absent did the Nationalists poll well, and the SNP's performance was, overall, inferior to its last major general election campaign, in 1935. But it did creditably in seven seats, mainly in central Scotland, and membership continued to double annually. In 1962 it had been 2,000; by 1966 it was 42,000. In that year the Liberal revival began to falter, with a drop of about 15 per cent in the party's Scottish vote, while the Nationalists doubled their overall poll. Although Scotland supplied half their parliamentary vote, the Liberals did not recover. Grimond resigned in 1967, having led his party in the direction of formal federalism. Although in 1968 this was endorsed by the Scottish Liberals, the Liberal Assembly, who favoured equating the position of Scotland and Wales with the English regions, repudiated it. Grimond could have mediated between the centre and the Scots, but he already led the latter, while the new Leader, Jeremy Thorpe, preferred to bid for the votes of the English suburbanites. By 1968 the choice facing the Scottish Liberals was fairly explicit: to compete with the Nationalists on home rule – an unenviable task given the latter's commanding position – or to back the revival of the party's chances south of the border. The ambitions of the ablest of the Scottish Liberal MPs, David Steel and Russell Johnston, were firmly oriented to Westminster and Europe, so their reaction was predictable, but other prominent activists, the party treasurer Michael Starforth and the broadcaster Ludovic Kennedy, threw their hands in with the Nationalists. By 1970, when the party lost a further two seats, the Liberal hour had passed.

IV

By 1970 the Nationalist hour seemed to have passed as well. Between 1967 and 1969 the SNP experienced a dramatic boom, followed by a scarcely less spectacular slump. In 1968 it had the largest party membership in Scotland, gained the largest proportion of the vote in the local elections, and looked poised to make significant parliamentary gains. A year later its fortunes had ebbed and it seemed unlikely to retain any of the ground it had made. How much was this oscillation the natural outcome of mid-term protest voting, how much was it the expression of a genuine will to independence, vitiated by the relative immaturity of the party? As late as 1973 the first interpretation would have won general assent, but both the resilience of the SNP and the growing support for devolution since 1970 now indicate that, even before the impact of North Sea oil changed the whole political agenda, the SNP had located and was ministering to (or exploiting) inadequacies in Scottish society which the other parties were constitutionally incapable of dealing with.

Mid-term unrest set in only a matter of weeks after the

general election of March 1966. The Right-wing and Liberal candidates gained 26 seats from Labour in the May local elections. The SNP was not assured of the Scottish protest vote, but the right wing was hamstrung by the difference between local and national political parties, while the SNP was given a fillip by Gwynfor Evans's victory in the Carmarthen by-election of 14 July. Then, in the autumn, the member for Labour's most marginal seat, Glasgow Pollok, died. Despite several Nationalist successes in local authority by-elections, the two main parties were preoccupied with each other. The Conservatives produced Professor Esmond Wright, who had been until then a seemingly detached commentator on Scottish politics for the BBC. The Labour Party approached Alastair Hetherington, the editor of the *Guardian* and son of a respected Principal of Glasgow University, who turned them down, and they eventually settled for Dick Douglas, a technical college lecturer. The SNP's choice, George Leslie, a Glasgow vet, was an unknown quantity, but turned out to be a fierce, impressive orator rather in the style of Maxton. On 9 March 1967, as expected, the Tories captured the seat, but the Nationalists polled 28 per cent and the Liberal just beat the Communist candidate to come nowhere. The Nationalists had now become news.[9]

Two months later they broke through in local politics, gaining 27 seats in the burgh elections and 42 in the counties, and increasing their share of the poll from 4·4 per cent in 1966 to 18·4 per cent. The right-wing revival was stopped in its tracks and the Labour Party, still clinging to office in the major cities and towns, was badly rattled. Hitherto polls had been around 30 per cent and results reflected the popularity of the major parties. Local issues mainly revolved round rents and rates, but council tenants who theoretically supported Labour tended usually to be reluctant to vote, even when a right-wing council was raising their rents. It was this apolitical mass which responded to the SNP's call to 'put Scotland first'. No attempt was made to formulate a Nationalist municipal policy or select experienced candidates: there was no need to.[10] One more than usually cynical Labour candidate remarked that the electorate in his ward would vote Nationalist 'even if the Nats put up pink-eyed rabbits'. Afterwards, there were a lot of pink-eyed rabbits around.

The new Nationalist councillors appeared out ot the blue. Mainly small businessmen, housewives and the self-employed, only about 40 per cent of a representative sample had more than three years' membership of the SNP and only 13·5 per cent had been members of other parties. If they offered a more varied alternative to Labour's trade unionists and the Progressive shopkeepers, it may only have been because they didn't know enough about the difficulties that the other parties had in finding members with the time to spare to attend council meetings. With the exception of several middle-sized burghs in central Scotland, the Nationalist councillors made little impact. Defections and resignations, and a Labour recovery in 1969, made the aftermath of the municipal coup an extended embarrassment. But in the summer of 1967 this was still in the future. An even greater victory was at hand.

Tom Fraser, the Minister of Transport, had not been a success and was dropped from the government in December 1965. In May 1967 he accepted the chairmanship of the North of Scotland Hydro-Electric Board, precipitating a by-election in the solid Labour constituency of Hamilton. The National Union of Mineworkers made it plain, to the distress of the various ambitious activists who turned up on the short list, that they were going to get their own man selected, although there were, in fact, no working collieries in the constituency. They got their way and Alex Wilson, an elderly councillor, became the Labour candidate. The Nationalist candidate was in direct contrast. Mrs Winifred Ewing, a prominent Glasgow solicitor with an ILP background, was attractive, articulate and, when circumstances required it, appropriately emotional. Her selection was also a comment on the neglect of women candidates by the other parties. Fortune was on her side. Although well backed up by canvassers and well projected by the SNP publicity organisation, the by-election, on 2 November, came at the absolute nadir of the Labour government's fortunes, with a disastrous balance of payments deficit making devaluation and deflation inevitable. The combination of circumstances was too much for even a 16,000 Labour majority. Mrs Ewing left Glasgow for Westminster on a special train. The last one the railways had run for politicians had carried Maxton and his Clydesiders south forty-five years before, to inaugurate Labour's conquest of the Scottish left. The point was not lost.

The Hamilton result registered with particular force in Downing Street, but it was the opposition which took action. In 1967 the Scottish Conservative Party set up a study group on devolution. Its report was endorsed by Edward Heath in May 1968, when a further and more authoritative 'Constitutional Committee' was set up under Sir Alec Douglas-Home. There was at this stage, little difference between this reaction and Churchill's endorsement of the Convention's activities in 1950; just as at that time, the Labour hierarchy in Scotland as well as the Secretary of State were against any concession. This – plus the government's manifold economic preoccupations – seems to have held Wilson's hand. A strongly pro-devolutionist manifesto by the Berwickshire MP Professor John Mackintosh, conceivably the ablest constitutionalist in the House, probably made attitudes even more rigid, as Mackintosh's relations with Ross and Wilson were notoriously icy. For a year Labour led with its chin, until Wilson announced the Crowther Commission in December 1968. This hiatus was to be critical in creating a new home rule consensus. Churchmen, lawyers and academics – representatives of the institutions which had, two decades before, aligned themselves with MacCormick's Convention – recaptured their devolutionist convictions. Symposia and conferences were organised. Devolution, if not the SNP, became respectable again, but, with Labour hostile and the Liberals weak, such publicity as it received went to enhance the appeal of the Nationalists.

With the election of Mrs Ewing the media, which had hitherto ignored the SNP, became almost indulgent. She was quickly signed up to contribute a weekly column to the *Daily Record*, the only Scottish daily which supported Labour, while the *Scottish Daily Express* reanimated its late master's patronage of Scottish nationalism and covered her Westminster activities with a weekly report 'Winnie in Westminster'. Roy Thomson's northern outposts shifted over to a strongly devolutionist standpoint, *The Scotsman* producing, in February 1968, a plan for the federal reconstruction of the United Kingdom, and even the Dundee diehards, the *Courier and Advertiser* and the *Sunday Post*, made sympathetic noises.[11] Alone of the major papers the *Glasgow Herald* remained hostile, providing a vehicle for high Tory and (oddly enough) extreme left-wing attacks on the Nationalists.

It was probably this combination of respectable fellow-travelling and the practical inexperience of the SNP in local government which provoked the intense hostility of the left. Although individual MPs and Labour activists supported devolution, like Andrew Hargrave, Scottish correspondent of the *Financial Times*, whose 'Devolution: the Third Choice', a Fabian tract of 1969, came close to anticipating what the Labour government eventually offered in 1976, the attitude of the rank and file was more appropriately summed up by a rather strident pamphlet, 'Don't butcher Scotland's future', produced by two MPs, Alex Eadie and Jim Sillars, in the same year. This came out firmly against a parliament of any kind, as a concession to a movement which was basically irrationalist and reactionary. Despite the endorsement of some leftish public figures like Sir Compton Mackenzie, Claud Cockburn and Cliff Hanley, who had a couple of decades earlier written 'Scotland the Brave', there were enough signs within the SNP that such suspicions were not without foundation.

'There's plenty of support among the Scots regiments,' an SNP official told the *Daily Telegraph* in early 1968. 'They haven't taken kindly to the disbandments and amalgamations wished on them by the English.'[12] Shortly after the Hamilton by-election the government announced the disbandment of the Argyll and Sutherland Highlanders, who had just come back from sorting out the Arabs in Aden. It was alleged that all sorts of War Office skulduggery had suppressed the regiment's tough and successful commanding officer. 'Mad Mitch' – Lieutenant-Colonel Colin Mitchell – was articulate, charming and even rather learned, reading philosophy in his spare time. Mitchell conformed to the traditional Scottish image of the popular fighting-man and he and his regiment came back to a hero's welcome, especially in their depot town, Stirling, now controlled by the Nationalists. A 'Save the Argylls' campaign was mounted by the *Scottish Daily Express*, and rumour had it that 'Mad Mitch' would stand as a Nationalist candidate. Mitchell turned out to be a Tory, and won West Aberdeenshire from the Liberals in 1970. (Subsequently he showed little taste for politics and so he didn't help them much.) But imperial nostalgia which the whole episode conjured up did not accord at all well with the SNP's radical pretensions.

The SNP was further embarrassed by the resurrection of its troubled past, in the shape of the 1320 Club. This group, founded in 1967 to commemorate the Declaration of Arbroath, sought to wean the nationalist cause away from the identification with the SNP and reconstitute a broader-based consensus, along the lines of the pre-1948 SNP. Douglas Young was a founder-member, along with veteran agitators like Wendy Wood, Oliver Brown and Hugh MacDiarmid. Remembering what its past history had been like, the SNP rapidly put it under an interdict, earning for itself the anathemas of the literary nationalists and the reputation of outdoing the other parties in philistinism. The ban turned out to be justified: the Club's conspiratorial and authoritarian tendencies came to the surface and in 1975 landed its secretary, Major F. A. C. Boothby, in prison on a conviction for terrorist conspiracy.

In 1969 the former editor of *Private Eye*, Andrew Osmond, and the private secretary of the Leader of the Opposition, Douglas Hurd, had the bright idea of writing a fantasy about a Nationalist takeover of part of the Scottish Highlands, which turned out in true Buchan style, to be backed by the Russians. Mastrovin redux! *Scotch on the Rocks*, thanks to a certain Oxford academic who shall be nameless, contained several fictional nationalists who were not wholly unrelated to the real thing, causing a mixture of annoyance (on the part of those parodied) and fury (on the part of those left out). Six years later fact caught up with fiction when the eccentric dictator of Uganda, Field-Marshal Amin, claimed to have had consultations with the provisional Scottish government, and telegraphed a very embarrassed William Wolfe to assure him of his support for 'the Scottish [who] are among the most brave people I have known in the world'.[13] His message coincided with the trial of some very real terrorists.

Apart from its backing of Radio free Scotland, which used to broadcast after hours on the BBC TV wavelength, the SNP as an organisation scrupulously kept to the letter of the law. Yet on the fringes of nationalism there was a fair amount of violence, and six trials, two in 1971 and 1972, three in 1975 and another in 1976, exposed the ramifications of its seamier side. Compared with Northern Ireland, illegality was trifling, but its very existence, along with a tendency for some SNP activists to slip out of the party and into illegal organisations, had ominous implications in the event of a constitutional break down. In 1972 three activists in a crazy little left-wing organisation, the Scottish Workers' Party, were handed out draconian sentences of over twenty years for bank robberies in Glasgow; in April and May 1975 the two 'Army of the Provisional Government' trials – resulting from an unbelievably inept bank raid – lifted up a corner of a bizarre world of death oaths, assassination squads, and plans for military subversion, in which the implication of at least one SNP activist could not be ruled out. In 1976 a further batch of activists, some of whom had been SNP local officials and most of whom were rather respectable middle-class men came before the courts on explosives charges. Legal ineptitude meant the release of two of them, and, although convictions were secured, the existence of a 'Tartan Army' remained as shadowy as before. As the *Guardian* commented, on 24 May 1975, the breaking of the Army of the Provisional Government 'does not mean the demise of all those intent on launching guerilla operations to take over Scotland by force. It is only the end of an important chapter.'

In 1986, however, the SNP's main problem was not the 1320 Club but its own policy. Independence was its traditional first step, but in its 1968 situation this had about the same relevance as the demand to open Joanna Southcott's Box. It had to sustain a role in local politics, and take advantage of the various qualified steps towards home rule that the government or the other parties might suggest. So, largely under pressure from Wolfe and the younger men in the party, policy formation groups were set up in 1968, to report back to the annual conference in 1969. The old guard acquiesced.

When the groups reported at Oban in 1969 the SNP moved to a formal position left of centre, subject to a degree of populism in matters of liberal reform and crime and punishment. However, largely because of the party constitution, which gives equal weight at conference to local associations, the adoption of policies was anything but logical. Conference refused to come to a decision on several important policy issues, and a division still remained between the 'freedom first' school and the 'social democrats'. The latter, however, secured the election of Wolfe as Chairman over the veteran Arthur Donaldson. But by then the party was in serious electoral trouble. In the May local elections its vote slumped from 30 per cent to 22 per cent; although twenty seats were gained, this was a fall of eighty on the

1968 performance. Labour was beginning to climb out of the trough. At an October by-election in Glasgow Gorbals, the centre of Catholic-Labour Clydeside (where the Labour posters were printed in green), the Nationalist vote fell to 25 per cent. Worse was yet to come: at the by-election in South Ayrshire in March 1970 caused by the death of Emrys Hughes, who had always been sympathetic to them and had sponsored Mrs Ewing at Westminster, their poll fell to 20 per cent despite a strong candidate in the shape of Hughes's former election agent. In May, Labour revenged its 1967 losses by recovering its position almost completely. The SNP, its membership shrunk to half its 1968 level, did not look forward to the general election.

Increasing political adversity produced a greater realism in SNP policies. By 1970 attitudes to independence were less absolute: a future was seen for some sort of association of British states, and at the very least a customs union. This moderation stemmed partly from the contradiction of one of the SNPs pet propaganda points: the calculation that Scotland was, through taxation, subsidising England at sums variously computed at between £30 and £120 million per annum. The destruction of this was the work of the regional economist Dr Gavin McCrone, in *Scotland's Future: The Economics of Nationalism*, published in 1969. McCrone calculated that Scotland remained indebted to England to the tune of £56–£93 million per annum and, as a strong critic of government economic policies for Scotland in his earlier book *Scotland's Economic Progress, 1951–1960* (1965), his analysis of Nationalist economics was authoritative. It was also, however, a two-edged weapon, as in the early 1970s it provided an accurate basis for calculations about the surplus that would accrue to Scotland through the extraction of North Sea oil.

V

The 1970 election was, predictably, a near-disaster for the SNP. Although it secured 11·4 per cent of the total vote – rather more than double its 1966 level – this was divided between 65 candidates (compared with 23), 42 of whom lost their deposits. In the cities, where the party had made its sweeping local election gains – and losses – its performance was poor. At Glasgow Gorbals, for example, its vote, which had been nothing great at 25 per cent the previous October, slumped to 7·4 per cent. At Hamilton Mrs Ewing was beaten by over 8,500 votes. The only consolation came with the last result to be declared. In the Western Isles – Lewis and Harris – the SNP candidate Donald Stewart, a popular local figure as provost of Stornoway, overcame a 40 per cent Labour majority to oust Malcolm Macmillan, the non-resident MP. The politics of the Western Isles had little to do with any national trends, but in their idiosyncratic way they ensured that a parliamentary presence continued.

However, there were compensations. The Liberal bid to remain third force was now at an end, with the loss of two of their five Scottish seats, and the retention of only 5·5 per cent of the vote. The Nationalists had still polled respectably in central Scottish county constituencies, and in seven seats – Aberdeenshire East, South Angus, Argyll, Banff, Galloway, Hamilton and West Lothian – they lay second. A solid presence had been established in a part of Scotland which economic developments, as yet only shadowy, were to make significant – the north-east – while the capacity to shock the two major parties, especially Labour, by delivering a protest vote in the cities still remained.

The rise of the Nationalists was not unique in late-1960s Britain. In early 1967 John Vincent, criticising the 'radical' programme of the Liberal Party, wrote in *New Society*:[14]

> There is definitely room in British politics for a party based on middle-aged opposition to the secular humanism (to use no more actionable term) of the Oxford Union, on the opposition of the less demoralised and modern areas to the solipsism of the

> M1 country. There is room for a party which puts locality before party conflict.

Scottish nationalism could, in these years, be seen to fit into a pattern which included the English as well as the Welsh, involving not only the success of some populist Liberals but the enormous popularity of Enoch Powell, which was transmitted at by-elections to other Tories who had convictions very different from his. Although the absence of an immigration issue differentiated Scottish from English populism, there were important similarities – the idea of a community under threat, the suspicion of bureaucratic machination. Powell was in some ways a throwback to the democratic, xenophobic nationalism of the late nineteenth century. In his denunciations of state intervention he set out to rile the Scots:[15]

> I don't think that because Scotland has five million people it has a right to that size of population . . . if you don't like your geographical position – being away from the dense population markets – get out of it . . . but don't ask people to give you handouts. That's the begging-bowl mentality.

But he was, on the other hand, blunt about independence. If the Scots wanted it, they should take it. Anything would be preferable to continued subsidy or devolution. English nationalism did not survive the 1970 election, but Scottish nationalism did.

The period of Conservative government after 1970 showed that the SNP decline had been temporary. Membership picked up, the party performed creditably at by-elections at Stirling (16 September 1971) and Dundee East (1 March 1973) and ultimately broke through to capture Glasgow Govan on 8 November 1973. All its successes were at the expense of Labour, which contrasted with the 1955–64 situation, when Labour had pre-empted the 'national' anti-Conservative reaction.

The SNP had matured. If it was an opportunist party, it was

no longer a populist one. It structured its appeal around issues which it could exploit, and which directed attention at its main goal of independence, not around issues which would anyway be popular in a conservative electorate, like law and order. It tapped available expertise on sensitive social and economic issues – like social deprivation, education, steel closures – and projected its findings at the electorate through its highly-geared publicity machine, something a populist party would never be capable of doing, as it could never gain the necessary intellectual support. For this reason, its vaguely left-of-centre line was virtually inevitable, as was the general imprecision of its policies in areas where there was no direct benefit to be gained from agitation. Policy subserved the need to provide a talented cadre of activists to exploit specific issues when the need arose. As a result, no party was better fitted to conjure with North Sea oil.

VI

From 1967 the ports of eastern Scotland started to fill up with odd-looking vessels, high-prowed and low in the stern, like floating lorries: these were the tenders for the oil drilling rigs. Old shipyards and warehouses sprouted the insignia of international oil and engineering companies; local grocers started to stock exotic American tinned foods; house prices rose. The hunt for North Sea oil was under way. It had started over a decade earlier, when the discovery of a natural gas field in Holland suggested the likelihood of oil-bearing strata under the North Sea. By 1965 gas was being piped from the sea off East Anglia, and in 1969, following the partition of the sea between the neighbouring states, a commercially viable field – the Ekofisk – was located in the Norwegian sector. As pressure on world supplies increased in the late 1960s, the rigs were towed north to the difficult and treacherous waters off the north-east coast. The finds would have to be rich indeed to justify

£1 million for a test borehole and up to £500 million for a production platform the height of the Post Office Tower. By late 1970, however, the investment seemed to be paying off. BP discovered a large field – the Forties – 120 miles north-east of Aberdeen. They talked in terms of a total output of 12 million tons a year in 1980.[16] Thereafter, however, a sequence of events occurred which resulted in output forecasts rising by a factor of 13, to 158 million tons a year in 1980.

'It's Scotland's Oil!' Whatever the ethics of the proposition, the SNP chose an opportune moment, 16 March 1973, to launch a sophisticated and well organised campaign. Just over a month later the United States government suspended quotas on oil imports, admitting that an oil shortage was in prospect, and the Middle East states were already beginning to show their bargaining strength.[17] A year later, after the Yom Kippur War, prices per barrel had risen by a factor of between 6 and 8 on their 1972 levels. The North Sea oilfield was no longer a marginal economic proposition, and the SNP, with a lot of informed advice from the universities, and a press department run by a former Fellow of the Royal Institute of International Affairs, Stephen Maxwell, was well placed to exploit the disquiet with which the Scots regarded the descent of the multinationals on their coastline. The other parties might denounce the demand for Scottish control of oil revenues as selfish but, in a Scottish context, the oil issue was more complex than crude. To an extent not appreciated by politicians in the south, it presented the Scottish economy with as many problems as opportunities, problems which ultimately brought, as no other issue did, the whole concept of the Union into question.

The central issue was the result of geographical chance, aggravated by government policy. The economy of north-eastern Scotland was still predominantly agricultural, industry was limited, and, following decades of emigration from the countryside, the surplus of labour available was very small. Thus the local economy could not respond to the stimulus offered by the oil, while the diversion of labour from existing industries and the land, and the increase in prices of houses and services, actually meant considerable economic disadvantages. The capacity to supply oil equipment existed in Scotland on the Clyde, where there was heavy engineering capacity – and unemployment – in abundance. But this required time and investment to re-equip and modernise, just as the north-east needed heavy investment in housing, transport and social services simply to survive. For the advantages of oil to outweigh the disadvantages, there had to be investment and a slowing-down of the programme of extraction. But a British government, obsessed with the need to overcome disastrous balance of payments deficits, and reluctant to increase public expenditure, could not be expected to agree.[18] The Heath government backed both the rapid extraction of oil and the dispersal of 'onshore' activities around the northern Scottish coast, a policy which seemed deliberately to exacerbate the situation.

Already apparent early in 1973, this threat was dramatised when an oil platform construction company, Taylor Woodrow, proposed to acquire land for platform building at Drumbuie, on the shores of Loch Carron in Wester Ross. The land had been covenanted by a previous owner to the National Trust for Scotland, yet the London government in early 1974 intended to ease the company's acquisition by enacting a bill which gave it general powers to acquire whatever land was needed around the coast for oil-related use. Drumbuie was not the first – or the last – area of great beauty to be threatened by oil developments, but the government's peculiarly insensitive response to the problem seemed to promise a gang-bang on the Scottish environment, while the credibility of the groups which had traditionally stood out for conservation was endangered by the wholehearted participation of the Scottish upper classes in oil developments.[19]

Although Scottish industry was increasingly dominated by the state, the native capitalist institutions had seen something of a revival in the late 1960s. The five banks were now reduced to three, but the two largest of these were now controlled from Scotland. Five merchant banks had also been set up, and the Bank of Scotland had played the key role in establishing in 1973 the International Energy Bank, with assets of £50,000 million, to finance oil exploitation. Yet the integration of the world of investment trusts and banks with the traditional rulers of Scotland was such that suspicions of incest inevitably arose. The left made much of the involvement of George Pottinger, who was jailed for corruption in February 1974, with the business empire of the first Hugh Fraser, and there were other examples in Local authorities and in the Highland Board. When Heath brought Lord Polwarth, Chairman of the Bank of Scotland and of the Scottish Council, into the government in March 1973 as 'oil supremo', he seemed to put the seal on an alliance of big business, government, Scottish institutions and the multinationals. That summer John McGrath's 7:84 Theatre Company punched the message home throughout the Highlands with *The Cheviot, the Stag and the Black, Black Oil*:[20]

> Now all you Scotties need have no fear,
> Your oil's quite safe now the trouble-shooter's here,
> So I'll trust you if you'll trust me,
> 'Cos I'm the ex-director of a trust company.

The Cheviot was the highlight of the Nationalists' annual conference at Oban in August. How can they put on a play like that and then say they are not Nationalists?' a *Scots Independent* reporter asked Wolfe. 'If we knew the answer to that, we would sweep Scotland tomorrow,'[21] was the answer he got. But for every one of McGrath's audience who was converted to his own Marxist position, ten saw the confrontation in national rather than class terms. Tactically, the SNP was in a very strong position. It could mobilise Scottish resentment against both the manoeuvrings of the multinationals and of the British state without committing itself to a positive policy, left or right. Oil had brought about what Muirhead had vainly hoped for in the 1930s: the equation of nationalism with anti-imperialism. But, when the Tories fell in 1974, it also left open to the SNP the option of being courted by businesses concerned about possible interference from the labour government, symbolised by the adherence of Sir Hugh Fraser in April 1974.

Inevitably, the oil discoveries reversed the gloomy prospects of the Scottish economy, and the Nationalists made the most of it. The choice 'rich Scots or poor British' appealed to some of the remaining industrialists and several of the fringe finance operators. But doubts remained. Would the huge balance of payments surplus that the oil would bring not prove a curse in disguise, pushing up the value of the Scots pound and strangling the exporting activity of Scottish industry? Had Scotland, anyway, an industrial infrastructure large enough to absorb the wealth? The Nationalist answer to this – a slower rate of extraction – might result in substantial redundancy among those involved in oil-based industry. After the initial impetus of 1974, in fact, the equation between independence and oil looked much less straightforward.

But the problem of industrial structure remained, and while it did the SNP's case remained plausible. The strategy of Oceanspan, with its prospect of the Clyde as a major European entrepôt for imported oil, was struck a fatal blow by the North Sea discoveries and by the slackening of European demand after 1973. The axis of Scottish economic development was no longer the Forth–Clyde isthmus, but along a south-west/north-east corridor.[22] Investment was also likely to be much more directed at oil-related developments. While encomiums of the Scottish economy like that in the Hudson Institute's notorious *The United Kingdom in 1980* (1974) looked flattering, on closer inspection economic revival seemed perilously restricted to oil and plentiful government investment. No party had any strategy about what could come after the oil, but at least the

SNP could promise that it could retain the revenue for industrial reconstruction. From late 1973 it could also make use of the political impetus towards devolution released by the publication of the Kilbrandon Report.

VII

The Royal Commission on the Constitution reported on 31 October 1973, about two years late. It had heard a great deal of evidence from individuals and institutions in Scotland which proved, if nothing else, that opinions on devolution bore little resemblance to the traditional polarities of British politics. The Communists, the Scottish Trades Union Congress, the Liberals, the Tories and the Kirk were in favour of an Edinburgh assembly, endowed with a greater or lesser degree of authority. The Labour Party and the Confederation of British Industry were against.[23] Practically every group also managed to produce its quota of eloquent dissenters. Only the SNP was straightforward about what it wanted, but its support was apparently on the slide. The Commission's reports came to 850 pages and the whole exercise had cost just under £500,000. Had this been paid to further devolution or to frustrate it?

Kilbrandon's conclusions were neither distinct nor unanimous. Although all its members were in favour of devolution of some sort, there seemed to be almost as many opinions as there were members, and several of the heavyweights originally appointed had dropped out, most notably Lord Crowther, who had died at the end of 1972, and two of the appointees representative of the 'grey' – and English – centre of the Labour Party, Douglas Houghton MP and David Basnett of the General and Municipal Workers Union. The nomination of the Scottish judge Lord Kilbrandon as Crowther's successor, and the stamina of the 'Celtic fringe Liberal' group on the Commission, meant that the bulk of the reduced Commission moved to the

Liberal 'home rule all round' position of backing legislative devolution to the 'historic nationalities'. There was some individual dissent from this position, and a coherent revolt by two English academics, Dr Norman Hunt of Exeter College, Oxford and Professor Alan Peacock, of the University of York, who backed a uniform system of regional executive councils throughout Britain. Hunt and Peacock were far apart in their politics – Hunt later joined the 1974 Labour government and Peacock, a Liberal, was a member of the free-market Institute of Economic Affairs – but their dissenting report was a coherent attempt to equate devolution with regionalisation. This came too late to influence local government reform; the majority report seemed a cosy exercise in Liberal revivalism; presumably both had been allowed to go through by default. No unanimity was required because no action would be taken.

This was evident in the reaction to the report. The Liberals and the Nationalists, Scottish and Welsh, were naturally in favour; the Conservative government was politely evasive, the party in Scotland sceptical (it had thrown out its Assembly commitment at its conference in May). The Scottish Council of the Labour Party was from the start bitterly hostile, finding the report 'at first glance totally unacceptable'.[24]

If not stillborn, Kilbrandon looked likely to become a victim of infanticide. But its time of peril was short. A week later there was a by-election in the safe Labour seat of Glasgow Govan, and the Scottish National Party candidate Margo MacDonald swept home. Nationalism, this time fuelled by oil, had again come to the fore. The miners' work-to-rule and the fuel crisis deflected English attention and the Liberals were having another revival (they captured Berwick on the day Govan fell) so that the SNP's breakthrough in the February general election was unexpected. Although it lost Govan, it captured Dundee West and Stirling East from Labour, and Argyllshire, Aberdeenshire East, Moray and Nairn and Banff from the Tories, polling 21 per cent of the Scots electorate, bearing out Wolfe's shrewd pre-poll estimate. The result was no freak: in five of the six seats the SNP had already gained second place, and had simply moved in, aided unquestionably by its oil campaign, which was particularly relevant to north-east Scotland. But it concentrated wonderfully the minds of the other parties, and the new Labour government.

Despite the warning of Govan, the Labour Party's manifesto in February went no further than restating its evidence to Kilbrandon – that it would explore the possibility of holding meetings of the Scottish Grand Committee in Edinburgh. But after February, with seven Nationalists in Parliament a more positive commitment was unavoidable. A group of four Labour MPs, John Robertson (Paisley), Alex Eadie (Midlothian), Jim Sillars (South Ayrshire) and Harry Ewing (Stirling), two of whom – Sillars and Eadie – had previously been committed anti-devolutionists, memorialised the party on 6 March, demanding an assembly on Kilbrandon lines. They took a resolution to the Conference of the Scottish Council of the Party at the end of March, where it was remitted. Willie Ross, back as Secretary of State, reserved his position. It was then that the going got interesting. On 8 May elections were held for the new regional and district council seats. Of 432 seats in the regions Labour won 171, the Nationalists only 18. On 18 May, addressing an apprehensive Scottish Conservative and Unionist Party Conference, Edward Heath promised a Scottish Assembly – indirectly elected from members of Scottish local authorities – and a Scottish Development Fund. Doubtless he calculated that in this way a coalition of Conservatives and Independents could stand a chance against Labour. These changes seem to have strengthened the anti-devolutionists within the executive of the Scottish Council of the Labour Party. However, on 3 June the government published a Green Paper on devolution, theoretically offering several options though in practice hinting at a Hunt-Peacock type of settlement – executive but not legislative devolution.

On 28 June, with only a third of its members present the Scottish executive of the Labour Party rejected all the schemes with the verdict: 'Constitutional tinkering does not make a meaningful contribution towards achieving socialist objectives.'[25]

This example of national insubordination was not allowed for long. On 25 July the Labour Party National Executive, meeting at Transport House, brusquely and unanimously commanded the Scots to toe the party line and back the assembly plan, by reconvening their annual conference on 11 August. At this conference the big unions, which had remitted the pro-assembly resolution in March, swung round in favour, and after only two hours of debate, an elected legislative assembly became the policy of the Scottish Council of the Party, only three weeks before the second general election campaign of the year began.

At the election of 10 October the Nationalist vote rose by 10 per cent to 30 per cent but Labour held on to its seats. The SNP gained Galloway, Dunbartonshire East, South Angus and Perthshire East from the Tories, reducing them to 16 seats and a total poll of only 24·9 per cent. The margin between the total votes of SNP and Labour was narrow – only 6·4 per cent – and in 35 seats the contest was now between the two. The state of parties in the new House, moreover, continued to put the Nationalist MPs in a strong position. However little it liked it, the devolution issue was going to preoccupy the Labour Party in Scotland throughout 1975.

The right wing of the Labour government – Anthony Crosland, Roy Jenkins, Shirley Williams, Reg Prentice – was silent on the issue and was thought to be hostile. No opinions were ever expressed which suggested otherwise. Social democracy, to which pluralism was supposed to be second nature, sought refuge in a sort of cataleptic trance. The orthodox left did not lack its 'democratic' alternatives to nationalism. It made much of the need to devolve authority vertically – to the workplace –

as well as horizontally. But in 1975 this mirage dissolved as well. The 'work-in' at Upper Clyde Shipbuilders in 1971 suggested a new and revolutionary *démarche*, and attracted the support of Labour notabilities, although it was an effective exercise in propaganda rather than a success for workers' control. Its much-advertised sequel, the takeover by a workers' cooperative of the Beaverbrook printing plant in Glasgow after the move south to Manchester of the *Scottish Daily Express* in February 1974, ended in a dispiriting fiasco. The *Scottish Daily News*, launched in May 1975 with government backing and the goodwill of the Nationalists (Wolfe was an auditor to the co-operative) as a 'left-of-centre' daily, succumbed to editorial lack of imagination and the forceful intervention of the 'socialist millionaire' Robert Maxwell, whom the trade secretary Tony Benn had allowed to take a minority shareholding. The damage to the Scottish press was as nothing compared to the damage to left-wing ideals of 'socialist democracy'. At the very least the lesson was rammed home that democracy at the workplace was no substitute for the devolution of government.

Both the Nationalists and the Labour left had backed the *Scottish Daily News*, but it was the latter which was hit most by its failure. The same thing happened with the left's pet project, the referendum on entry into the European Community. The Nationalists managed to achieve almost total unanimity on their opposition to entry: 'NO – ON ANYONE ELSE'S TERMS', as their posters put it, although many of their leaders were known to be privately pro-EEC. Labour conducted its disputes in public, with full comradely venom, and a fairly sharp division between the views of MPs and their constituency parties. The Scottish vote in favour of entry was 60 per cent, about 6 per cent less than in England on a low poll of about 62 per cent. It could plausibly be claimed that only a minority of the electorate voted in favour of entry, but so sweeping had been the claims of the SNP and Labour to command a majority against entry that the result was received with silence. The Nationalists, who could at least claim the success of an overwhelming 'anti' vote in the Western Isles, rapidly and unobtrusively reversed their policy, and Mrs Ewing went to Strasbourg as their representative at the European parliament. Labour was left to self-recrimination. For a time the right in the Cabinet may have seen the vote as an excuse for ditching the devolution commitment, but the Nationalists held their position in the polls and at a Lothian regional council by-election in August they reduced Labour to third place with 18 per cent in a seat which had hitherto been solidly socialist.

The Labour government had promised a White Paper on devolution early in 1975, but the period of party conferences passed and nothing was forthcoming. There certainly seemed to be little unanimity about it in the Labour Party. Tam Dalyell, having endorsed devolution in November – 'There is really no backsliding of feeling on the Assembly'[26] – and forecast the Assembly meeting by Autumn 1976, opposed it in April, and the Scottish Council of the Labour Party pressed in June to have its powers reduced to the minimum. Two of the Assembly's protagonists – Alex Eadie and Harry Ewing – were now in the government, leaving Jim Sillars and John Robertson rather isolated, and even more vociferously devolutionist. Yet there were good grounds for the doubts expressed by many of the Scottish Labour MPs, after 1974 more impressive and ambitious than they had been for a long time. They feared a reduced representation at Westminster, and its consequences. The more powers that were devolved, they sensed, the less chance there was of gaining office in the departments in which they were interested, as the convention was already that promotion would not be given to a Scottish MP in departments like Education or Environment, which had no authority in Scotland. The Labour members at Westminster had no wish to end up like the Ulster Unionists.

The White Paper *Our Changing Democracy* appeared on 27

November, offering a legislative Assembly to Scotland and an executive Assembly to Wales. It was a very strange document, evidently more the product of an inter-departmental power struggle in Whitehall rather than of any desire to settle the political issue permanently. Edward Short, the minister responsible, seemed to take away with one hand what he gave with the other. The Assembly would have 142 members. It would be housed in the Grecian Hall of the old Royal High School, a late flowering of classical Edinburgh perched above the city on Calton Hill. But its powers were limited and drastically qualified. They would cover local government, health, education (except universities), social work, transport (except railways), economic development agencies (except the Scottish Development Agency), natural resources (except most of agriculture), private and criminal law (except the courts) and tourism (except tourist promotion abroad). Further, it seemed that the authority of the Secretary of State was being increased to counterbalance such concessions. Representing the Westminster government, his control over economic policy was strengthened. He continued to supervise electricity, police, agriculture and fisheries and judicial appointments. Moreover, he carried out much of the organisation of the Assembly, appointed its executive, and adjudicated on the legality of its enactments. As one commentator wrote, William Ross would have 'the powers over the Kingdom of Scotland of the Secretary of State for India and the Viceroy combined'.

The Assembly lacked the 'real measure of economic power' the Labour party had promised in August. It lacked even the power to raise any revenue other than that allocated by Westminster in a block grant, although the White Paper rather unenthusiastically suggested the possibility of a rates surcharge. Reaction to it was far from enthusiastic, not only on the part of the Nationalists but from within the Labour Party. In mid-December, Jim Sillars gave notice of his intention to found a 'parallel' party – the Scottish Labour Party. Although hostility to Sillars was immense – saturated with that venom which socialists tend to reserve for ideological disagreements with their colleagues – his challenge stimulated the Labour Party to abandon its restrictive attitudes. By its conference at the end of March 1976 all but two of its MPs were united behind demands for a much greater range of powers, embracing the economy, the universities and the Scottish Development Agency. A month later Willie Ross, having led his party to devolution, followed his master, Harold Wilson, into the shadows.

This conversion did Labour little electoral good. The SNP continued throughout 1976 to win sweeping victories in local elections, even when Labour tried to convert them into plebiscites on separation. The new Scottish Labour Party set up by Sillars gained only one other MP, John Robertson, an unexciting middle-of-the-roader from Paisley. It signed up about 2,000 members in some forty branches, probably about a tenth of the paid-up Labour membership in Scotland, and attracted a lot of support from dissident Labour office bearers, journalists and the New Left – Tom Nairn and Neal Acherson were early members, and from the Nationalist Party came dissident left-wingers like Hamish Henderson and Bob Tait. Alex Neil, Labour's Scottish research officer, became its first general secretary. But although polls showed it might take as much as 28 per cent of the Labour vote, it seemed like an army of officers looking for a rank-and-file. Attempts by militant left-wingers from the International Marxist Group to infiltrate brought about clashes at its first conference in October 1976, and a rather brutal purge of the Left. Like its nineteeth-century predecessor, it seemed destined to end as 'a sorry spectacle of self-indulgent sectarianism'.

By the time the Devolution Bill was tabled on 13 December, the Conservatives were in comparable disarray. It had been evident for some time that Mrs Thatcher had little time for the measure, and that her rival, Mr Heath, was prepared to accord it high priority. It was not at all clear how much this commitment owed to Mr Heath's enthusiasm for devolution (which had been far from evident between 1970 and 1974) and how much to his desire to recapture, or even break up, the Tory party. Mrs Thatcher's declaration that Tory MPs would be put under a three-line whip to defeat the Bill was followed by Mr Heath's avowal of apostasy and the resignation of the Tory spokesmen on Scottish affairs, Alick Buchanan-Smith and Malcolm Rifkind, to be replaced by the apostle of redneck Unionism, Teddy Taylor. The threat that Labour dissidents had posed to the Bill seemed mitigated by the growing reality of fissures on the right.

On 17 December the bill passed its second reading by a majority of 45. Out of the 71 Scottish MPs, 55 voted for it and only 7 against, 6 of them Tories. However, in order to win over the dissidents in his own ranks, the Leader of the House, Michael Foot, conceded their demand for referendums in Scotland and Wales after the bill had become law, probably in November 1977. It was difficult to see what logic, other than that of securing party unity, lay behind this decision. Some Welsh MPs were against any measure of Welsh devolution, and believed that their line would be confirmed by a popular vote, but the case was quite different in Scotland, where a write-in poll held by the *Daily Record* a month earlier had shown 45 per cent of respondents supporting independence.

'History repeats itself', wrote Marx, 'first as tragedy, then as farce'. Despite the warnings of Michael Foot about the fateful consequences of the rejection of Irish home rule in 1886, little of the dignity that had attended the earlier crisis was in evidence when, in January and February 1977, the Devolution Bill was destroyed. There was no clash of principles; the bill was killed in Committee, the victim of mediocre leadership by government, Conservative frondeurs, and sectional pressure groups. Foot himself, after a successful tenure of the Ministry of Labour, proved a spent force as Leader of the House; the new Scottish Secretary, Bruce Millan, was competent but totally unmemorable; his team was second-rate. The Scottish Labour MPs who favoured devolution did little to save it.

The initiative passed to the English and Welsh opponents of the bill. Foot and the whips proved incapable of controlling the sectional groupings which emerged, especially in North East England. Tam Dalyell, Scots Labour's most determined unionist, seemed determined to immolate himself, as well as the Bill, on a pyre of amendments. Nor was the Government any more successful in gaining the support of Conservative dissidents or Liberals. Mrs Thatcher had, anyway, trumped Mr Heath. Conservative opposition was provided, not by a concerted front-bench assault, but by gadfly factions sanctioned by the leadership. Liberal support for devolution depended on the bill moving in the direction of formal federalism and proportional representation – which would benefit them nationally. When such concessions were not forthcoming, they became hostile.

In all, 350 amendments had been tabled when the Bill went into Committee on January 13, and a month later virtually no progress had been made on them. The Bill could not succeed save by the introduction of a timetable or 'guillotine'. Foot attempted to buy support for this by sanctioning the referendum but did not include a poll on the option of outright separatism (the only reason Scots Labour MPs had for wanting it). Then the referendum became consultative rather than decisive. To no avail. On Tuesday, 22 February, the guillotine motion was lost by 29 votes.

This was not, as might have been expected, a regional revolt or a rejection of the principle of devolution. Labour dissidents came from throughout the country and were strongest in London constituencies. On the whole, objections to the bill were very disparate and were, from the Liberals and some Tories, fairly directed at its inadequacies as a settlement. Could, they asked, devolution stop short of federalism? Michael Foot with a veneration for Parliamentary sovereignty which surpassed A. V.

Dicey's, was scarcely the man to answer this. Yet, as inter-party consultations began, in the aftermath of 'Black Tuesday' some form of federalism seemed increasingly to be the only alternative to separation. But this, of course, was not a problem that concerned the SNP.

VIII

The remarkable thing about the rise of the SNP, which was until 1973 completely unaided by external circumstances, has been the strength of its organisation. Not only has it proved almost impervious to the challenges of other parties but it seems to have exercised a mysterious deterrent effect on those of its opponents who are well fitted to 'play politics' with it. Although there are distinct left- and right-wing groups in the party, and although members of, say, the left, can be heard to prefer a left-wing Labour MP to a right-wing candidate of their own party, solidarity wins out in a way that no longer seems possible elsewhere. The SNP has not achieved its position by intellectual dominance: its parliamentarians are about par for the Scottish course, and certainly less impressive than some of the younger Labour MPs. The future of some of them may well be in the balance at the next election. Under the oil and the publicity, the party remains a coalition between the intransigent tradition of political nationalism and the consensus politics of Scottish Convention. Yet, as each year goes by, it retains a large proportion of members who have never been anything other than Nationalists: those who joined the party during the boom years of the late 1960s are now veterans of ten years. And there are more of them than there are members of any other Scottish party.

The other parties, one suspects, do not 'play politics' with the SNP because, one one side, their structures of authority and policy making are English-dominated – on the Labour side by the power of the trade unions and on the Conservative side by the numerical weakness of the Scottish Tory MPs, under a fifteenth of the parliamentary party. On the other side, there is a certain subconscious reluctance to 'go for' the SNP. Given the violent denunciations of the other parties, this sounds surprising, but in a way these are no more than ritual. Scottish politicians know that the rise of the SNP has given them a status and a bargaining power they would not otherwise have. While concerned about any threat to their own votes, the eclipse of the SNP would also be a threat to them.

At another level the character of the SNP candidates and policy makers is now very close to that of the other parties. All are now dominated by young professional people, mainly educated in Scotland. Political activity is now a matter of personal conviction and inclination, no longer of class and status and life-style. Within this group, there are few of the profound fissures which alienated party from party in the past; there may be reasoned dissent about the Assembly, but this will not prevent an overwhelming commitment to it. Whether this new political class is any better fitted to cope with the problems of the mass of the Scottish people than the old civil society, or the young Whigs who entered on their millennium a century and a half earlier, remains to be seen.

Chapter 8

Conclusions: Forward from Nationalism

Nations, races and individual men are unified by an image, or bundle of related images, symbolic or evocative of the state of mind, which is of all states of mind not impossible, the most difficult to that man, race or nation.

W. B. Yeats

I THE RISE AND FALL OF CENTRALISATION

In 1977 the main question in Anglo-Scottish politics is no longer what to do about the Scottish National Party or about North Sea oil, but how to prevent a total disintegration of the relationship between the two peoples. While this book was being written, layer after layer of the paintwork which overlay the Union settlement has been shaken off. What has become visible is not a mechanism for the systematic exploitation of the Scots by the English, as in nationalist mythology, but a complex range of institutions and assumptions which have in the past linked, not fused, the two nations. The corrosive factor has not been the rise of political nationalism or the discovery of oil. Both were only catalysts in the dissolution of a relationship which pivoted on the joint exploitation of industry and empire, a relationship which has been for most of the two hundred and seventy years of particular benefit to the prizewinners in the achieving society of the north.

This book has attempted to study the terms on which the Union survived, as an institution which was throughout its existence as much nationalist as assimilationist. For its first century the Scots élite considered it a type of federation, in which it took its own decisions. Then, with the changes in that élite, relative political autonomy was given up for proper representation, increased industry and imperial involvement. The balance was always difficult to maintain, but the discipline of the traditional institutions and a cosmetic nationalism made it possible to make the new industrial mass society conform. The crisis came, both for the Scottish élite and for its southern counterpart, when the masses acquired the possibility of independent political power.

This crisis occurred in 1885–6. Radicalism presented a revolutionary threat to both elites. Throughout Britain, it sought a total restructuring of society: the destruction of the power of the landed aristocracy and the established church and the devolution of power to prestigious regional authorities: 'home rule all round', in other words. This was what radical politics had all been about since the 1830s; democracy had become too big for Westminster and the political élite of the day. Sensing the threat to both, Gladstone's response was to hijack the Liberal Party by tying it to a policy of virtual separation for Ireland which he knew would split the radicals, frustrate the revolution and preserve him in power. Devolution, which as MacDiarmid later alleged would complete the Union, was postponed for nearly a century.

Gladstone's coup coincided with changes in the British political élite which ensured the continuation of its control. Oxford and Cambridge, now reformed, provided government with its administrative and policy-making cadres. The English 'traditional intelligentsia' – in Gramsci's phrase – pre-empted and then incorporated the 'organic intelligentsia' of capitalism, creating the embryo of the social democracy – welfarism and centralisation – which dominated the twentieth century. The Scots who did not join in were left on one side to mope in their kailyard.

Centralisation, under threat in 1914, was saved by one war and enhanced by a second. Labour politicians and centre-left theoreticians became in 1941 the new Whitehall establishment. Some deeper desire for structural change stirred before 1945, in the by-election successes of Common Wealth and the resurgence of Scottish nationalism, but this was channelled into the orthodox parties. As Anthony Howard has written: 'Far from introducing a social revolution the overwhelming Labour victory . . . brought about the greatest restoration of established values since 1660.'[1] It was the 'restoration politics' of social democracy, with its fairly simple view of human nature and decision taking, that was to collide with a growing Scots distinctiveness, engendered by the rapid decline of the Scottish economy after the First World War and reinforced by administrative devolution during the Second.

Although in the 1950s and 1960s the concentration of capital and the apparently homogeneous nature of British politics and publicity seemed to diminish Scottish national characteristics, the future of assimilation was tied to the success of efforts to regenerate the Scottish economy through an efficient combination of regional and national planning. This was the Sphinx's riddle of the social democrats, and their failure to answer it bore a fatal penalty, especially as it was the only question they turned out to be capable of answering. Successful regional planning would diminish Scots distinctiveness. Failure simply indicated that the élitism of the social democrats inhibited their understanding not only of Scottish politics but of the sort of politics necessary in a society which could no longer count on economic growth.

Mrs Q. D. Leavis, contrasting in 1941 the Bloomsbury group with Edwin Muir, forecast the nature of the conflict between the faltering élite and its new opponents. Bloomsbury was[2]

> a little world in which social life made the exercise of critical judgement bad taste; every member accruing to the group became entitled to eminence as it were. To be born outside any such group and to have to make his way by hard work and native endowment has its own reward.

The heirs of Muir have yet to create a sustained intellectual and political revival in Scotland. Devolution could still lead back to the Kailyard. But the 'little world' of the social democrats no longer counts, and the Scots intelligentsia has moved into the vacuum it has left. One of the ablest of the present Scottish MPs, Robin Cook, whose conviction about the need for devolution is significant because reluctant, has written that:[3]

> There now is indeed a specifically Scottish dimension to domestic politics. This is more than just a matter of the vote gathered in by the SNP. The rediscovery of a national identity has permeated all walks of public life, and the Scottish media, trade union movement, and lobby groups display an assertiveness and confidence which they lacked three years ago.

Since the early 1960s, in response to a range of factors – declining industry, the failure of socialist organisation to create a coherent politics in a working-class nation – a critique of Scottish society has emerged, albeit belatedly. Rejecting the premises of the Nationalists – the myth of Scottish democracy, for example – this has attempted to comprehend a complex society which has contrived to remain distinct from England. There has not been anything like it for over 150 years.

Significantly, however, this revival had not directly led to endorsements of independence. Although the scepticism of the Scottish intelligentsia about traditional Westminster politics is total, there are, as the *Red Paper* proves, few plaudits for the SNP. The movement in favour of devolution has implied a much more fundamental questioning of the basis of modern British politics, and one which is far closer to the 'semi-independent' spirit of the Scottish Enlightenment. Beyond the constitutional implications of current legislative proposals lie fundamental questions whose relevance extends far beyond Scotland.

II THE CONSTITUTIONAL OPTIONS

Maintaining the *status quo*: there is no possibility of maintaining the *status quo*. Within the Union, Scotland has been, since the Second World War, steadily gaining administrative autonomy; at the same time, relations between administrators and Scottish power-groups pose almost insoluble problems for a Secretary of State who may represent only a majority in Westminster. Both administrative logic and Scottish opinion concur that some sort of representative supervisory body is now required. The collapse of the National Plan and its regional components in 1967–8 meant that the 'central planning' alternative was lost for ever. To suggest that power be devolved to the regions rather than to a Scottish authority will simply make matters worse for the Scottish administration which must co-ordinate their activities. But the difference between sincere upholders of this view, like Tam Dalyell, and anti-devolutionist English MPs remains considerable. All too frequently the latter represent superannuated regional oligarchies whose opposition to Scottish devolution stems from the fear that, if successful, it will lead to demands for elected authorities which will end their own power.

Independence: with oil flowing onshore, the SNP's claim for all the benefits of total sovereignty appears particularly plausible. But the Nationalists still have to gain a Scottish consensus, and then negotiate for independence with a British government whose economic situation and external problems are likely to make it aggressive. Finally, if successful, they must create a political framework which will overcome the socially fissile nature of the country. Where SNP members have committed themselves to a coherent view of society and the state – and this is a relatively recent development – they have shown contradictions and ambiguities which could prove awkward in the circumstances of independence.

For a start, there is no unanimity about the 'mandate for independence'. Is it a majority of Scottish seats, or a majority of the Scottish vote? The SNP programme asserts the former, but the constitutionalist Professor Neil MacCormick backs the latter 'as an article of democratic faith'. That this was dismissed out of hand as 'humbug' by a member of the SNP national executive does not, for a start, bode well for the continuance of the alliance between the MacCormickite home-rulers and their more fundamentalist brethren.

The SNP rejects the primacy of class in Scottish politics and regards left/right divisions as irrelevant. If it has done nothing else, I hope this book has disproved both contentions: Scotland's class system is all the more rigid for being sanctioned by the inertia of the working class and masked by the myth of Scottish democracy. The Nationalists have managed to mobilise an atavistic 'Scottishness' among the working class; but, after independence, they will be expected to provide the positive improvements which the Labour Party attempted, and failed, to achieve. Whether they can do this is another matter. The Nationalists have tended to draw support from more prosperous areas of the country like the New Towns and the north-east, regarding Strathclyde, Labour's principal redoubt and Scotland's prime social problem, with fear as much as with hope.

After independence, the traditional Nationalist areas will want their loyalty recognised, but the Strathclyde latecomers will need an extremely expensive programme of rehabilitation. This tension could tear the country apart.

During the late 1960s the Nationalists liked to call themselves 'social democrats'. But they were not nineteenth-century revolutionaries or Butskellite élitists. They liked the name because it carried, in Stephen Maxwell's words, 'a public relations gloss of moderation and even of conservatism which is convenient to a Party which is proposing a major constitutional upheaval'.[4] It sounded vaguely Scandinavian, at a time when the SNP made much of Scandinavian precedents. More recently, however, it has laid particular stress on its 'radicalism', meaning by this the dispersal of power to local authorities and co-operatively-owned industries. With the tide running in its favour, the tension between the two claims has been muted within the party, and unnoticed outside it, but, when action has to be taken, it must provoke conflicts. When does the decentralist millennium come about? Is the Scottish government to impose its own control, before it decentralises? Otherwise, what happens to the Scottish element of British nationalised industries, which include the shipyards, steelworks, coal-mines, British Petroleum, Ferrantis, Rolls Royce and British Leyland? What happens if a group or corporation, allowed virtual autonomy, decides to ally with a powerful external interest – like a multinational company or even the English government – after a clash with the Scottish government or one of its prefectorial Area Development Officers? How are multinational oil companies, with £9,100 million invested by 1980, to be persuaded to go slow on oil extraction?

In its 'opportunist' challenge the SNP has backed any and every cause of discontent. It has always been early on the scene when factories are closed and wage claims denied. Such is the prerogative of every opposition party. But in the economic changes that will follow independence the party's performance is bound to betray its promises. It announces that 'a self-governing Scotland will not need to over-emphasise production for export';[5] this may simply be a euphemistic way of saying that exports of everything except oil are going to be priced out of world markets by the appreciation of the Scots currency. The SNP visualises an economy producing high-technology and luxury goods, largely catering for the home market, 'a future economic structure . . . more like Switzerland's than Detroit's . . . very little dependent on large-scale assembly industry',[6] yet the fate of the British television tube industry scarcely augurs well for this, and one can doubt whether the post-industrial world will have much need of Switzerlands. Using the oil wealth to tidy away Scotland's Detroit may be all very well, but what if the price of oil were to fall? The notion of a cosy little autarchy kept on the go by international trade in a single commodity promises even less resilience than at present.

Despite its claims, the policy-making dynamic within the SNP is corporate rather than radical, directed by middle-class activists in the interests of their professions. Doctors prescribe for medicine, teachers for education, economic consultants for industry. They represent an enfeebled projection of the old civil society, purged of the wide social and governmental claims of its institutions. There is no 'radical' questioning of the role of doctors or teachers. So far political success has inhibited any exposure of these contradictions, but for how long can this last? The Parliamentary Party leader, Donald Stewart, can commend the views of the party's token environmentalist, Dr Malcolm Slesser, to the Annual Conference, and get applause for the proposition that:[7]

> A new economic order is on the way when the countries with a reasonable balance between population, land and resources [i.e. like Scotland] will have the capacity to flourish, and states with a preponderance of manufacturing, a lack of land and high population density are simply in trouble.

Yet Slesser's bitter attack on the party's industrial policy as wasteful of resources and tending to create a 'mini-England' is overwhelmingly defeated.[8] The party can still command the loyalty of pacifists while its defence policy group, under the defence economist Dr Gavin Kennedy, can suggest a defence budget of £450 million a year, roughly six times that of Eire.[9]

Since 1970 sections of the Scottish middle class, following the line of least resistance, have backed independence where they would, twenty years earlier, have been Unionists or Scottish Convention home-rulers. But the motives which cause mass support for the SNP – the attempts of a disoriented working class to establish its own identity – are far different. This parallels the divergence George Orwell noticed in 1947 between an 'English or anglicised upper class' and

> a Scottish working class which speaks with a markedly different accent, or even, part of the time, in a different language . . . a more dangerous kind of class division than any now existing in England.[10]

After independence, the more opportunistic politicians would not fail to exploit this atavism as a means of polarising politics along lines which do not threaten the distribution of wealth. And by then the rocky road to freedom may have set the stage for the sort of ideological paralysis which gripped Eire for forty years.

Devolution: this means home rule and the granting of a parliament. Whatever it is called during the process of legislation, the Scots will unquestionably call the Assembly in the old Royal High School their parliament and the leader of its majority party their prime minister. Will it be a stepping-stone on the road to independence or a terminus? At the present time it is impossible to say. So much depends on the way the concession is made, and on the atmosphere in which the legislature gets down to work.

In the short run devolution is the most difficult option. Most federations were set up as means of securing unity, and the powers of the constituent states have been progressively subordinated to central authority. The proposals for Britain run against this trend. They are open to all the objections advanced against home rule or federalism by Dicey and Anson at the end of the last century – and that was an age of very limited governmental activity. They come, furthermore, at a time when the Scots seem to stand to gain little from continued involvement in the United Kingdom. The arguments made by opponents of devolution like Tam Dalyell and Ian Sproat, that Scotland will suffer grotesquely from over-government, cannot be dismissed lightly.

Scotland will have 150 representatives in Edinburgh, 71 in Westminster and 9 in Strasbourg, as well as 432 regional, and 1034 district councillors. With full-time parliamentarians, and councillors giving anything up to half their time to local government, the diversion of effort from industry and the social services could scarcely be recompensed by even the most enlightened government. A country in which one in every 3,000 is an under-employed legislator would not be a particularly stable place, and matters might be even worse if these are people of real talent and ambition. One thing can certainly be guaranteed: devolution will not bring tranquillity to the Scottish political scene. Indeed, the first years of the Assembly will be occupied largely by conflicts with its competitors, the Secretary of State on one hand and the regions on the other. The Assembly has to win to survive, so either or both its competitors will have to go. Westminster's present concession, if granted, will certainly not be its last. Even after this upheaval, however, it is still difficult to be optimistic about the stability of devolution if the current social structure survives.

Ultimately, this shows the inadequacy of regarding the

problem purely in a Scottish light. For if the demand for devolution has been a response to the collapse of the social democrat/centralist consensus, then the vacuum resulting will be felt elsewhere and the reconstruction of British politics implied will have to be correspondingly drastic. The value of the Scottish experiment will be the extent to which it changes not only Scottish politics, but the whole structure of politics in Britain.

Devolution will not succeed if the Assembly assumes that by invoking the Scottish democratic tradition sweet reason will descend on the Royal High School Hall. Faith alone will produce few results. Nor will more cash – from whatever source – buy off the problems which face the existing administrative and entrepreneurial system. Resources were not lacking in 1960s Scotland; they were misapplied by incompetent or irresponsible authorities. What is needed is not the decentralisation of government within Scotland but a radical improvement in the quality of government. The Scottish Assembly must sustain firm, fair, well-informed and open government, and its members must be hard-working, enlightened and incorruptible. Given this, the difficulty of its task may produce, as in the eighteenth century, a mature politics of 'semi-independence'. The Scottish intellectual tradition – with its emphasis on ideology, its transmission and application to government – is important here. Scottish democracy may be a myth, but the elitist oligarchy which has dominated politics in the south is still absent. Ideas and criticism still have an independent value. The problem will be to integrate them into the governmental process.

This is best done at the centre. Although all parties are enamoured of directly elected single-chamber legislatures, there is much to be said for a senate which scrutinises and initiates legislation, but does not impede it. Most second chambers have been thought up as checks on radicalism; but they can have a valuable role as an 'alternative civil service' for the elected members, a standing royal commission to draft and report on the working of legislation, to examine controversial planning and development proposals, to scrutinise government departments, authorities, and state and private industry. They can also give a voice to minorities and cultural groups which elected members cannot always represent. Too often advice had been 'bought' from experts – who often have material interests in the subjects on which they are advising – when the expert ought instead to be incorporated in the legislative process. Choosing the members of a senate will inevitably be contentious. A formula which, say, allows the political parties to nominate a third (numbers being in proportion to the party's percentage vote); universities, churches, trade unions, etc. to nominate a third; and local authorities the remainder, might be found equitable and workable. Such a body could both perpetuate and control the tradition of detached, imaginative administration and innovation which the Scots exported in the years of empire.

III ALTERNATIVE FUTURES

Possibly the most promising option for Scottish politics is that revenues from oil go to Britain, but that the Scottish legislature be allocated power and cash adequate for a total recasting of Scottish society. In 1953 the socialist writer Naomi Mitchison wrote to Roland Muirhead:[11]

> It seems to me that you are bound to assume that a self-governing Scotland is going to be immediately morally better, and I don't see it *unless there has also been a revolution.* I can't see how the people who are likely to govern Scotland under any democratic system are going to be any different from the undoubted Scots who are in positions of local power.

The point remains valid today. No guarantees should be given about the retention by any social class of any past privileges.

The mandate of the legislature must be the creation of a society capable of coping democratically with the austerities of the post-imperial, post-industrial age. This is a strategy relevant to the whole of Britain, but it is one which the Scots – given their unique experience – are capable of initiating. On the success of their experiment the future of British society will depend.

The factors which have propelled Scotland towards devolution are not the same as those which will make a devolution settlement work. The desire of the post-imperial intelligentsia for posts and political authority – as big fish in a small pool – has hitherto been important, but it is not something that the new state can tolerate for long. A revolution in political authority, creating a new politics of participation in place of the unquestioned political, religious or corporate loyalties of the past, should not benefit the traditional hierarchies. The situation of lawyers or teachers or administrators will not be better under the new dispensation; but it will be a challenge. Responsible no longer to their own corporations, but to the needs of the community, they will have to earn their status. They may have to change their priorities radically to do so.

Likewise with the working class. The patronage state has provided an eccentric mixture of kicks and handouts, which has brought neither tranquillity nor articulate protest. There is no more radicalism among Scottish workers than there is real conviviality – in the sense of living together and for one another – in the booze-culture which has moved in to sop up the fitful affluence of recent years. Things are more likely to get worse than better, whatever the outcome of constitutional change. The current crises in employment, public services and social medicine are likely before long to be compounded by large-scale deterioration in the multi-storey public housing which was run up by Glasgow and other local authorities in the 1960s. The road to a real working-class democracy is going to be painful, especially for a leadership whose rhetoric of class-consciousness has traditionally been accompanied by executive ineptitude and deferential acceptance of the goals of social democracy. In Father Anthony Ross's words, the hegemony of Labour created

> an illusion of socialism, depending on American capital on the one hand and exploitation of the Third World on the other . . . If we're going to create any radically socialist society we've got to reduce our standard of living in a way I see very few people prepared to do.[12]

In such a situation, devolution and the institutions it produces must create goals, of responsibility and self-discipline, and organisations, especially for working-class education, which will make our common culture richer and our sense of interdependence greater.

In this transition oil should be used by a Scottish government as the quid pro quo for autonomy: a bequest which will enable the rest of Britain – whose problems will be much more complex than those of Scotland – to make the same evolution. If the move forward from social democracy is achieved, the future relations of the two countries – as constituents of a federation or as friendly neighbours – can amicably be settled. But, whatever happens, the old politics of welfarism, centralisation and corporatism – of the amelioration of inequality and alienation through economic growth – will be at an end. Deeply committed to them though all the political parties are, there is no way – oil or not – that they can survive.

Paradoxically, the main appeal of the Scottish National Party is that independence and oil will enable it to defer this uncomfortable process; that the political goals of the 1960s and the certainties of social democracy can still be obtained north of the border when they are impossible in the south. The most serious charge that can be levelled at the SNP is the naivety of its combination of *machtpolitik* and conservatism, and its failure to realise where its strategy could land it. The rhetoric of its speakers at its National Conference is now totally unlike that of any other national movement: the stress is not on struggle but on the inevitability of a rapid triumph, something which the adoption of positive policies for the aftermath of independence, rather than the old declaratory nationalism, has tended to increase. Mrs Margo MacDonald is typical of the more moderate group:[13]

> The Scots want an Assembly with the ability to create long-term employment, to negotiate international fishing limits, to use Oil Revenues to improve our standard of living and to generate the dynamic to regenerate our social, cultural and political life. These expectations cannot be met by Devolution – they will be met by Independence alone.

But it is speeches which concentrate on the *when* rather than the *if* that get the loudest cheers.

The SNP denies the division of society on class lines, but posits another – and potentially much more frightening – confrontation by asking Scots to choose between being 'rich Scots or poor British'. It has singularly failed to explore the consequences of this, which could fairly easily amount to 'rich Czechs or poor Germans'. The SNP's implicit hope that English MPs will, by throwing out devolution, give it a Scottish majority, and then tactfully cease being unreasonable, betrays considerable immaturity. The rules of the game have never been as gentlemanly as that, and an England faced with political collapse through the removal of the expected oil revenues can scarcely be expected to concede independence gracefully, especially as a substantial minority in Scotland, with relatives and property in England and fears about the possible outcome, will always be there to play the part of the Sudeten Germans. SNP commentators have argued that such a constitutional crisis would precipitate a run on sterling; it seems more likely that creditors will insist on seeing a British government uphold its title to the oil on whose security it has borrowed so heavily. There are plenty of precedents – not all of them remote – for the sort of 'police' action that might be canvassed and, in a world where authoritarianism is likely to become more rather than less prevalent, no guarantee that it will not be taken.

The intellectual proponents of British democracy in the nineteenth century, like Leslie Stephen and James Bryce, believed that it was in the interest of a political elite to offer its popular opponents extensive concessions in order to preserve the fabric of the state and their hegemony over it. An illustration of this was the granting of the wider franchise in 1867, despite the protests of widely read defenders of elitism like Robert Lowe and Walter Bagehot. In a violent confrontation the elite, having access to organised force, would doubtless have won, but it saw that the destructiveness of the clash would nullify its gains. It is this sort of situation that now confronts the British political elite.

The questions that must now be asked are these: Has the elite any longer the power to secure a settlement? It not, can it realise this and make the alliances necessary to gain one? In Scotland the will to make devolution work still exists. A collaborative effort to establish a new politics in Britain is still possible. There is no guarantee that the British elite will survive the subsequent process of devolving power to the English regions, but the transition to a democratic and decentralised Britain will be a fitting final accomplishment. The alternative could be a descent into the reassertion of activistic loyalties, and possibly into violence, in which all the gains of a unique partnership could be lost.

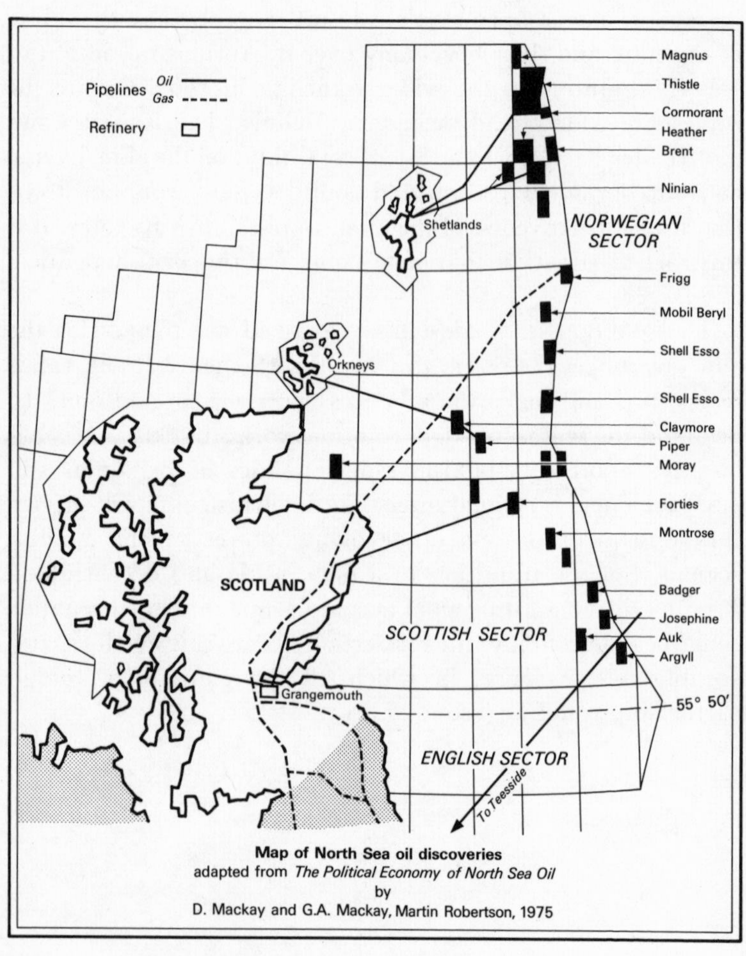

Map of North Sea oil discoveries
adapted from *The Political Economy of North Sea Oil*
by
D. Mackay and G.A. Mackay, Martin Robertson, 1975

APPENDICES

Further Reading

Notes

Index

Further Reading

Where, in the course of this book, quotations, interpretations and detailed statistical evidence have been used or alluded to, references can be found in the note which follow. These should also provide a reasonably comprehensive guide to available literature for those who want to follow up, or take issue with, the points *Scotland and Nationalism* has raised. However, the core of the book has relied on the factual information provided by several authorities. They are given here as a select list of works for further reading.

POLITICAL HISTORY

Gordon Donaldson, *Scotland: James V to James VII*, Oliver and Boyd, 1965.

William Ferguson, *Scotland: 1689 to the Present*, Oliver and Boyd, 1968.

H. J. Hanham, *Scottish Nationalism*, Faber, 1969.

James Kellas, *Modern Scotland*, Pall Mall, 1968.

James Kellas, *The Scottish Political System*, Cambridge, 1973.

ECONOMIC HISTORY

Alexander Cairncross, ed., *The Scottish Economy*, Cambridge, 1954.

R. H. Campbell, *Scotland since 1707*, Blackwell, 1965.

T. L. Johnston, N. K. Buxton and D. Mair, *Structure and Growth of the Scottish Economy*, Collins, 1971.

S. G. Lythe and John Butt, *An Economic History of Scotland*, Blackie 1975.

Scottish Council, *Inquiry into the Scottish Economy, 1960–1* (The Toothill Report), Scottish Council, 1961.

T. C. Smout, *A History of the Scottish People*, Collins, 1969.

CULTURAL HISTORY

David Craig, *Scottish Literature and the Scottish People*, Chatto & Windus, 1961.

G. E. Davie, *The Democratic Intellect*, Edinburgh U.P., 1961.

A. L. Drummond and J. Bullough, *The Age of the Moderates*, St Andrew's Press, 1973; *The Church in Victorian Scotland*, St Andrew's Press, 1974.

Duncan Glen, *Hugh MacDiarmid and the Scottish Renaissance*, Chambers, 1964.

Henry Grey Graham, *Scottish Men of Letters in the Eighteenth Century*, Black, 1901.

Wallace Notestein, *The Scot in History*, Cape, 1946.

Notes

INTRODUCTION

1 Harold Nicolson, *Diaries and Letters, 1939–45*, Collins 1967, p. 449.

CHAPTER 1

1 Quoted in 'Andrew Fletcher, 1655–1716 in *Dictionary of National Biography* (by George F. R. Barker).
2 Reproduced and translated in A A. M. Duncan, *The Nation of Scots and the Declaration of Arbroath (1320)*, Historical Association, 1970, p. 36.
3 'Robert Burns, 1759–96' in *Encyclopaedia Britannica*, 11th ed. New York, 1910 (by John Nichol).
4 Elie Kedourie, *Nationalism*, Hutchinson 1960, Chapters 1–3.
5 Frederick Engels, 'The Magyar Struggle' in *Neue Rheinische Zeitung*, 13 January 1849, translated in D. Fernbach ed., Karl Marx: *The Revolutions of 1848*, Penguin 1973, pp. 221–2.
6 Hugh Trevor-Roper, 'Scotching the myths of devolution' in *The Times*, 28 April 1976.

[7] For a sustained effort to sustain a nationalist interpretation of Scottish history, D. H. MacNeill, *The Scottish Realm*, A. & S. Donaldson, n.d. (*c.* 1948) Chapters 15 and 16.

[8] Wallace Notestein, *The Scot in History*, Jonathan Cape, 1946, p. 150.

[9] The First Book of Discipline (1560) quoted in Notestein, op.cit., pp. 131–2.

[10] A. V. Dicey and R. S. Rait, *Thoughts on the Union between England and Scotland*, Macmillan, 1920, pp. 323–6.

[11] Nicholas Phillipson, 'Scottish Public Opinion and the Union in the Age of the Association' in N. T. Phillipson and R. Mitchison, eds, *Scotland in the Age of Improvement*, Edinburgh 1970, pp. 125 & 142.

[12] W. E. Gladstone to Sir John Cowan, 17 March 1894, quoted in John Morley, *Life of Gladstone*, 1903, Lloyd's Two-Volume Edition, 1908, vol. II, p. 582.

[13] See Kenneth O. Morgan, *Wales in British Politics*, University of Wales Press, 1963, p. 54.

[14] James Kellas, *Modern Scotland*, Pall Mall, 1968, pp. 192–5.

[15] Kellas, op.cit., p. 125.

[16] H. J. Hanham, 'The creation of the Scottish Office, 1881–7 in *The Juridical Review* vol. 10 (New Series), 1965, p. 209.

[17] W. E. Gladstone, *The Irish Question*: I *The History of an Idea*. II. *Lessons of the Election*, 1886, pp. 36–7.

[18] Conor Cruise O'Brien in *The Shaping of Modern Ireland*, Routledge, 1960, p. 2.

[19] H. A. L. Fisher, *James Bryce*, Macmillan, 1927, vol. I, p. 201.

[20] Kenneth O. Morgan, *Keir Hardie*: *Radical and Socialist*, Weidenfeld and Nicolson, 1975, p. 43.

[21] John Vincent, *Pollbooks*: *How Victorians Voted*, Cambridge, 1967, 49.

[22] H. J. Hanham, *Scottish Nationalism*, Faber, 1969, pp. 97–8.

[23] Percy M. Young, *A History of British Football*, Stanley Paul, 1969, pp. 122–3.

[24] H. J. Hanham, 'Mid-Century Scottish Nationalism: Romantic and Radical' in R. Robson, ed., *Ideas and Institutions of Victorian Britain*, Bell, 1967, pp. 143–79.

[25] Nicholas Phillipson, 'Nationalism and Ideology' in J. N. Wolfe,

ed., *Government and Nationalism in Scotland*, Edinburgh U.P., 1969, pp. 167–88.

26 Hanham, *Scottish Nationalism*, Chapter 4.

27 Tom Nairn, 'Old Nationalism and New Nationalism', in Gordon Brown, ed., *The Red Paper on Scotland*, Edinburgh University Student Publications Board, 1975, pp. 37–42.

28 F. S. Oliver, *Federalism and Home Rule*, 1910.

29 William Ferguson, *Scotland: 1689 to the Present*, Oliver and Boyd, 1968, pp. 351–2.

30 Hanham, *Scottish Nationalism*, pp. 110–17.

31 Archie Lamont, *How Scotland lost her Railways*, Scottish Secretariat, 1945, pp. 6–10.

32 C. M. Grieve, *Albyn, or Scotland and the Future*, Kegan Paul, 1927, p. 55.

33 Duncan Glen, *Hugh MacDiarmid and the Scottish Renaissance*, Chambers, 1964, Chapter 2.

34 Kenneth O. Morgan, *Wales in British Politics*, pp. 302–4.

35 Edwin Muir, *Scottish Journey*, Heinemann, Gollancz, 1935, p. 234.

36 Hanham, *Scottish Nationalism*, p. 159.

37 Membership figures established from financial returns, 1941 in Scottish Secretariat MSS, National Library of Scotland: Acc. 2712, file 203.

38 Kellas, *Modern Scotland*, p. 135.

39 Douglas Young MSS. National Library of Scotland, Dep. 6419, Young to Muirhead, 1 August 1940.

40 Herbert Morrison, *Autobiography*, Odhams, 1960, p. 199.

41 Thomas Johnston, *Memories*, Collins, 1952, p. 169.

42 Paul Addison, *The Road to 1945*, Cape, 1975, p. 278.

43 James Kellas, *The Scottish Political System*, Cambridge, p. 86.

CHAPTER 2,

1 Grieve, op.cit., p. 46.

2 H. J. Paton, *The Claim of Scotland*, Allen and Unwin, 1968, p. 196.

3 Harold J. Laski, *Studies in the Problems of Sovereignty*, Yale 1917, p. 208.

4 Ibid, p. 65.

[5] Deutsch, op.cit., Knopf, 1969, p. 113.

[6] Letter of Defoe to Robert Harley, Earl of Oxford, quoted in W. Ferguson, *Scotland: 1689 to the present*, Oliver and Boyd, 1968, p. 54.

[7] Speech of November 4, 1707, quoted in C. H. Dand, *The Mighty Affair: How Scotland lost her Parliament*, Oliver and Boyd, 1972, p. 147.

[8] Letter of Earl of Roxburghe to George Baillie of Jerviswoode, 28 November 1705, quoted in Ferguson, op. cit., p. 52.

[9] Gordon Donaldson, *Scotland: James V to James VII*, Oliver and Boyd, 1965, p. 347.

[10] Quoted in Christopher Hill, *Reformation to Industrial Revolution*, 1967, Pelican 1969, p. 166.

[11] Nicholas Phillipson, 'Nationalism and Ideology', in Wolfe, op. cit., pp. 167–9.

[12] Geoffrey Best, 'The Scottish Victorian City' in *Victorian Studies*, vol. XI, 1968, p. 337–44.

[13] Quoted in 'Sir James Dalrymple, first Viscount Stair, 1619–95' in the *D.N.B.* (by Aeneas Mackay).

[14] Adam Smith, *The Wealth of Nations*, 1775, Encyclopaedia Britannica Ed., 1952, p. 354.

[15] Michael Hechter, *Internal Colonialism: The Celtic Fringe in British National Development, 1536–1966*, Routledge 1975, p. 33.

[16] 'Thomas Moore 1779–1852' in *D.N.B.* (by Richard Garnett).

[17] Francois Crouzet, 'England and France in the Eighteenth Century: a Comparative Analysis of two Economic Growths', in *Annales*, vol 21, no. 2., 1966, trans., Sondheimer and published in R. M. Hartwell, ed., *The Causes of the Industrial Revolution*, Methuen 1968, p. 155.

[18] Geoffrey Best, *Mid-Victorian Britain*, 1851–75, Weidenfeld & Nicolson, 1971, p. 98.

[19] Adam Smith, *The Wealth of Nations*, p. 318.

[20] T. C. Smout, 'The Landowner and the Planned Village in Scotland, 1730–1830', in *Scotland in the Age of Improvement*, pp. 73–98.

[21] Quoted in 'Thomas Telford, 1759–1834', in the *D.N.B.* (by Francis Espinasse).

[22] Figures from Newman A. Wade, *Post-Primary Education in the Primary Schools of Scotland*, University of London Press, 1939, pp. 25–33.

23 Lyon Playfair, 'The Universities and Professional Education', in *Subjects of Social Welfare*, London, 1889.

24 Quoted in R. H. Campbell, *Scotland since 1707*, Blackwell, 1965, p.229.

25 William Cobbett, *Rural Rides . . . together with tours of Scotland and Letters from Ireland*, ed. G. D. H. & M. Cole, Dent, 1930, vol. III, p. 765.

26 T. C. Smout, *A History of the Scottish People*, 1969, Fontana ed. 1972, p. 475.

27 E P. Thompson, *The Making of the English Working Class*, Gollancz 1963, p. 13.

28 Quoted in 'Glasgow', *Ordnance Gazetteer of Scotland, 1896*, vol. III.

29 E. J. Hobsbawm, *Industry and Empire*, 1968, Penguin 1969, p. 308.

30 Quoted in W. Ferguson, 'The Reform Act (Scotland) of 1832'. Intention and Effect', in *The Scottish Historical Review*, vol. 45, 1966, p. 105.

31 Ferguson, art, cit., pp. 105, 114.

32 Cockburn – T. F. Kennedy of Dunure, 5 May 1832, in *Letters on The Affairs of Scotland*, Ridgway, 1874, p. 385.

33 Henry Cockburn, *Journal*, Edmonstone and Douglas, 1874, Vol. II, p. 181.

34 J. B. Mackie, *The Life and Work of Duncan McLaren*, Nelson, 1888, vol. I, p. 281.

35 Cockburn, Journal, pp. 294–5.

36 Andrew Dewar Gibb, *Scottish Empire*, Maclehose, 1937, p. 310.

37 Charles Dilke, *Greater Britain*, 1868, MacMillan 1885 ed., pp. 365–6.

38 Quoted in Annie Dunlop, *Scots Abroad in the Fifteenth Century*, Historical Association, 1942, p. 3.

39 Figures from R. Mitchison, *A History of Scotland*, Methuen, 1970, p. 183; W. Ferguson, *Scotland: 1689 to the Present*, p. 178.

40 Thomas Carlyle, *Chartism*, 1839, Fraser 1840, p. 112.

41 Gordon Donaldson, *The Scots Overseas*, Robert Hale, 1966, pp. 113, 142, 162, 178. These calculations are roughly borne out by 'D. P.' in '*The Scot Abroad*', in *The Scottish Geographical Magazine*, vol. I, 1885, pp. 372–5.

42 F. J. Turner, '*The Significance of the Frontier in American History*', 1893, Holt ed., 1962.

[43] Alexander Somerville, *The Autobiography of a Working Man*, 1848, MacGibbon, and Kee, 1967, p. 125.

[44] Marx, 'The Magyar Struggle', p. 222.

[45] H. J. Hanham, 'Religion and Nationality in the Mid-Victorian Army', in M. R. D. Foot, ed., *War and Society*, Elek 1973, pp. 160–72.

[46] Hugh Cunningham, *The Volunteer Force*, Croom Helm, 1976, p. 50.

[47] Percival Spear, *A History of India*, 1965, Penguin 1970, vol. II, Chapter 8.

[48] Philip Woodruff, *The Men Who Ruled India*, vol. I., *The Founders*, 1953, Cape 1963, pp. 204–5.

[49] George Elder Davie, *The Democratic Intellect*, Edinburgh University Press, 1961, pp. 42–5.

[50] Goldwin Smith, *Reminiscences*, Macmillan, 1911, Chapter 25.

[51] Quoted in Keith Sinclair, *A History of New Zealand*, Penguin, 1959, pp. 94–5.

[52] Quoted in Donaldson, *The Scots Overseas*, p. 159.

[53] Quoted in Donaldson, op. cit., p. 117.

[54] Scottish Secretariat MSS, National Library of Scotland: A Donaldson – R. E. Muirhead, 5 January 1931, (Acc. 3721, File 80).

[55] A. C. Ross, 'Scottish Missionary Concern, 1874–1914: A Golden Era?', in *Scottish Historical Review*, vol. 51, 1972, pp. 52–61.

[56] Quoted in A. Vidler, *The Church in an Age of Revolution*, Penguin, 1961, p. 248.

[57] M. A. Laird, 'Alexander Duff and Scottish Educational Influences in Bengal during Bentinck's Administration, 1828–35', in *Scottish Educational Studies*, vol. 2, No. 1, May 1970.

[58] 'Central Africa', in *Encyclopaedia Britannica* 11th ed.

[59] S. G. Lythe and John Butt, *An Economic History of Scotland*, Blackie, 1975, pp. 146–50.

[60] Quoted in F. Turrentine Jackson, *The Enterprising Scot*, Edinburgh University, 1968 p. 297.

[61] J. A. Hobson, *Imperialism: a Study*, Nisbet, 1902, pp. 91–9.

[62] J. M. Reid, *Glasgow*, Batsford, 1950, p. 120.

[63] 'Scotland', in *Encyclopaedia Britannica*, 11th ed., (*War Supplement*) vol. 32.

64 W. Ferguson, *Scotland: 1689 to the Present*, p. 353.
65 Figures from Gollan, *Scottish Prospect*, p. 5.
66 J. A. Bowie, *Scotland's Future*, Chambers, 1939, p. 23.
67 George Malcolm Thomson, *Caledonia on the Future of the Scots*, Routledge, 1926, p. 41.
68 Quoted in H. J. Hanham, 'The Development of the Scottish Office', in J. N. Wolfe, ed., *Scotland, Government and Nationalism*, p. 62.
69 I. McLean, 'Red Clydeside, 1915–19', in J. Stevenson and R. Quinault, eds., *Popular Protest and Public Order*, Allen and Unwin, 1974.
70 J. G. Kellas, *Modern Scotland*, p. 186.
71 Bowie, op. cit., p. 237.
72 A. Lothian, 'Glasgow', in *Picture Post*, 1 April 1939.
73 Johnston, *Memories*, p. 90.
74 J. A. Bowie, *Principles of Reconstruction*, Saltire Society/Oliver and Boyd, 1941, p. 31.

CHAPTER 3

1 A. J. P. Taylor, *The Hapsburg Monarchy, 1809–1918*, Penguin 1976, p. 33.
2 Karl Marx and Friedrich Engels, *The Communist Manifesto*, 1848, translated and reproduced in D. Fernbach, ed., *The Revolutions of 1848*, Penguin, 1973, p. 77.
3 Quoted in E. Abbott and L. Campbell, *Benjamin Jowett*, John Murray, 1897, vol. 1, p. 399.
4 See C. T. Harvie, *The Lights of Liberalism*, Allen Lane, 1976, p. 50.
5 Quoted in Phillipson, 'Nationalism and Ideology', p. 178.
6 Neil M. Gunn, *The Green Isle of the Great Deep*, Faber 1944, p. 181.
7 Hobsbawm op. cit., p. 294.
8 David Caute, *Communism and the French Intellectuals*, Deutsch 1964, p. 12.
9 Antonio Gramsci, 'The Intellectuals', in *Prison Notebooks*, Lawrence and Wishart, 1971, p. 18.
10 R. H. Tawney, *Religion and the Rise of Capitalism*, 1926, Penguin, 1961, p. 135.

[11] George MacKay Brown, 'The Broken Heraldry', in Karl Miller, ed., *Memoirs of a Modern Scotland*, Faber, 1970, p. 146.

[12] Quoted in Douglas Young, 'Introduction', in *Edinburgh in the Age of Reason*, Edinburgh University Press, 1967, p. 10.

[13] Quoted in David Craig, *Scottish Literature and the Scottish People*, Chatto & Windus, 1961, p. 43.

[14] See Duncan Forbes, 'Adam Ferguson and the Idea of Community', in *Edinburgh in the Age of Reason*, pp. 40–7.

[15] Quoted in Young, op. cit., p. 13.

[16] Charles Dickens, *Hard times*, Oxford, 1955, p. 8.

[17] J. G. Lockhart, *Life of Sir Walter Scott*, Blackwood, 1836–8, vol. II, p. 299.

[18] Quoted in W. L. Langer, *Political and Social Upheaval*, 1832–52, Harper and Row, 1969, p. 547.

[19] See John Gross, *The Rise and Fall of the Man of Letters*, 1969, Penguin, 1973, pp. 210–13.

[20] Thomas Carlyle, 'Signs of the Times', in *The Edinburgh Review*, vol. 49, June 1829, reproduced in C. T. Harvie, Graham Martin and Aaron Scharf, eds, *Industrialisation and Culture*, Macmillan, 1970, p. 22.

[21] Quoted in Elie Kedourie, *Nationalism*, p. 45.

[22] Frank Field, *The Last Days of Mankind: Karl Kraus and his Vienna*, Macmillan, 1967, p. 67.

[23] John Davidson, *The Testament of an Empire-Builder*, Grant Richards, 1902, pp. 81–2.

[24] H. G. Matthew, *The Liberal Imperialists*, Oxford 1973, p. 289.

[25] Noel Annan, 'The Curious Strength of Positivism in English Social Thought', Oxford University Press, 1959, p. 9.

[26] Rudyard Kipling, 'MacAndrew's Hymn', in *From Sea to Sea*, 1894. Hugh MacDiarmid, 'John Davidson', in *Scots Unbound*, 1932.

[27] For the Kailyard see George Blake, *Barrie and the Kailyard School*, Arthur Barker, 1951.

[28] Henry Cockburn, *Journal*, Vol. II., p. 296 (10 July 1853).

[29] Quoted in Hugh MacDiarmid, *The Company I've Kept*, Hutchinson, 1966, p. 81.

[30] Hugh MacDiarmid, *Selected Poems*, Penguin, 1970, p. 33.

[31] MacDiarmid, *Albyn*, pp. 44–5.

32 See Maurice Lindsay, *The Lowlands of Scotland*, Robert Hale, 1953, pp. 213–17.

33 Tom Nairn, 'Culture and Nationalism', in *Scottish International*, April 1973, pp. 7–8.

34 'A Drunk Man. . . .' in MacDiarmid, op. cit., p. 45.

35 Loc. cit.

36 Ibid., p. 61.

37 MacDiarmid, 'Growing up in Langholm', in Karl Miller, *Memoirs of a Modern Scotland*, p. 167.

38 See Lewis Grassic Gibbon, 'The Land', in Gibbon and MacDiarmid, *The Scottish Scene*, Jarrolds, 1934.

39 Muir, *Scottish Journey*, p. 232.

40 MacDiarmid, *Selected Poems*, p. 29.

41 'Third Hymn to Lenin', 1957, in op. cit., p. 110.

42 *Scots Independent*, January 1944, p. 8.

CHAPTER 5

1 Edwin Muir, *Scottish Journey*, p. 1.

2 Kellas, *The Scottish Political System*, p. 75.

3 Sir Winston Churchill, *Speeches*, vol. VIII, Chelsea House, 1974, p. 7937 (delivered at Edinburgh, 14 February 1950).

4 H. J. Hanham, 'The Development of the Scottish Office', in Wolfe, ed., *Scotland, Government and Nationalism*, pp. 68–9.

5 See J. M. Reid, *James Lithgow*, Hutchinson, 1964, and W. J. Reader, *Weir: Architect of Air Power*, Collins, 1966, especially Chapter 6.

6 A. Cairncross, ed., *The Scottish Economy*, Cambridge, 1954, pp. 3–4.

7 A. M. Robb, 'Shipbuilding', in *Glasgow: The Third Statistical Account*, Collins, 1958, p. 192.

8 G. D. N. Worswick and P. H. Ady, *The British Economy in the 1950s*, Oxford, 1962, p. 349.

9 John Firn, 'External Control and Regional Policy', in *The Red Paper on Scotland*, p. 158.

10 Andrew Hargrave, 'Economy and Industry', in D. Glen, ed., *Whither Scotland?* Gollancz, 1971, p. 32.

[11] Farquhar Gillanders, 'Crofting', in Derick Thomson and Ian Grimble, eds, *The Future of the Highlands*, Routledge, 1968.
[12] John Berry, 'Hydro-Electricity' in H. W. Meikle, ed., *Scotland*, Nelson, 1947, p. 99.
[13] Kellas, *Modern Scotland*, pp. 164–5.
[14] Cairncross, *The Scottish Economy*, p. 1.
[15] Scottish Council, *Annual Report*, 1959.
[16] Inquiry into the *Scottish Economy, 1960–1961* (The Toothill Report), Scottish Council, 1961, p. 184.
[17] *The New Statesman*, 8 October 1965.
[18] J. P. Mackintosh, *The Devolution of Power*, Penguin, 1968, p. 81.
[19] David MacKie, 'By-elections of the Wilson Government' in Christopher Cook, and Brian Ramsden, eds, *By-Elections in British Politics*, Macmillan, 1973, pp. 237–46.
[20] *Scotland's Older Housing*, HMSO. 1967, p. 12.
[21] Peter Jay, 'A Distinct Economy', in *Investing in Scotland's Future*, Scottish Council, 1974, p. 22.

CHAPTER 6

[1] 'Room at the Top', Chapter 18 of David Keir, ed., *The City of Edinburgh*, Collins, 1966, p. 464.
[2] Scottish Council, *Annual Report*, 1947–8.
[3] Kellas, *Modern Scotland*, p. 115.
[4] *New Society*, 1 July 1965, p. 4.
[5] *The Scotsman*, 16 February 1974.
[6] J. P. Mackintosh, *The Devolution of Power*, Chapter 9.
[7] See Christopher Harvie, 'The Motorway Interest', in the *New Statesman* 16 November 1973, pp. 274–5.
[8] Vincent Cable, 'Glasgow: Area of Need', in *The Red Paper on Scotland*, p. 239.
[9] *Church of Scotland Annual Report*, 1974; *Catholic Directory*, 1975; Kellas, op. cit., p. 510.
[10] John Highet, *The Scottish Churches*, Skeffington, London, Chapter 2.
[11] Anthony Ross, 'Resurrection', in Glen, *Whither Scotland?*, p. 123.

12 G. E. Davie, *The Democratic Intellect*, p. 336.
13 op. cit., p. 11.
14 T. R. Bone, 'Education', in *Whither Scotland?*, p. 76.
15 D. G. Macrae, 'More means less', in *New Society*, 27 May, 1971.
16 Kellas, *The Scottish Political System*, pp. 169–80.
17 Russell Braddon, *Roy Thomson of Fleet Street*, Fontana, 1968, pp. 160–224.
18 Edwin Muir, op. cit., Routledge 1936, p. 21.
19 Alexander Scott, 'Literature', in *Whither Scotland?*, p. 187.
20 Edwin Morgan, 'Scottish Poetry in the 1960s', in *Essays*, Carcanet Press, 1974, p. 177.
21 Gibbon, op. cit., Jenkins, 1932, p. 193.
22 Ian Munro, *Leslie Mitchell: Lewis Grassic Gibbon*, Oliver and Boyd, 1966, p. 177.
23 Quoted in MacDiarmid, *The Company I've Kept*, p. 234.
24 Oscar Wilde, 'The Soul of Man under Socialism', in *Plays, Prose Writings and Poems*, Dent, 1960, p. 270.
25 Hugh MacDiarmid, 'Introduction' to *Contemporary Scottish Studies*, Scottish Educational Journal, 1976, p. vi.
26 Stanley Eveling, interview in Edinburgh Student magazine *Gambit*, summer 1964, p. 6.
27 Lawrence Daly, 'Scotland on the Dole', in *New Left Review*, winter 1962, p. 23.
28 Norman Buchan, 'Politics', in *Whither Scotland?*, p. 90.
29 Raymond Williams, *The May Day Manifesto*, Penguin, 1968, pp. 162–3.
30 V. G. Kiernan, 'Notes on Marxism in 1968', in *The Socialist Register*, Merlin Press, 1968, p. 180; Tom Nairn, 'The Three Dreams of Scottish Nationalism', in Karl Miller, ed., *Memoirs of a Modern Scotland*.
31 The *Ecologist*, January 1972, p. 21.
32 Neal Ascherson, 'Return Journey', in *Question* no. 2, November 1975.
33 John McGrath, 'Scotland: Up against it', in *The Red Paper*, p. 138.
34 V. G. Kiernan, 'A Scottish Road to Socialism', in *New Left Review*, 1975.

CHAPTER 7

[1] Hanham, *Scottish Nationalism*, p. 175.
[2] McIntyre, speech reported in *Scots Independent*, May 1975.
[3] Scottish Secretariat MSS: Muirhead – Dunnett, 11 October 1957.
[4] *Scots Independent*, August 1944, p. 5.
[5] MacCormick, *The Flag in the Wind*, pp. 118–23.
[6] Scottish Secretariat MSS.: Muirhead – MacCormick, 16 August 1957.
[7] William Wolfe, *Scotland Lives*, Reprographia, 1973, p. 10.
[8] Wolfe, op. cit., pp. 38–9.
[9] David McKie, 'The By-elections of the Wilson Government', p. 240.
[10] Iain McLean 'The Rise and Fall of the Scottish National Party', *Political Studies*, vol. XVIII, no. 3, September 1970.
[11] Kellas, *The Scottish Political System*, p. 184.
[12] William Greenberg, *The Flags of the Forgotten*: *Nationalism on the Celtic Fringe*, Clifton Books, 1969, p. 93.
[13] The *Guardian*, 16 May 1975.
[14] *New Society*, 26 January 1967, p. 121.
[15] Speech of June 1969 quoted in Alasdair Buchan, *The Right to Work*, Calder and Boyars, 1972, p. 40.
[16] Hagrave, 'Economy and Industry', in *Whither Scotland*?, p. 35.
[17] See Nicholas Dekker, *The Reality of Scotland's Oil*, SNP, March 1973.
[18] D. I. MacKay and G. A. MacKay, *The Political Economy of North Sea Oil*, Martin Robertson, 1975, Chapter 6.
[19] Christopher Harvie, 'Scottish Oil Illusions', in the *New Statesman*, 27 April 1973.
[20] John McGrath, *The Cheviot, the Stag, and the Black, Black Oil*, West Highland Publishing Company, 1974, p. 30.
[21] *Scots Independent*, July 1973.
[22] Andrew Hargrave, 'Whatever happened to Oceanspan?', in *Business Scotland*, April 1976.
[23] Kellas, *The Scottish Political System*, pp. 143–4.
[24] *The Times*, 1 November 1973.
[25] *The Scotsman* 28 June 1974.
[26] The *Guardian*, 18 October 1976.

CHAPTER 8

1 Anthony Howard, 'We are the Masters now', in M. Sissons and P. French, eds, *The Age of Austerity*, Penguin, 1964, p. 33.
2 Q. D. Leavis, 'Edwin Muir', in *Scrutiny*, vol. IX, 1940–1, p. 172.
3 Robin Cook, 'Scotland before the Flood', in the *Guardian*, 18 August 1976.
4 Stephen Maxwell, 'Beyond Social Democracy', in G. Kennedy, ed., *The Radical Approach*, Palingenesis Press, 1976, pp. 7–8.
5 SNP Industrial Policy: Annual Conference Resolution no. 16, 1976.
6 The *Guardian*, 2 September 1975.
7 Donald Stewart, MP speech to SNP Annual Conference Motherwell, 29 May 1976.
8 Dr M. Slesser, speech to Annual Conference, 28 May 1976.
9 *The Times*, 28 April 1976.
10 George Orwell, 'As I Please', *Tribune*, 14 February 1947.
11 Scottish Secretariat MSS.: Naomi Mitchison – R. E. Muirhead, 23 April 1953.
12 Anthony Ross, interview with Bob Tait, *Scottish International*, no. 10, May 1970, p. 26.
13 Margo Macdonald, speech to Annual Conference 29 May 1976.

Index

Some of the entries in this index have been concentrated in subject areas like 'industry', 'newspapers' and so forth. Thus, for 'steel industry' look up 'industry: steel'. I have given the dates of various Scots historical personalities mentioned in the text, and where the mention is brief, a word or two of description has been added.